THE DODGER

Eimear Ní Bhraonáin is a journalist deeply rooted in her community. She previously worked as midlands and south-east correspondent of the *Irish Independent*, and in more recent years spent almost a decade working as a local broadcaster with KCLR (Kilkenny Carlow Local Radio). Since leaving her presenting role in May 2023, Eimear has been running her communications firm, Eimear.ie, based in County Carlow. She is mother to Róise, and is married to Alan O'Reilly, better known as 'Carlow Weather'.

THE DODGER

DJ CAREY AND THE GREAT BETRAYAL

EIMEAR NÍ BHRAONÁIN

First published in 2025 by
Merrion Press
10 George's Street
Newbridge
Co. Kildare
Ireland
www.merrionpress.ie

© Eimear Ní Bhraonáin, 2025

978 1 78537 490 6 (Paper)
978 1 78537 491 3 (eBook)

A CIP catalogue record for this book is available from the British Library.

All rights reserved. No part of this publication may be reproduced, stored in a retrieval system, or transmitted, in any form or by any means (electronic, mechanical, photocopying, recording or otherwise), without the prior written permission of both the copyright owner and the publisher of this book.

Typeset in Sabon LT Pro and Century Gothic

Cover design by Fiachra McCarthy

Front cover image: DJ Carey © Inpho
Back cover image (top): DJ Carey lifts the Liam MacCarthy Cup after Kilkenny's All-Ireland Senior Hurling Championship win over Cork, 14 September 2003 © Ray McManus/Sportsfile

Merrion Press is a member of Publishing Ireland.

CONTENTS

	Author's Note	vi
	Prologue	1
	Introduction	3
1	Little DJ	10
2	Lovely Hurling	23
3	Life Off the Field	50
4	DJ the Video Star	74
5	Enter the Dragon	96
6	High-fliers	114
7	'It's all in his head'	141
8	Falling for DJ	159
9	Hurler on the Rich	188
10	Terminal Illness	215
11	Family Drama	248
12	Full-Time	265
13	DJ the Malingerer	278
	Buíochas	289

AUTHOR'S NOTE

Some of the names in this book have been changed to protect the identity of those involved in certain incidents.

PROLOGUE

DJ's phone was ringing, but it didn't sound like he was abroad. That was strange. He had recently explained how he was in Seattle getting treatment.

Tom Brennan turned into The Avenue off Granges Road on the outskirts of Kilkenny city. He didn't get out of the car, he just watched the house and waited. There was no answer.

Moments later, the front door opened. DJ walked out with an attractive woman. She looked younger than him and had dark, straight hair.

Tom sent DJ a text and the reply came swiftly. He had an explanation for the normal dial tone – his calls were being diverted to his Irish number for privacy reasons, but he was travelling, on his way back from Seattle.

Tom read the text and lifted his head. He could see DJ right there but decided not to confront him. It was a summer's day in August 2021. DJ and his female companion strolled a few doors up. Maybe they were joining their neighbours for a barbecue?

The realisation was dawning on Tom that his hard-earned money was probably never going to be paid back. He had heard stories, he had his own theories, but he had needed to see for himself.

He knew in that moment that DJ Carey was a liar. He wasn't in America where he was supposed to be getting treatment for his cancer. In fact, he had never been too far away. All this time, he had been in Kilkenny city.

One of the best hurlers who ever lived, one of the leading Irish sports stars of his generation, a man who had also attended Tom's alma mater, St Kieran's College, had conned him.

INTRODUCTION

'Is it true that DJ is dead?'

Not for the first time, the rumours about DJ Carey were flying. Just before 9 p.m. on Wednesday, 25 October 2023, a concerned Kilkenny woman sent a text to DJ's local radio station, KCLR, asking this question. It was never read out, but the rumour had already been circulating for a few hours on WhatsApp.

The story of DJ's apparent death by suicide spread like wildfire, mostly through social media. People frantically texted each other speculating over whether there was any substance to it. One woman said her brother had heard the story in Tramore, County Waterford. A man in Belfast said he had gotten a text from New York City. A businesswoman's son had phoned her from a holiday in Italy to ask if it was true. A barman heard it from a reliable source in Goresbridge, County Kilkenny.

By the following day, the reports were showing up all over the web, on Twitter, Facebook, WhatsApp and even retrievable by Google searches linking to various websites. There was even a 'Rest in peace DJ Carey' message written on a Facebook page for the Kilkenny diaspora. Many believed the news, as the reports looked official, although some wondered why the mainstream media was not carrying any details.

If ever there was an example of fake news travelling fast, this was it. It would later turn out that the story had been picked up from a website called snbc13.com, where a report in the 'home/obituary' section carried the headline 'DJ Carey Death: Former Kilkenny hurler has died from suicide following cancer cash fraud'. The byline Jazmine Woods appeared in the article, with a photograph and details of the well-known Kilkenny man's 'death': 'Irish former hurler player tragically passed away after viral cancer funding case. Learn more about Denis Joseph Carey death and obituary.' The end of the piece stated, 'DJ Carey Obituary and Funeral Arrangements Will be Released by the Family'.

It was a work of fiction, most likely generated by artificial intelligence. But who was behind it? And why? Surely the original story was sparked by a human somewhere along the line? Emails to the snbc13.com website, registered in Iceland, asking for their source went unanswered.

For people who have followed the story of DJ Carey's life in recent years, this level of drama was hardly surprising. In fact, it was par for the course. It was not the first time he had been the subject of this type of nasty story, much to the distress of the people who care about him. In 2012, when he was under huge financial pressure, he collapsed in Kilkenny Garda Station and, following this, he claimed his then thirteen-year-old son read about his father taking his own life online. DJ revealed what a 'horrible experience' this was for his child, and he blasted social media and anonymous users who spread the story.

INTRODUCTION

And now it was happening all over again.

Yet perhaps it was not surprising that these things happen to DJ Carey and that the rumours about him are usually devastating, involving sudden death or terminal illness. After all, this latest rumour came just nine days before he was due before Dublin Circuit Criminal Court, charged with twenty-one fraud offences, nineteen counts of deception and two counts of using a false instrument with the intention of inducing another person to accept it as genuine in the period from 1 January 2014 to 18 September 2022 at an unknown location within the State. These offences were connected to Carey's own lies that he had been suffering from a rare form of cancer.

Although an escalation in severity, feigning illness was not a new ploy for DJ. He had been doing this since he was a young man. It started with the normal things that children do as an excuse to get out of school. However, from those relatively benign beginnings, it seemed to become more about being the centre of attention, and he moved on to disrupting the odd night out with his Gowran friends by ending these, more than once, with a fainting episode. Then there were the many times he wore bandages on and off the field. The more he got away with, the more his lies grew.

In his court case he was accused of 'dishonesty by deception' for inducing Irish businessman Denis O'Brien to give him money to pay for cancer treatment on unknown dates between 1 January 2014 and 18 September 2022 contrary to Section 6 of the Criminal Justice (Theft and Fraud Offences) Act 2001. Two well-known retired hurlers had also been due to be named as victims: Wexford's Larry O'Gorman and Clare's Tony Griffin. However, before the case came to trial, O'Gorman would confirm that he had withdrawn his statement against Carey, despite being named in the initial complaint. 'Now it's sorted and I'm happy,' was all he would say about the matter.

Carey was also accused of 'dishonesty by deception' against Ann Kelsey, Owen and Ann Conway, Mark and Sharon Kelly, Peadar Hughes, Aidan Mulligan, Edwin Carey, Donal Carroll, Christy Browne, Margaret and Ger Kirwan, Thomas Butler, Jeffrey Howes, Noel Tynan, Brendan Fleming, Sean Murray, Patrick Somers, Aonghus Leydon and Tom Brennan. The offences were all alleged to have occurred in a period ranging from 2019 to 2022.

The people involved in the case were rattled when they heard the rumours about Carey's death. Some had already felt conflicted about going through with a complaint, and this unsettled them further. I found it interesting that when I started interviewing people for this book, it proved not to be as straightforward a task as expected. Despite what had happened, often the people I spoke to were torn. Some had barely discussed with their own family and friends that they had given Carey a loan. Many wanted to tell the truth about their hurling hero but feared doing this in public. It was not just the embarrassment of having handed over money to him. Some didn't want DJ to know they had talked about him. Others didn't want to be seen as kicking somebody who was already down. And, although they knew his actions were wrong, many still showed concern for and loyalty to the hurler. This reluctance to turn on Carey

INTRODUCTION

is why so many of the sources in this book are anonymous and why his crimes went unreported for so long.

As well as interviews with some of the people named in the action against Carey, the book also includes details from many sources who did not make a statement to gardaí. There are various reasons why these people cannot come forward and cannot be named. Some are still loyal to him, despite knowing the truth. Others fear Revenue repercussions, having given him sums of cash. There are also people who don't need the stress it would bring, and they have already resigned themselves to the fact that they will never get their money back. There are privacy issues too, such as where husbands did not tell their wives that they had loaned DJ money.

Whatever reasons people have given for not coming forward, there is an abundance of evidence that DJ Carey's lies have long been an open secret in the GAA. Indeed, there are many people out there who have known the truth about the 'Dodger' for quite some time.

My purpose in writing this book is that I believe the public deserves to know the truth. I am a strong believer in the idea that when someone does something wrong, they should not get away with it simply because of who they are. As a journalist, my main responsibility is to gather the facts for you, the reader. But I also have a responsibility to be fair when scrutinising somebody's life. In order to be fair to DJ Carey, I interviewed over a hundred people who know him, as well as carrying out major secondary research, which included reading interviews published in newspapers over the years and using accounts from DJ's own autobiography, which he wrote with Martin Breheny and published in 2013. DJ himself is one of the biggest sources of my research, as he gave so many interviews to media throughout his life until his fraud was uncovered. He also sent many emails and text messages to people close to him who provided some insights into what was happening. I am especially grateful to the ordinary decent members of the GAA who were deeply embarrassed and hurt by Carey's actions but were not afraid to tell me what happened. It is not an easy thing to do, with or without your name, in Ireland. We have a culture of protecting our heroes, even when those heroes need to be held accountable for their crimes.

From the very beginning, when I started meeting some of DJ's old acquaintances, I realised he lived in a different universe to most of us. His natural talents made him different to other sportspeople. He was born with gifts that opened many doors for him. However, patterns quickly emerged in the accounts people gave of DJ. They told almost identical versions of stories about him, whether they came across him during his youth, the Celtic Tiger years or in more recent times. There were signs that DJ had been deceiving the people who loved him for a long time. He was good at it, so people didn't always see him coming.

People high up in the GAA have privately told me that they thought DJ Carey lacked intelligence. I find this an interesting viewpoint, considering just how long he was able to con people. His actions required skill, aptitude and planning. Maybe DJ is not book-smart, but he is able to read people and situations so

INTRODUCTION

he can stay many steps ahead. Exacerbated by what appears to be a complete lack of conscience, this made it easy for him to take advantage of those who adored him.

1

LITTLE DJ

Growing up in Gowran, Denis Joseph Carey, or DJ for short, ran the two miles home from his national school every day. Up the quiet rural road to his parents' house, he'd go toe to hand with a ball and keep soloing for the run home if it was football season. The rest of the time, it was the sliotar and hurley in hand until he reached the farm. He'd open the door, throw the school bag in a corner and run back outside gripping his hurley. Every day was the same. Once the cows were looked after, hours were spent belting a sliotar off the gable wall until it got dark and he had to go inside. This was DJ's imaginary hurling field. It is where all the action happened and where he honed his craft.

The second child of Maura and John Carey, DJ was born on 11 November 1970. He is the eldest of his surviving siblings: Jack, Kieran, Martin, Catriona, Liz and Aisling. There is a twenty-one-year age gap between DJ and his youngest sister, Aisling. He was very close to his brothers growing up, with just one year staggering each of them. He also had two other brothers, both of whom died tragically. When DJ was three or four, a younger brother, Thomas, was killed in a farm accident after getting caught on a power take-off shaft between a tractor and large manure spreader on the farm. He was trying to climb up to his father, who was cleaning out the machine. A couple of years earlier, DJ lost his older brother, John, as the result of a cot death. DJ later recalled that the memory of these events never left his parents, and especially his father in relation to Thomas's death.

DJ's parents were a huge influence on him growing up, as they struggled to provide for their family. They worked hard, and locals recall them trying their hand at various enterprises at different times: running a chip van, opening a hardware shop in the village, as well as running their farm. At one time Maura, who was a McGarry from County Kilkenny, worked as a cook in St Kieran's College. Some years earlier, DJ's father, John, had moved to Gowran with his father and family from Galmoy, a mining area in north Kilkenny. His family received land in Gowran from the Land Commission, and this is how John Carey got into farming what amounted to around sixty acres. It was on this farm that DJ was brought up, and for much of his childhood it was the only source of income for the household, so money was scarce.

Some described the family as well regarded and a big sporting family. Many said DJ's father was a great character, 'a gentleman', and that the Careys were 'wonderful neighbours'. They recall chatting to John either at the house buying a hurl, or at Mass, which the family regularly attended. They said you could hardly drink a cup of tea in a friendlier house or a more welcoming kitchen than that of DJ's parents. Others affectionately noted that Maura was a 'rogue' and laughed as they remembered the time she chanced pushing a full trolley of shopping out of a supermarket. When the security man stopped her, she explained that she had completely forgotten to pay. People who knew them also say that it was Maura who 'definitely wore the trousers' in the relationship. She was often seen driving when John was the passenger in their van, and she made all the financial decisions in the household. According to one friend, 'She used to hand him out a tenner for his lunch money when he was going off on deliveries for DJ's cleaning business for the day.'

However, there are some who disagree with this benign assessment of the family. They remember the Careys growing up and describe them as being 'as odd as ditches'. For many years, if an outsider mentioned the Careys in Gowran, the place from where the great DJ hailed, there were those who exchanged looks. They didn't say a bad word. They simply said nothing. One thing that did emerge were stories about John's temper, and more than one witness recalled how he could turn from placid to madman if provoked. In a documentary on DJ's life, aired in 2003, DJ himself mentioned feeling the lash of a rubber tube against his backside as a youngster after he accidentally broke a window while hurling at home, but he made light of the incident. He didn't mention which parent gave him the beating, but it wouldn't have been considered unusual at that time for children to be disciplined in this way.

There was also talk of a land dispute in DJ's family. It was said that John Carey inherited land in the Galmoy and Lisheen mines area from a man known to the family as 'Uncle Dinny'. A source said John and Maura had regularly visited this man, helping to take care of him. They also said that John put the land he inherited into his son Kieran's name. This later became an issue when the land was sold for a substantial sum and there was a falling out over how the money was divided. John Carey was apparently not happy with his share.

Hurling was DJ's religion growing up in Gowran. He doesn't remember when he started playing, but he got a black Cooper helmet from Santa when he was four years old. It was the only one he ever had throughout his playing career, and he explained in his official autobiography, 'Now, it was either too big for me back then or too small for me when I became an adult but, either way, it was my constant companion all through my career.' DJ had it taped and mended many times, having grown too attached to it to replace it. The best Christmas presents the Carey children got were hurls from their Uncle Martin every year.

There was only one form of entertainment at birthday parties around Gowran when DJ was growing up. Usually around thirty children turned up, and they would go outside for a game of hurling. Play would only stop for one of two reasons: either there was a row over the score, or somebody needed to go to the doctor for stitches. When play was suspended, they would often go inside for a bottle of Coke and all would be well again.

As children, DJ and his brother Jack would go to the woodlands of south Kilkenny to look for the perfect ash tree. The root of the ash is what makes the best hurling stick because of its curve and strength. A nice sun-ripened grain with no knots and as little sap as possible was what the boys searched for to take home to Gowran. Then they would dry it out for nine months before Jack would carve DJ a hurl. Jack was a year younger than DJ, but he was a gifted craftsman from the time he was a child. It didn't matter that they already had hurls from their Uncle Martin; the Carey boys couldn't get enough when it came to their favourite sport. They had their favourite hurls, but DJ was never fussy as long as it felt light in his hand.

Hurl in hand, standing in front of the gable wall of the farm, little DJ would pretend he was playing alongside his heroes, Ger Henderson and Eddie Keher. He imagined he was wearing the Black and Amber and was ten points down in an All-Ireland final. Aiming at the chimney, every time the ball came back to him, he scored that goal. If he missed, the ball went sixty yards down the field and he'd lose it or have to spend hours looking for it, so hitting the target really mattered. He'd go to bed and dream of playing for Kilkenny and scoring those crucial goals in his make-believe All-Ireland final. He even hurled in the bedroom. It was said that his mother was so fed up replacing smashed windows in their home that DJ's bedroom window was left broken. Maura thought there was no point in putting in a new one.

In July 2002 Canon Liam Devine wrote a column in the *Roscommon Herald* about bringing a young lad, Keith, from Sligo with him to visit the Carey farm. DJ was Keith's great hero. Devine couldn't believe the time and attention that the famous hurler gave to the young boy. He showed him his medals, his All-Star awards, signed autographs and answered all Keith's questions. When Keith asked what it took to make a great hurler, DJ replied, 'Come on and I will show you.' He brought him outside with a hurl and sliotar to that same gable end, plastered smooth like the front wall of a handball alley. He hit the ball against the wall and each time killed it dead on the hurl. He told the priest and Keith of how he had spent hours doing that as a young lad.

It has been suggested by some that DJ's initial interest in hurling was sparked by his granduncle on his father's side, Paddy Phelan, an iconic hurler of the 1930s. Others believe his inspiration came from Peggy Muldowney (née Carey), an aunt who won four camogie All-Irelands for Kilkenny. DJ himself claimed that the ferocious enthusiasm for the sport was in his immediate family and that his skills came, not from some inherent talent, but from his work against that gable wall, learning to control the ball. One thing he did learn from his family was that if you wanted to be a better hurler and to be fitter, you didn't drink or smoke, so DJ did neither. His parents, his Uncle Martin and his Aunt Peggy set the example by never drinking alcohol. On this subject, DJ once said, 'I always had in my head that if I wanted to be a good sportsman I shouldn't drink, and I stick by that.'

In 1975 DJ started in Gowran National School, where he was heavily influenced by two of his teachers, John Knox and Dick O'Neill. DJ has described how they helped to grow him into the game and were 'marvellous hurling men'. Under these two teachers and coaches, there was an incredible group of hurlers in the school. During DJ's time there, he found himself competing with the likes of Charlie Carter and Pat O'Neill in the playground. As a young boy, he was tiny, but his slight stature never held him back – he made up for it with his speed. Once he got the ball, he was gone.

When DJ was about ten years old, he was part of a special team from the school that emerged in his parish. For two years in a row in 1982 (with DJ) and 1983 (without DJ), they never lost a league or a championship match in Kilkenny. They went undefeated, completing a unique double-double (1982 Championship: Gowran 7–2, St Patrick's 1–2; League: Gowran 3–3, Thomastown 3–2; 1983 Championship: Gowran 3–8, Freshford 1–4; League: Gowran 3–8, Freshford 2–4). Everybody was talking about Gowran National School and how a small country school was producing these brilliant hurlers. They were all around the same age and hurling was huge for them. All their friends played, and the young boys looked up to the Senior hurlers, whom they worshipped.

John Knox started teaching in Gowran National School in 1967, and as far as he was concerned there was no better parish in the country, as he always had the support and cooperation of parents. It made his job enjoyable and easy, and he was only too happy to focus on cultivating the next generation of Kilkenny hurlers. He remembered DJ as a shy and self-effacing boy. When the class travelled on school trips to Croke Park in Dublin to watch big games, instead of sitting down the back of the bus to have fun with his classmates, DJ opted to sit at the front of the bus next to the teachers. Knox described young DJ as an average scholar, 'not a great man for the books', but he was 'intelligent, clever and articulate' all the same. He couldn't recall DJ being particularly weak or strong in any subjects; he just did his lessons when he was in school.

People would regularly tell Knox to 'play him, sir', because they enjoyed watching this tiny boy race across the field. The sidestep and the handpass were two of DJ's early signature moves, and it was during this time, John said, that classmates started calling him 'The Artful Dodger'. The teacher never had to worry about DJ getting to a match on time, as his parents would bring him. 'Maura was a real lady, she was the mainstay of the family, holding down various jobs, including working in St Kieran's College,' John said. A huge chunk of DJ's primary school day revolved around hurling. 'He'd hurl on the way into school, before school, then they'd hurl at break at 11 a.m., again at 12.30 p.m., and they'd be hurling at 2 p.m. and hurling again on the way home.' His teacher also said DJ 'wasn't the best attender at school', and if there was a match on, DJ would often be missing until five minutes before throw-in. 'He'd get a touch of nerves before the school matches … he'd be absent all day and miss the school, but suddenly he'd be there for the match.'

DJ was not only a great hurler; he was also a talented footballer, handballer and soccer player. He had been an all-rounder with a ball from a young age. A neighbour who was bringing his own son to play handball in Goresbridge had also brought DJ and his brother Jack from the time they were around eight or nine years old. News of DJ's handball exploits appeared in print as early as 1982. On 26 March that year, the *Kilkenny*

People reported that 'D.J. Carey of Goresbridge teamed up very successfully with James Delaney of O'Loughlin's at the weekend when they clinched the under-12 Leinster doubles title in Drogheda. They had a very easy victory over their Louth opponents.' By May, DJ had made history for Goresbridge. He won the first ever juvenile 60x30 Leinster title for the club and went on to win world handball titles. DJ would later credit handball for his footwork and anticipation on the hurling field. This stood to him more than anything else in the game.

By the time he was eleven years old, DJ had won an All-Ireland medal for under-12 handball. He brought the medal to school, where his teachers made him go around and stand at the front of the classes to show it off. As Michael Foley put it in *The Sunday Times* in November 2013, when DJ reflected on this episode, 'No one in Gowran has an All-Ireland handball medal. No one in Gowran will visit America eight times for handball tournaments before they turn 20 either, or get offered a handball scholarship by a school in North Carolina. They know he's special and sensitive and needs minding and encouraging, but the talk still starts. Jealous, small-town stuff.'

Word about DJ began to spread. His handball prowess at this time brought him into contact with Tommy O'Brien, a teacher in Kilkenny CBS Primary School and the mentor of another emerging handball talent in Michael 'Ducksie' Walsh. O'Brien, the president of the Handball Association at the time, watched the 1983 All-Ireland hurling final, a victory for Kilkenny over Cork, from the Ard Chomhairle seats in Croke Park's Hogan Stand with the diminutive DJ on his knee.

In school, DJ did enough to get by and moved from Gowran National School to St Kieran's College in Kilkenny city for his secondary school education. He would probably have gone to the Kilkenny CBS, except for the fact that Fr Tommy Maher, a legendary hurling coach who taught at St Kieran's, called out to the house in Gowran with a bribe – a new hurley and sliotar for DJ. On the very same day that DJ started in St Kieran's, in September 1983, Adrian Ronan and Pat O'Neill also began their secondary education. The trio went on to win All-Ireland Colleges, Minor, Under-21 and Senior medals. Ronan once joked that DJ was never in school unless there was a match on. People noticed how obedient he was as a youngster, particularly at hurling training. He trained hard and did what he was told. He didn't like to get into trouble in school as, if he did, he knew he would also get into trouble at home.

In his first year in St Kieran's, DJ lined out for the juvenile hurling and football teams and won provincial honours in both. He was once described as a beautiful footballer, small but skilful. At this point DJ was still small, but he was deceptive, with a great sidestep. Fr Paddy Bollard, the hurling coach, paid individual attention to every member of the team bar one. DJ was told to do his own thing. There was nothing Fr Bollard could teach him.

Hurling folk around Kilkenny began to notice young DJ. One of his teachers, Nicky Cashin, said he stuck out like a sore thumb on the field. When he played Féile games around the country, people would ask from the sidelines, 'Who's the little fella?' Apart from his obvious talent, they commented that if he would only grow and fill out a bit, he would be brilliant. But it wasn't only on the field where his small stature could lead to him being underestimated. There was a story that some of the bigger lads in St Kieran's were taking and eating his sandwiches. He wasn't happy about this but was too small to confront them, so instead he put Sudocrem in them once; after that, he had no further bother.

DJ's slight build didn't stop him from cleaning up as a young hurler. He won under-14, under-16 and under-18 championship medals with St Kieran's. Everybody was watching this hurling star rise. Expectations had already started to build. During his school holidays in 1987, he got a job in Dunnes Stores on Kieran Street in Kilkenny. When he was stacking the shelves, customers would constantly come up to him to praise his performance in some match or other. His co-workers assumed that, as a young man, DJ was mortified by all the attention he got, but he was always pleasant to those who approached him. His parents had brought him up to always open the door for people, to be courteous and to be mannerly, and this part of his upbringing always stayed with DJ.

On the day of the 1988 All-Ireland Colleges final in Waterford, the legendary broadcaster Mícheál Ó Muircheartaigh noticed DJ and checked the programme for his name. In *DJ: The Story and the Skills*, a documentary produced in 2003 by Barbara Galavan, Ó Muircheartaigh recalled how he realised DJ was special from day one, describing him as 'something different'. In the same documentary, Clare star Jamesie O'Connor remembers being a second-year pupil in school the first time he came across DJ. St Flannan's College in Ennis had a super team back then, and he remembers them playing St Kieran's in the 1987 All-Ireland Colleges final and winning on the day. All the Flannan's supporters were roaring 'mind the child' every time the small corner-forward got the ball.

In May 1989 St Flannan's met St Kieran's again in the All-Ireland Colleges final. DJ scored a massive 3-3 that day, and the Kilkenny school won on a final scoreline of 3-5 to St Flannan's 1-9. This was St Kieran's ninth win, but their first back-to-back All-Irelands. A match report stated that after DJ scored two goals in the searing heat for Kieran's in the first five minutes of the second half, the Noresiders never looked back. His performance left the spectators under no illusions about how good he was.

In his Leaving Cert year, seventeen-year-old DJ, who had grown six inches taller over the course of the previous year, made his Senior hurling debut for Kilkenny. He never hit six feet, but that didn't really matter. He was at his fittest and strongest, standing five foot eleven inches and weighing twelve stone seven pounds.

DJ knew he was different to the rest of his teammates, a special talent. Even at this early stage in his career, he saw himself as a role model and so didn't go out much. In media interviews, he often talked about the importance of behaving off the field so you don't let your teammates down. Despite this remarkably serious attitude to the game, there were those who said DJ was too young at the time to be on the Kilkenny Senior panel. This argument did not wash with then Kilkenny manager Diarmuid Healy, who was overheard saying, 'If he's good enough, he's old enough.'

Hurling was DJ's life in school and nothing else mattered. He had so many games, he was having to get grinds from teachers in between training sessions. Healy, who made DJ his mission, told him to go home to study for his Leaving Certificate three weeks before the big exams, as he was afraid DJ wouldn't pass. He also made sure DJ had time to eat after school and before hurling training. Unlike other boys who might eat their leftovers from lunch, DJ was regularly sent to a local hotel in Kilkenny, Langtons, for the best of steak and fish dinners to bulk him out. Healy's efforts proved to be worthwhile, and DJ's adult hurling career would fully justify the manager's faith in him.

2

LOVELY HURLING

DJ was known to be good-natured when it came to doing people a turn. He was never rude or arrogant, despite the constant demands on his time. On one occasion in 1989, he called to Dunnes Stores in Enniscorthy, County Wexford, to visit a former colleague, bringing a pair of handball gloves he had worn while winning an All-Ireland title for their son who loved handball.

He would go anywhere for anybody. One evening during the 1989–90 college year, a student at Carlow RTC stuck out her thumb as she waited on the roadside. She was trying to hitch a lift home to Thomastown, County Kilkenny. She hadn't been waiting very long when a young man in a flash company car pulled up. He told her to jump in. He was going home to Gowran. Instead of dropping her there, however, he insisted on continuing the extra eight miles to Thomastown. When they arrived at her front gate, she went to get out, but he insisted on bringing her up the driveway to the front door. The young woman had recognised her driver, her own father having played Minor hurling for Kilkenny. She invited DJ in for a cup of tea, but he politely declined. They said their goodbyes and he drove off. She went inside and said, 'Dad, you'll never guess who gave me a lift home. DJ Carey!'

DJ was once referred to as the Daniel O'Donnell of hurling for both his pulling power and temperament. By the time he was just twenty years old, he was already established as a 'clean hero' and 'the darling of Kilkenny followers'. Modest, polite and approachable, he'd give anybody the time of day. For somebody who appeared to be shy, he was good at small talk. Even non-hurling people knew his name. He was a two-dinners-a-day man; he couldn't play or train on an empty stomach, and he'd munch through a packet of biscuits with his tea. The public could relate to him; he was one of them. As the *Kilkenny People* reported back then, 'Sure, he is the type of fellow every girl would love to bring home to meet mammy.'

Hurling has few superstars. There was Christy Ring in the 1940s and 1950s, Eddie Keher in the 1970s, and Tipperary's Nicky English in the 1980s. Then DJ Carey came along. He was an instinctive hurler. He was good in the air and on the ground. He had scorching pace. If he was in trouble, he could handpass a ball brilliantly. Left side or right – it didn't matter. DJ had fine-tuned his coordination skills in the handball alley, so he didn't have a weak side on the hurling field.

Kilkenny sports journalist John Knox (a cousin of DJ's teacher of the same name) had his eye on DJ from the time he was a boy. He did not see greatness the very first time he saw DJ but realised the possibility was there. In the *Kilkenny GAA Yearbook* for 1990, the year Kilkenny had become unexpected

Under-21 All-Ireland hurling champions, Knox wrote: 'Carey, of course, has had his problems with leg injuries, but on his day he shows such natural talent he would have you wondering can he outstrip our own Eddie Keher. Yes, he suggests he has that kind of enormous potential.'

Two years earlier, an action photograph of a youthful Carey had featured as the front cover of the *Kilkenny GAA Yearbook 1988*. Inside the cover was this description: 'D.J. Carey of the Young Irelands (Gowran) club heads towards the Cork goal during the Minor hurling All-Ireland final. The year was one full of good tidings for D.J. He helped St. Kieran's College win the Colleges Senior championship, and also won a handful of handball honours.'

Knox remembers one occasion when DJ was playing at full-forward in an All-Ireland Colleges semi-final in Nenagh. He notes how the young player's feet seemed to be anchored to the ground as he knocked the full-back and made contact with the ball. Apparently, it was a sight to behold. Knox also recalls being told how DJ, when only seventeen, had started off at Senior level in goal with his club, Young Irelands: 'I don't remember that, but I do remember when he got into his twenties, he was doing magical things. It was a joy.'

Watching Carey closely, after a prolonged period he came to believe that DJ was the real deal: 'DJ was no ordinary hurler. He came at a time with Charlie Carter, who was very good as well. He was just one of the greats, full stop – the excitement factor was all there.' Knox observed how DJ could handpass the sliotar almost as far as others could hit it with a hurley. Like any special player, he had vision and an ability to find space. 'He was able to create space. It's always a great sign of a special talent. Henry Shefflin could do it. Messi can do it. They can work in tight spaces and have the accuracy of the touch. Carey had that.'

Sometimes DJ seemed to be nervous before matches, which surprised people observing him. For a star player, Knox remembers how accessible he was. 'People said he loved the publicity, but it is part of the promotion. There was a promotion factor for the GAA and certainly DJ made himself available. He was the sort of ambassador you'd want, he always conducted himself well.' The 'DJ factor' helped to pull in the crowds for county finals, when people came across the Kilkenny border from counties Laois, Tipperary, Carlow and even further afield to see him in action. There was always pressure on DJ and expectations on his shoulders. If Carey performed, Kilkenny performed. John Knox firmly believes that DJ took the pressure off his teammates by telling players, especially those less experienced, not to worry about how they passed the ball – he'd instruct them to simply get the ball to the forwards and 'we'll do something with it'.

DJ understood the team ethic and was dedicated to his sport. Expectations in Kilkenny were always high, to the extent that they were sometimes unrealistic. 'DJ would have carried the expectations to be the main man, the one to deliver the most. He had to live with that. When Kilkenny were in the valley period, maybe he wasn't surrounded by some of the greatness that came with Brian Cody's team. He did carry it and he didn't shy away from it.'

Enda McEvoy, a native of Kilkenny city, former hurling correspondent of the *Sunday Tribune* from 1996 to 2001 and subsequently a columnist with the *Irish Examiner* (2001–present), saw many of DJ's games from the late 1980s onwards. He makes the point that Brian Cody had three great forwards to call on during his twenty-four years as Kilkenny manager: Henry Shefflin, TJ Reid and DJ Carey. 'Henry and TJ were both brilliant in different ways, but DJ was something different again. He was like no hurler we had seen before or since. He was otherworldly.'

On 21 July 1991, the morning of Carey's first Leinster final, a photograph of two schoolboys appeared in the *Sunday Independent* alongside an article by McEvoy. The photo, taken in 1989, showed DJ sitting next to Adrian Ronan in St Kieran's. McEvoy wrote about how Carey was the 'gonna-be-hurler-of-the-nineties'. 'Is he everything the publicity suggests?' asked McEvoy, before giving his own response: 'Yes, actually; maybe even more. The guy is totally brilliant.' He described how Carey had Carl Lewis's speed, Olga Korbut's balance, Gary Lineker's level-headedness, and the handpassing ability of the handball champion he'd been many times over, with a Japanese bullet-train of a shot. 'All this and modest with it! When he says he knows he could never be as good as Eddie Keher, he seems to genuinely believe it himself.'

According to Enda, everything DJ did had a touch of drama about it. The victories were big. The defeats were big. 'In the 1990s, whether Kilkenny were winning or losing, it was almost always about DJ. Either he did something spectacular and they won, or he had a quiet match and they lost. One way or another he was usually the story, which wasn't a good thing. On a personal basis he was a pleasure to deal with. Always so polite and low-key and amenable. If he had an ego, it was very well hidden. But it's a good job he played when he did. Imagine how much bigger the attention and pressure would have been had he played in the age of social media.'

Before we had selfies, DJ signed autographs. Attendances at matches soared, and when the rest of the hurlers had gone home, DJ would still be there with a queue of eager youngsters in front of him, waiting to get his signature. The GAA loved him, he attracted corporate sponsorship of a kind that the game had never seen before. He was almost too willing to be interviewed, at times, always at the end of the phone for the media. It's hard for people who didn't know DJ Carey in the 1990s to fully grasp the power of his enormous profile.

An example of this was when DJ was watching a handball game in County Tyrone. His great friend Michael 'Ducksie' Walsh of Kilkenny and Walter O'Connor of Meath had battled it out for two hours on the court. They were covered in sweat. It had been an epic match. When they looked out, they laughed when they saw the crowd. The spectators weren't waiting to talk to them about the action on the handball court. They had spotted DJ and there was a line of people waiting for him to sign autographs.

In 1992 John Knox wrote about how our nation was re-energised by the sheer joy that only sporting achievements can bring. We were enjoying the exploits of Jack Charlton's 'army', and Michael Carruth had won gold in the Olympic Games boxing. The reawakening was felt in Kilkenny too. The county had suffered. Previously, All-Irelands may have been taken for granted by Kilkenny fans, but there's nothing like having to wait nine long years to appreciate the sweetness of victory once again.

In desperate wind and rain, there was ecstasy and excitement for young DJ when the Cats beat Cork 3–10 to 1–12 in the 1992 final. Enda McEvoy remembers the moments after the win, when Kilkenny supporters who rushed onto the field at Croke Park started chanting 'DJ, DJ'. It was only his third full season on the panel, yet DJ was already acknowledged as the star. After this win, John Knox penned an article entitled 'The pain of defeat made hurling men of Ollie's army'. In it, he wrote: 'DJ Carey played with such belief that you had to remind yourself he is still only 21.' DJ has often said that the 1992 All-Ireland win holds a special place in his memory.

In the 1993 All-Ireland final against Galway, Kilkenny were again triumphant, giving them their first back-to-back wins for a decade. That year, DJ picked up Leinster and All-Ireland medals, an All-Star award, and he was also named Texaco Hurler of the Year. But from this point on he felt the pressure 'beginning to build'. In the aftermath of the 1993 final he was prickly about the newspapers referencing how he had been 'off-colour'. 'Unless I scored 2–7 or 2–8 in every game, I almost had to explain myself. What did people expect? I landed some pressure frees against Galway, worked as hard as I possibly could, yet people seemed to want more. The 1993 final would later be used to support the theory that I didn't play well in All-Ireland finals, an argument which simply doesn't hold up.'

Fans were always hanging off the edge of their seats during championship season because they never knew who would lift the Liam MacCarthy Cup come September. Kilkenny had DJ, but you could never take anything for granted, especially in an All-Ireland final. After the wins of 1992–3, there was a hiatus in Kilkenny's success. By 1995, just two years after doing the double, Kilkenny supporters were already feeling bereft. In other counties expectations are never quite as high, but in Kilkenny the fans are reared on success. Barrie Henriques, the editor of the *Kilkenny GAA Yearbook*, remarked in 1995, 'The fact that Kilkenny won the Church and General National Hurling League, Leinster Minor, Junior and Under-21 titles, the All-Ireland Junior final, the All-Ireland Masters final, the All-Ireland Colleges camogie final, and reached the All-Ireland final stages of all hurling competitions except Senior, not to mention a bucketful of handball All-Irelands, does not prevent people from saying to me, "Ye won't have much for the *Yearbook*, this time!"'

There were four years in the mid-1990s when Kilkenny didn't reach Croke Park on All-Ireland Sunday, and the weight of those expectations were felt by the team, and most especially by DJ Carey, who was constantly in the limelight. Kilkenny supporters were disappointed in 1996 with just two Leinster titles, at Minor and Junior level. However, the year brought some highs for DJ, who captained his club, Young Irelands, in their epic clash with James Stephens. Gowran and James

Stephens created a jersey industry in the county that year, with teenagers proudly wearing their club colours on the streets of Kilkenny. They chased their hurling heroes for autographs after hurling sessions. The 1996 county final between the two clubs went to a replay, and attendances soared. Normally a county final in Kilkenny would attract a crowd of 8,000 to 10,000. DJ's presence in 1996 ensured an attendance of around 16,000, which meant double the entrance fees – he was the sole reason many of the spectators were there.

So many of DJ's finest moments were captured on camera and in the press. On 3 August 1997, Peter Finnerty wrote in the *Sunday Independent* about Kilkenny's All-Ireland quarter-final clash with Galway in Thurles seven days earlier. 'Priceless DJ' was the headline. 'The man of the day and the game was DJ. The point he scored under pressure while tearing down the left wing and striking off his lefthand side was as good a score as I have ever seen. At this stage it has all been said about DJ and there is very little I can add to it. Jonah Lomu, who dominated the 1994 Rugby World Cup, wasn't as awesome as Carey was last Sunday. Lomu is worth millions but Carey is priceless.' The Cats won by two points that day on a final score of Kilkenny 4-15 to Galway 3-16. Carey was the hero of the day with a tally of 2-8. However, they would lose to Clare in the semi-finals.

Just six months after this formidable performance, DJ delivered a bombshell when he announced that he had lost his 'appetite' for hurling. On Wednesday, 4 February 1998, his local newspaper, the *Kilkenny People*, confirmed the story that the most decorated player in the modern game was walking away from intercounty hurling. Headlines of 'DJ Carey about to call it a day' (*The Irish Times*), 'Hurling world is bewildered' (*Irish Examiner*) and 'Mystery surrounds DJ Carey's retirement' (*Belfast News Letter*) were splashed across the press. The abrupt decision was the talk of the country, with Kilkenny supporters in disbelief. They couldn't understand why, at twenty-seven, DJ was leaving the game he loved. There was a flurry of interest in what was behind the announcement. Questions swirled over whether pressure close to home was at the centre of his decision, as DJ's club, Young Irelands, were beaten by Dunnamaggin in the 1997 county final. He had taken a break soon after this but was expected back once the National Hurling League resumed on 8 March 1998.

When DJ announced his retirement at a press conference, there were a few reasons given for the decision: he felt mentally exhausted from hurling non-stop for club, college and county since he was a child; his batteries were flat. A report by Enda McEvoy appeared in the *Munster Express* on 3 April 1998. In it, DJ is quoted as saying that the people who got the biggest shock at the news were his family. They were the most disappointed of all, especially his wife, Christine. She had known his feelings all along, according to DJ, but probably didn't think he would actually go ahead and retire.

During interviews with journalists in the weeks after his announcement, DJ hinted that pressure from the public and the media had also contributed to his decision. He seemed to have had the weight of the world on his shoulders, dragging him down. Reflecting on 1998 in his autobiography, he said it wasn't all about 'highs and glory'. 'There was another side too, one which left me feeling so flat and disillusioned that I felt I had no option but to walk away from the game I loved at the age of 27.' The roar of the crowd was all very well, but when the game was over, he had to go back to his personal cares, worries and stresses. He explained how running the new business he had set up, DJ Carey Enterprises, was 'brand new territory' for him, and that it came with pressures he hadn't experienced before. 'Trying to balance the books was mighty difficult and however hard I worked at putting it to the back of my mind so that it would not interfere with my hurling, it just wasn't possible.'

Years later, DJ would say, 'Nobody can separate their work and sporting life to the degree where they don't interact. So if my overdraft facility was overheating in a week before a big game and I was trying to get money in to cool it down, hurling had to take its place in the queue of priorities.' DJ described how he was leaving his cleaning supplies company on a Friday wondering how he would pay his bills on a Monday morning. He was hitting frees on Sunday but always thinking about Monday and balancing the books. While he was enjoying the benefits of being one of the highest-profile sports stars in Ireland, he admitted that running his business was stressful. 'I had no formal training for running a business which made it all the harder. Learning as you go along is all very fine, but you make mistakes and they can be costly. Having said that, I had plenty of good times too, but the stress was there all the time.' He also explained that there was nothing exclusive about his business and it was a competitive sector to be in. People didn't care if their supplier was a sports star, they were more concerned with price, quality and service.

While DJ attributed his decision to work pressures and the responsibility he felt every time he played for club and county, it didn't quell the rumours and gossip. Journalists reported that there appeared to be more to the story than 'meets the eye'. An article in the *Evening Herald* on Thursday 5 February stated, 'Kilkenny was one big rumour machine yesterday'. The press reported on a theory that DJ wanted to devote more time to golf, which he denied. There was even a suggestion that the sportsman, who was a 7 handicapper in 1998, ultimately wanted to turn pro, and there was talk of him signing with ProActive Sports Management Agency. Two years earlier, in November 1996, he had attended the launch of the agency and was photographed with its co-founder, former Republic of Ireland international Kevin Moran. DJ admitted he had sought advice from the agency but denied signing with them.

Other rumours centred on his relationship with the Kilkenny manager, Kevin Fennelly. Fennelly took over from Nickey Brennan in November 1997, after Brennan had managed the county team for the two previous years. Some people had the impression that DJ had fallen out with Fennelly, stemming from the fact that Fennelly had been a manager of DJ's Young Irelands club and had omitted one of his brothers, Martin, from the team for the 1997 county final. Martin had been in goal when Gowran won the county final for the first time in 1996 but didn't want to play in that position in 1997. Instead, he wanted to go into the forward line, and DJ was dispatched to deliver the news to the manager. While Fennelly wanted Martin to stay in goal, he decided to allow him to challenge for a new position. By the time the county championships were hotting up, Martin had changed his mind again and wanted to get back in goal as his new position wasn't working out. However, by then Gowran's replacement goalkeeper was doing well.

DJ denied the rumours, saying he and Fennelly never had a cross word. When addressing the controversy in his autobiography, he added, 'The beat on the gossip drums claimed that I was annoyed with Kevin for not restoring Martin to the goalkeeping position for the county final. Not true. Martin had made his choice and it hadn't worked out so he had to live with the consequences.' DJ insisted he had never had an argument with his manager and said there was no bad blood between himself and Fennelly.

But no matter what was said, the parish kept talking, as they were observing the dynamics from the sidelines and suspected the pair didn't get along. Stories circulated in Gowran, where some locals recall how John Carey marched down to Loughlin's pub ahead of the 1997 county final. A young woman had painted an impressive mural of the Gowran superstars – Pat O'Neill, Charlie Carter, DJ Carey and their manager, Kevin Fennelly – on the side of the building. DJ's dad was said to be furious that Fennelly featured on the wall and told the artist to 'take it down'. Locals said the woman had done a 'grand job on it', but John was bitter over Martin being dropped from the Young Irelands team.

Other stories were concocted by locals, such as how Fennelly looked the other way when DJ fell to the ground in apparent agony during a training session. People analysed the body language between the pair at matches, and many were convinced there was no love lost between the two men. Despite the rumours, when DJ had a spare ticket to the 32nd Ryder Cup at Valderrama Golf Club in Sotogrande, Spain, in September 1997, he invited Fennelly. The pair didn't seem to socialise on the trip, however, with DJ spending most of the time in his room. He told people he had food poisoning.

Soon after DJ's retirement announcement in February 1998, Nickey Brennan rang the hurler. The call was more in a personal capacity than any formal intervention. 'Jaysus, DJ, don't throw it all away,' Brennan pleaded, asking the player to see sense and not to do something drastic. He couldn't believe that a guy at the peak of his career would give up everything.

He wasn't the only one pleading with the hurler to come to his senses. In the days after DJ made his decision known, the postman delivered thousands of letters to his home in Gowran from hurling fans across the country, begging him to come back. DJ had boxes stuffed with cards, faxes, notes and letters from people asking him to change his mind. One letter came from a Kilkenny man who had lived in Canada for the past thirty-five years. The man had daughters and was hoping to bring them home to see DJ playing for Kilkenny in an All-Ireland final. About two hundred of the letters had come from schools around the country, many of them signed by young children who had difficulty writing their names but who, their teachers explained in a covering note, had lost interest in hurling since the Gowran man retired. Hurling fans lit candles in churches and said prayers for him to return.

DJ hadn't expected this kind of reaction to his departure – it was overwhelming. Reflecting on it years later, he admitted it was one of his more stupid decisions. Many players made the decision to give up hurling over the years and were never asked back. In DJ's case, the country was almost plunged into mourning, and hurling fans and the Kilkenny County Board wanted him back. It was also pointed out to him that his son, Seán, who was eight months old at the time, might never see him hurl. As DJ said, 'You have to take all these things into account.'

Nickey Brennan was one of the few who read the tea leaves correctly. When DJ announced his retirement, the former Kilkenny manager predicted he'd be back for the National League match against Laois. So it proved. On 20 March 1998, Radio Kilkenny was on standby for a breaking news story, and that afternoon Ned Quinn, the vice-chairman of Kilkenny County Board, gave hurling fans the news they were craving. DJ would be rejoining the panel. Quinn was eager to point out that there was no angle to the story – DJ 'just felt he had lost his appetite'. The county board had decided to leave him alone, as he had been through a lot, according to Quinn, who also said DJ's family had urged him to go back. 'We all wanted him back. I don't think I realised the impact it would have on people; Kilkenny fans were devastated.'

The next day, the front page of the *Irish Independent*'s sports section featured a photograph of DJ wearing the black and amber under the heading 'Back on the Prowl'. Liam Horan wrote about 'Kilkenny joy as superstar Carey decides to hurl again'. Horan reported that the announcement of his return came as Carey, Christine and Seán were 'winging their way to New York for a family holiday'. He stated that DJ had made no public comment on his reasons for coming out of retirement.

There were headlines about the return of the 'prince of hurling' everywhere, but soon afterwards the focus shifted to talk of DJ being paid to return. There were rumours all over Kilkenny that money had been offered to lure him back into the fold, and the press reported the speculation of 'cash for play'. At one stage, there was even a suggestion that Kilkenny's sponsors, Avonmore, had paid him to return, but that was vehemently denied. Despite this, while officials said it didn't happen, there are those who say there is no doubt that 'DJ was looked after'.

At a special press conference held by the Kilkenny County Board in Langtons Hotel in Kilkenny at the end of March 1998, they desperately tried to quell suggestions that DJ had been paid to return. Ned Quinn opened with a prepared statement to address the rumours. He stated unequivocally that no money from any source was offered to DJ to return to the game. He said it was important that a clear line of distinction continued to be drawn between all GAA players, who were amateur and receiving no financial reward for playing hurling and football, and contracted professionals in other sports. Quinn stressed that not only had no inducement of any kind, financial or otherwise, been offered to DJ to return, but the player was due expenses dating back to the previous July. This seemed to contradict the idea that people had that DJ was money-hungry and mad for endorsements. Instead, he was being chased to claim for his expenses.

That day, in Langtons, DJ talked to the gathered media about how he was going to become more thick-skinned, as it was clear the rumours were getting to him. He also said he would no longer be on the road six or seven nights a week, but he would still do his best for people. Quinn explained how there were extraordinary pressures on DJ, who was in high demand to attend events such as medal presentations, and he made no apologies for saying DJ needed to be 'protected'. The Kilkenny County Board would screen all requests for his attendance at functions from then on. Quinn said journalists would be able to speak to the hurler before and after matches as usual, but the subject of his retirement was now closed.

Not quite. In August 1999 DJ Carey told Vincent Hogan of the *Irish Independent* about his struggles around the time of his brief retirement. Things were very bad and he heard all sorts of stories through the grapevine, from his business being gone to family trouble and affairs. Nobody was thick-skinned enough to ignore all of that, and DJ recalled how he couldn't take the persistent rumours that he'd hear constantly. Even when he occasionally challenged the stories he was being told about himself, he found some people didn't believe his denials. He described the gossip as small-town Ireland 'poison', and he said he was getting a vibe from people that there was no smoke without fire. He revealed how he attacked people over this, 'people that were in company of very close friends of mine'. The hurling star said he knew he shouldn't be taking these things personally, but it was very hard not to when he was on the receiving end. According to him, his head was ready to explode with everything he was hearing from people he met.

In this interview, DJ explained that he had retired because of the many rumours going around about him, claiming his mind wasn't clear. He also addressed the stories about his comeback and the claims that he got a fat cheque to play again: 'When I came back out of retirement, some of the media were trying to make out that the reason I came back was because money was shoved under the counter. The word was I got £50,000 from Avonmore. It was all total nonsense, but certain people kept pushing it. I didn't get a penny to play. Not one penny. I don't earn anything from the game. I'm not a professional hurler or GAA player. My profession is out there selling detergents and paperware.' Despite his denials, to this day people still discuss the rumour that DJ was looked after by Avonmore. Sources say that his company, DJ Carey Enterprises Ltd, had lucrative contracts with the Irish milk giant, and that, while he wasn't paid to play hurling, there were many businesses out there that were finding ways to reward him.

The year 1998 was not a good one for DJ. Neither was it a good year for Kilkenny hurling. Carey's short-lived retirement had thrown hurling in the county into disarray. A retirement of this magnitude, coming from such a young player, and with no convincing reason, had cast a long shadow. Tensions had developed that were still there by the time the All-Ireland final came around, to which Kilkenny had made it despite the problems. On the morning of the day when the scheduled Kilkenny press event before the All-Ireland final would take place, a story ran in a tabloid quoting an unnamed county board official running DJ down. Carey was said to be incensed, and he confronted all the leading board officers, who denied saying anything. He then rubbished the story at the press event, describing the source as a phantom county board officer. Some days later he received a letter from the reporter providing detail that verified the story.

Reflecting on the day of the 1998 All-Ireland final, a source said it was a 'shit show'. Just hours before the biggest game of the year, DJ was organising a game of golf with the owner of the Back Door pub in Dublin. The rest of the players watched as he seemed more interested in scheduling a tee time with Nick Faldo than he was in the coming game. Kevin Fennelly was overheard asking the publican not to be annoying his star player, saying, 'We're playing an All-Ireland today.'

Former players and those involved in the Kilkenny set-up remember that at half-time during the game, Fennelly walked onto the field and had a few words with DJ and Brian McEvoy. McEvoy was having a terrific game, but only two points separated the sides at half time. Fennelly asked the two men to swap positions and they agreed, but when the manager turned his back, DJ motioned to the crowd by putting his hands in the air. The manager confided in people afterwards that he got the impression DJ was turning the crowd against him. Certainly, the gesture got the spectators riled up, and there was no shortage of people asking Fennelly afterwards, 'What did you say to Carey at half time?' Some were even heard abusing the manager. There is no doubt that Carey was able to get under Fennelly's skin.

Kilkenny were beaten by Offaly 2–16 to 1–13. Nobody was more devastated than Fennelly, but Carey was overheard in the dressing room telling him, 'It's not the end of the world.' In the *Kilkenny GAA Yearbook* of 1998, Liam Horan said that, at the time of writing, it was possible to label the job of managing Kilkenny as the poisoned chalice of intercounty hurling, as some who might be suitable for the job were turned off by the pressures it brought from fans.

There were several people in the room when Kevin Fennelly went to the Kilkenny County Board after the 1998 final. He had been expected to stay in the Kilkenny job, given his two-year contract, but he had something on his mind. Fennelly asked the board officials to have a word with DJ, as he felt he was not getting the best out of him. He feared Carey's behaviour would have a negative impact on some of the other players. The officials told Fennelly to just 'do the job', insisting that Carey had 'no problem' with him. A source recalls how, before walking away, Fennelly told the county board, 'It's your job now – I'm not doing it.' After just one year, he resigned.

The *Kilkenny People* reported on 16 October, just over a month after the All-Ireland final loss, that a last-minute hitch had left Kilkenny without a Senior hurling manager. 'Incumbent Kevin Fennelly was due to be installed in office for a second term, but it didn't happen. But no one is able to explain why, because all parties involved are singing dumb. The *People* has learned that there was an 11th hour call from Mr Fennelly asking that the Co. Board hold off on making the appointment. Via well connected sources, the *People* learned Mr Fennelly won't take the job on the same terms as last year. He wants more scope and full control of matters relating to the senior panel.'

Years later, in an interview with Pat Nolan published in the *Irish Mirror*, Fennelly alluded to what happened saying, 'I asked a question of the county board that night and they didn't give me the answer I wanted.' Fennelly added, 'I'm never going to discuss what that was, but people often wondered what it was and some people knew, but it didn't suit me, certain things weren't suiting me.' People close to Fennelly knew the real reason he left was that DJ was being allowed to do his own thing. When it came down to it, the county board put their star player ahead of the manager's concerns.

At the time, there was no clear favourite to succeed Fennelly as manager of the Cats, with many potential contenders, including Georgie Leahy, Noel Skehan, Diarmuid Healy and Paddy Johnston, ruling themselves out. Clubs were asked to make nominations for the job. On 13 November, the newspapers reported that the Kilkenny hurling succession stakes appeared to be coming down to a head-to-head between Brian Cody of the James Stephens club and Nicky Cashin of Clara. The clamour for an All-Ireland title was growing stronger every day in Kilkenny, as the team hadn't lifted the Liam MacCarthy Cup since doing the double in 1992 and 1993. Wexford, Clare and Offaly had all had a slice of the action in recent years. Kilkenny supporters were growing impatient, but they didn't have long to wait for their golden era, with Brian Cody, Kevin Fennelly's cousin, about to step into the role.

Cody's arrival signalled a new awakening for Kilkenny hurling. In his first season, he tweaked the team that had reached the 1998 All-Ireland final. Some observers thought he lacked the enthusiasm of his predecessor, but others said this was no bad thing. The change also coincided with a massive improvement in DJ Carey's form. The mood in the Kilkenny camp was better, too, since DJ had rediscovered his appetite for the game. He was hungry for goals again and his breakneck speed had returned. He was once more able to turn a game on its head. DJ's intercounty hurling pal, John Power, was back in the panel, and this helped. John, who was a few years older than DJ, was given credit for inspiring his teammates and getting stuck in selflessly to help them.

Another change was that DJ was no longer taking frees and instead focused on his open play. In the days leading up to the 1999 All-Ireland final between Kilkenny and Cork, the *Evening Herald* printed an interview with him, in which Carey explained that when Brian Cody came in, he asked him to bring in someone to hit the frees, 'because I wanted to concentrate on my own way and leave that to someone else'. Cody brought in a new young star for this – Henry Shefflin. DJ said this meant that, instead of going out every night for an hour or an hour and a half practising frees, 'you can actually spend that time putting the ball over the bar on the run, hitting penalties, scoring goals and doing other things'. He revealed that taking a free was not an easy thing, especially not in Croke Park on a big day.

All-Ireland hurling final day came around on Sunday 12 September. Expectations were high in Kilkenny, but the terrible pain of the previous year's loss to Offaly was felt all over again, when the Cats lost out by a single point, 0–12 to 0–13. There were tears in the eyes of many Kilkenny players when they got off the train for their homecoming a day later. As DJ disembarked in MacDonagh Station in Kilkenny, supporters loudly chanted his name, before his son, Seán, was passed into his arms. The players swallowed hard as they boarded the open-top bus for the trip through the city to wave at their heartbroken fans. 'All we can do is put our chins up and go on, hopefully come back next year with the MacCarthy Cup,' Brian Cody remarked, as published in the following day's *Irish Examiner*. A photograph of a sombre DJ holding Seán appeared in the same report, with the caption quoting Carey: 'We will be back, as long as we all stay together and there is no reason why we shouldn't.'

There is nothing like a good homecoming parade after an All-Ireland win in Kilkenny, but when there is no cup it is more like a funeral. Players drown their sorrows and go through the motions. The pain and sorrow are visible, the smell of drink is strong in the air. Bishop Laurence Forristal told the crowd gathered for the 1999 homecoming that the last time Kilkenny lost a two in a row was 1945 and 1946, 'but they came back in '47, to beat Cork by a single point in the final. Wouldn't that be justice next year?'

In 2000 Kilkenny were going for the worst kind of three in a row, having lost the previous two finals. The tension around the city and county was palpable, with fans terrified at the prospect of DJ and the boys making the wrong type of history. They feared Offaly might snatch victory in the first All-Ireland hurling final of the new millennium. On the streets of Kilkenny they talked about the weather, the price of cattle – anything but the match.

The Hurling Team of the Millennium had been chosen earlier that year, selected by former presidents of the GAA, and included Offaly's Brian Whelahan, DJ's great rival and contemporary, but not DJ. This was a sore point with Kilkenny fans, who believed DJ was carrying the can for the defeats in the 1998 and 1999 All-Ireland finals. Some thought an injustice was done, that DJ was robbed and that he had earned his place on that special team. Rev. Martin Ryan of Muckalee, County Kilkenny, was seventy-one years old when he penned a letter to the *Kilkenny People* about the decision. 'I have never seen a hurler as skilful as D.J. Carey. Neither have I seen a hurler as unselfish as D.J. I have never seen a hurler like D.J. Carey, who, under severe pressure, can be so totally aware of the availability of a colleague and lay on a perfect pass for him. Have you ever seen a hurler scoring goals with the magic of D.J.? Have the Millennium selectors done [an] injustice to D.J.?' All fifteen of the players who made the Team of the Millennium featured on An Post stamps. Four of them were from Kilkenny: DJ's granduncle Paddy Phelan, Lory Meagher, Jim Langton and Eddie Keher.

This all meant that DJ was very much in the spotlight in the run-up to the 2000 final. Far from keeping a low profile, as might have been the case with another player, he appeared at the Kilkenny media night in Langtons, where he spoke at length. Kieran Shannon of the *Sunday Tribune*, who was there, reckoned that DJ might have even more to say if pressed, so he went up to him quietly afterwards. Lo and behold, DJ gave Shannon an hour-long, one-on-one interview at his home place in Gowran the next day. Given the intense pressure on him in the circumstances, why did he do it? Nobody would have blamed him for turning it down, Shannon concluded. In fact, many a manager would have insisted that DJ not touch the media with a bargepole ahead of the 2000 final. But DJ was an obliging individual. Sometimes he didn't know when to say no. Was it that he lacked a mentor he could trust, someone who'd look out for him? Someone who would occasionally say no on his behalf? Or did he quietly crave the limelight at all costs?

After days of torture for Kilkenny hurling fans, Sunday 10 September arrived, and Brian Cody's men were hell-bent on a win. Fans watched as DJ raced through for the opening goal inside the first six minutes, and that was that. As the Offaly manager, Pat Fleury, remarked afterwards, 'that goal was worth more than just three points to Kilkenny'. In the closing stages that afternoon, DJ lost his footing and fell on his back as a teammate was passing him the ball. He still managed to catch the ball, jump up and put it over the bar. 'And it wasn't that he was showing off,' as Enda McEvoy noted. 'He never played to the gallery. It was simply that he was able to do things people hadn't seen before.'

After the final, Eamonn Sweeney of the *Sunday Independent* described how even the doubters could give themselves over to sheer admiration of the 'great man'. He described the showbiz elements to DJ's hurling and wrote that Carey had been taken for granted, but on that All-Ireland Sunday his pace suggested he had been propelled from the barrel of a gun. 'He came into the game with a colony of monkeys on his back. Hopefully they'll find good homes.'

After the bitter disappointment of losing two All-Ireland finals in a row, the millennium win was savoured in Kilkenny. Twenty-nine-year-old DJ was named man of the match and proved he was still deadly on the field, especially while on the rampage with young Shefflin. In the aftermath of the 2000 All-Ireland final, the newspapers lapped up DJ's 'solo bonanza', talking about how Kilkenny brushed Offaly aside easily with 'flamboyant skill and awesome finishing'. Did the expectations of fans bring on the pressure that DJ referred to after his brief retirement in 1998? If they did, he didn't admit to it when he was asked how he felt after the victory. He smiled, saying he 'did not feel under any great pressure – it's a great day for us altogether'.

DJ Carey's early goals in All-Ireland finals were one of the things that were crucial to Kilkenny's success. 'It's been forgotten that DJ scored the opening goal in three All-Ireland finals. Kilkenny went on to win all three. Not a coincidence,' explained Enda McEvoy. In the 2002 All-Ireland final against Clare, DJ scored another trademark early goal. Henry Shefflin hit the ball in, and DJ, watching it all the way, diverted it back the other way with a beautiful soft touch, back across Davy Fitzgerald, the Clare goalkeeper, and into the net. It sent out the signal: 'Daddy's here. Everything is going to be okay.'

Yet, despite his incredible success, what DJ craved, more than anything, was to be wanted. On the field, we saw a man who was calm and unflustered, and when in the limelight he exuded confidence. Underneath it all, though, he obsessed about the things people were saying. Others in his place would shrug off these comments, but they mattered to DJ.

3

LIFE OFF THE FIELD

DJ's high profile came from hurling, but it was not a sport that would provide him with a living. His success in handball offered one possible career path, when Wake Forest University in North Carolina offered him a fully paid handball scholarship on their physical education programme. However, DJ didn't give much thought to this, as a permanent move to the United States would have killed his dreams of becoming a Kilkenny hurling hero.

So DJ, like everyone else, had to find a way to make ends meet. He had his part-time job in Dunnes Stores on Kieran Street in Kilkenny city while at school, but once he finished his education, he went straight to work. He was employed briefly as a sales representative with international confectionery company Cadbury. People remember him back then and that they envied his position, as Cadbury was a great company to work for and the world was his oyster. He was only young, but already he had a nice company car.

During the early days of his sales career, DJ met Christine O'Keeffe from Railyard, near Castlecomer, County Kilkenny, after offering her a lift home from a disco in October 1990.

They didn't know each other before that night, despite growing up just twenty-five miles apart. In April 1994, when DJ was twenty-three years old, he got engaged to Christine. The young woman didn't initially have a huge interest in hurling and had never played any sport, although her dad, Pat, would have gone to matches. From her early days dating DJ that changed, and by the time they married Christine could be seen shouting on the sidelines with the rest of the supporters. However, because of his sporting and work commitments, DJ and Christine didn't see as much of each other as they would have liked in those first few years.

DJ's Cadbury career came to an end because of his hurling. He got knocked out in a game against Wexford and was out of work for three weeks after suffering a concussion. His job depended on driving, but for those three weeks he was not allowed to do so. As he explained, 'I was told – politely but firmly – that I either wanted to work for Cadbury or hurl, but that I couldn't have time off every time I got a belt. Fair enough. They were paying my wages.' After he left Cadbury in 1991, DJ moved on to another sales role, this time with MF Kent.

By 1993 he was working for Three Rivers Oil, and it was around this time that he was introduced to the game of golf. The Kilkenny Supporters Club organised a golf classic; a guy called Louis Fitzgerald was looking for a caddie and DJ obliged. He had shown no interest in golf before this, as he didn't see it as a game that was open to people like him. His caddying experience changed this outlook. His first game was with John

O'Dwyer, a former hurler and past captain of Callan golf club. DJ had applied to some clubs for membership but received no response, so when John asked him if he wanted to join Callan, he jumped at the chance. Callan was a nine-hole club back then; when it was being extended to eighteen holes, DJ took advantage of an offer to become a lifelong member. He said the skill level and the satisfaction of the long drive appealed to him. He could drive the ball huge distances. When he first started playing golf in the mid-1990s, he was still training twice a week with Kilkenny and playing matches on Sundays.

After leaving Three Rivers Oil, DJ joined Moynihan & Moynihan in Cork, again in sales. The company sold hygiene products and chemicals, and it was during his time there that DJ got the idea to set up his own business. People were always telling him he should go out on his own, although a few who knew him better than the rest thought this was a mistake. One man, who knew DJ in the early days of his sales career, said he thought people shouldn't have put those ideas into DJ's head. This man said DJ wasn't book smart, so running his own business wouldn't suit him. Former co-workers also noted that DJ, despite his status, struggled to bring in big contracts for some of his employers. They said he wasn't cut out for a nine-to-five job – he had too many other commitments and couldn't be depended on to turn up consistently for his shift.

DJ's employment record shows he had many jobs over the years but didn't stay with any company for a prolonged period. He didn't like being tied down or having to take on the responsibility of full-time work. Yet many of his employers were glad to have somebody like him on the payroll because of his reputation as a sports star, and one of them thought that offering DJ the job secured them a row of seats at the All-Ireland final – he was disappointed to find out otherwise. A former colleague of DJ's thought he should have kept his regular job with Cadbury, the one with the company car and good income, and should have stayed away from going out on his own. This person suggested DJ was seduced by the idea of being a businessman.

In June 1994 DJ set up his own cleaning company, DJ Carey Enterprises Ltd. He supplied toilet paper, paperware and cleaning chemicals to schools, restaurants, factories and pubs. Initially, he concentrated on selling products in his own area and worked from his garage at home in Gowran. As the business expanded, he turned cow sheds on the family farm into warehouses for storage. Other unused buildings on the farm were converted into offices.

His fiancée, Christine, and his family helped him to get the business off the ground in the early days. 'In the beginning, I went to the bank for an overdraft, sold a load of products, and then found I owed a big VAT bill, so I had to go back to my bank manager to see if he would give me another overdraft. I owed money to the VAT man, and that obviously had to be paid. I basically started with no experience of running a business,' he told the *Kilkenny People* as he reflected on the early days of his business in an interview published in January 2004. He also received support from the Kilkenny Enterprise Board in the form of two employment grants. Early into his business growth,

DJ employed Christine, his father, his brother Jack, and his Kilkenny hurling teammate Willie O'Connor.

DJ was twenty-four and Christine was twenty-three years old when they married in Moneenroe church on Thursday, 5 October 1995. The reception for 300 guests was held in Langtons in Kilkenny. There was lots of media attention on the couple, and the *Kilkenny People* ran their wedding photograph on the front page. The newlyweds built a large, detached, two-storey house across the road from DJ's family homestead at Gowran demesne. But between hurling and work commitments, DJ didn't get to spend much time in his new home, being constantly on the road. When he was at home, he could barely peel potatoes, and he never changed a nappy. Christine took care of the everyday things, such as cooking and cleaning, as well as helping him with the day-to-day running of the cleaning business.

The couple welcomed their first son, Seán, in August 1997. The little boy was the first grandchild in the family; local media described him as the 'baby heir for King D.J.' Their second child was born in April 1999, another boy, named Michael ('Mikey'). DJ's mother, Maura, often helped with minding the children while Christine was working in DJ's business. However, sources close to the family recall how Christine was 'never good enough' for DJ in the eyes of his mother. They say that Maura was a hard woman to please and that she gave Christine a hard time.

As DJ's popularity was increasing, he became more involved in commercial deals, and he was much sought-after by corporate

Ireland. He was signed up to work with Guinness from the start of their sponsorship of the Senior Hurling Championship, despite the fact that he never tried the drink or any of their products. He said he loved how they marketed hurling, describing their campaign as 'slick'.

In 1999 there were significant off-the-field developments in the GAA world. The Gaelic Players Association (GPA) was founded after a meeting in Belfast, with the aim of becoming the representative body for players across the island. Several GAA stars readily gave their backing to the GPA, including Armagh's Kieran McGeeney, who said the association was not about payment for players but about looking after players. DJ was also one of those who supported the organisation from the start. He explained his reasons for doing so in his book, emphasising that, for him, it was not about pay-for-play – he thought this would be a 'betrayal of the principles on which the Association is founded'. Instead, he supported a system that recognised the players as the most important people in the association. 'Without them, there are no massive crowds, no big stadiums and no GAA. Generations of players come and go but the principle is the same – at any given time the players are the ones who really matter.'

He also cited a 'bad experience' he had as a player when he was out of work for 'six or seven weeks with a broken leg'. 'For some strange reason, my claim form for insurance got lost a number of times and, in the end, my time to claim had elapsed so I was entitled to nothing. From what I heard afterwards, that sort of thing was rampant around the country, but there were other problems too over gear, travelling expenses, match tickets and even little things like getting into the players' hospitality area in Croke Park after games.' This kind of thing really got under DJ's skin, and he described how he might have played in front of a full house but still only got one ticket into the players' area afterwards, which he found deeply insulting. DJ was aware that the gate receipts from the All-Ireland Championship by 2000 had reached the equivalent of nearly €9m, yet players still found themselves begging for an extra person to be allowed into the lounge.

Less than a year after the GPA's inception, DJ found himself in the middle of a battle between it and Croke Park, which did not officially recognise the association in its early years. It was seen as operating outside the official realm of the GAA, and some feared it secretly wanted to turn the games professional. In April 2000 Carey handed the organisation a massive vote of confidence when he publicly declared his support for it and called on the GAA to meet with the players. 'For me, as a player, I see the GPA as the first step to realism,' he said. The GAA president, Joe McDonagh, claimed that the Kilkenny forward had been pressured into joining the GPA, but DJ strongly refuted this in media reports, saying it would be wrong for people to think he was coerced into membership. On 4 April 2000, the *Evening Herald* reported how Carey's support for the new players' union was 'a huge blow to the Croke Park hierarchy as he had been a high-profile member of their Players Advisory Group'.

The GPA soon became embroiled in a controversy with

the GAA's official agents. 'Players' rift with GAA grows over sponsor deal' was the headline in the *Irish Independent* on 10 August 2000. Grainne Cunningham reported on a controversial £50,000 sponsorship deal between the Marlborough group of recruitment consultants and a group of hurling and Gaelic football stars. When the deal was announced, the players who were at the launch were Brian Whelahan (Offaly), Peter Canavan (Tyrone), Brian Lohan (Clare), Jarlath 'Ja' Fallon (Galway), Brian Corcoran (Cork), Stephen Melia (Louth), Paul Flynn (Waterford) and Derek Duggan (Roscommon). DJ didn't attend, stating years later that the reason he didn't go was that Kilkenny were due to play Galway in the All-Ireland semi-final on the Sunday after the launch, and he reckoned Brian Cody wouldn't have been happy to see him 'perched up at the top table for the launch of a controversial sponsorship deal four days before I was due to tangle with the Galway defence'.

Under the Marlborough deal, to which DJ's participation was seen as central, the players were to receive sums of money in return for four public appearances over the following twelve months promoting the recruitment company. The GAA saw this as an affront to their own endorsement policy, and the rift between the two organisations deepened, with the chairman of the GAA Players' Committee, Jarlath Burns, expressing disappointment after the launch. He doubled down on earlier claims of the GPA being 'elitist' and only representative of 'a greedy minority', saying the sponsorship announcement may have vindicated the GAA in its criticisms. DJ resented the accusations of elitism and greed, saying that in all his years playing for Kilkenny he had only put in travelling expenses for three seasons. 'That was when I was going to Dublin to get treatment from the great AK, Alan Kelly,' he said in his official autobiography.

When DJ and Christine's children were toddlers, and the couple were running the cleaning supplies business together, DJ was travelling long distances, the length and breadth of Ireland, but not just for business purposes. He presented medals to children, gave talks to clubs and officially opened sports facilities. He rarely, if ever, charged for these appearances. There were other hurlers who wouldn't turn up without a minimum appearance fee, but when clubs offered him money, DJ just waved the hand and said the cup of tea was grand. He once said he had enough crystal clocks – when they were all the rage – to open a jewellery shop, and revealed that, while Hurler of the Year in 2000, he made the equivalent of just €1,400 from his sport. At the height of his fame DJ undoubtedly enjoyed the perks – free cars and free trips – but it was still just an amateur sport, so he didn't get a wage from his hurling. American golfers and sports stars who met him found this remarkable.

To the outside world, DJ Carey had it all – natural sporting talent, a supportive wife and two beautiful children. To top it all off, he experienced incredible success in 2000. Not only was he an All-Ireland and Leinster hurling champion, but he also picked up many more accolades, including the Gaelic Writers' Association Hurling Personality of the Year and Eircell Hurler of the Year; by then he had also accumulated a record eight All-Stars. Training under Brian Cody was getting harder than ever, but DJ felt he was in a good place. The GAA was also experiencing a boom in attendance at matches; in *The Munster Express* in January 2001, DJ described the period as a 'golden age for hurling and for the GAA in general in terms of the quality of games played and the rising attendances of recent years, and long may it continue'. Finally, DJ had silenced some of the noise about him not performing in All-Irelands, and things were looking up.

One of the rewards that nobody begrudged the Kilkenny hurlers was their holiday to celebrate the All-Ireland win in 2000. There was a lot of excitement among not just the hurlers but their wives and entourage of supporters. Businesses like Hotel Kilkenny handed over cheques, while supporters raised funds for the well-earned break for the Kilkenny panel and their wives and partners, along with the backroom team. They were joined on the trip by ordinary supporters, who paid their own way.

On Monday, 8 January 2001, just days before the trip, a front-page story under the heading 'DJ nets £115,000 in libel settlements' appeared in the *Irish Examiner*. It stated that Carey had sued both the *Sunday World* and the *Sunday Independent*, claiming he had been seriously defamed. Legal sources told the newspaper that DJ settled the cases for a combined total of £115,000, adding that he was believed to have 'netted approximately £70,000 tax free after legal fees'. 'This means the amateur sportsman DJ earned, from libel cases alone, almost exactly the same amount last year as full-time professional rugby stars Brian O'Driscoll and Ronan O'Gara did through their contracts with the IRFU.'

THE DODGER

So DJ must have been a happy man on 16 January, as he jetted off with the rest of the Kilkenny panel to Thailand for twelve days. The trip was organised by Killester Travel's Sean Skehan, the man who introduced to Ireland the concept of organised golf trips abroad. DJ was described as one of the main instigators of the choice of location for this holiday, as he had already been to Thailand on a golfing trip the previous October. The trip provided a rare chance for him and Christine to spend some time together as a couple, while Seán and Mikey were looked after at home by their granny, Maura. The group stayed for the first couple of nights in Bangkok, followed by a week in the seaside resort of Pattaya.

The trip was a big hit with the victorious hurlers and their supporters. The pressures were lifted and the dark clouds of 1998 were finally dissipating for DJ. There was lots of golf, and in the evenings the group would kick back and relax. The younger hurlers would head to downtown Pattaya, while the older ones mostly stayed around the hotel and its vicinity. Friendly golf competitions had been arranged for some of the group, and one of the main attractions for ordinary supporters going to Thailand was the opportunity to play alongside some of the hurlers. However, they got more than perhaps they expected. One man who was on the trip recalls how DJ got involved in organising the golf, describing him as a 'control freak'. 'Once Carey came in, the prizes all of a sudden were only for hurlers. We were excluded from the competition. He was a bossy fucker.' Another who was there agreed: 'Carey came along and tried to run the show and that was that.'

There are people who distinctly remember spotting a Thai beauty sitting at a table with DJ Carey and Christine during this trip. She was introduced to others in the group as 'Jan', an au pair. The young Thai woman accompanied the Careys home from the trip. One man remembers her sitting on the team bus on the way back. A non-EU national needs a special work permit from the Department of Enterprise before they can apply for an employment visa in Ireland. DJ had organised the visa before the trip, telling a journalist that a young Thai woman would be staying with himself and Christine for a year.

Once the hurlers returned home, word about the au pair spread throughout Kilkenny. The woman was seen on the sidelines at matches. People were asking questions about her, the kind you hear in a small village. Was everything in the marriage okay? Was Christine happy with this new arrangement or did she feel threatened by the arrival of the young woman? 'I think Christine got suspicious and thought maybe DJ was having an affair. She was not happy about this situation at all,' said one woman who recalls those times. There were murmurs that the marriage was in trouble. People presumed the au pair eventually went back to Thailand, as there came a time when she was no longer seen around the village.

Whether or not there is any truth in the rumour that DJ was having an affair with the au pair, it seemed that when the couple returned from the Thai holiday, the marriage was under strain. Stories flew around Gowran about how Christine changed the locks on their house and threw DJ's clothes out of the window. Christine, who had been listed as a director of DJ Carey

Enterprises since its establishment in 1994 and had worked alongside her husband and his family in the cleaning supplies business since then, had her name removed from the company accounts in August 2001. DJ's sister Catriona replaced her. DJ denied his marriage was in trouble, and outwardly the couple appeared to stay together, but there was no doubt that there were signs of a rift at this stage. Otherwise, why would DJ have replaced Christine as director of his company, when she had been involved from the start?

In hurling, months of social functions, illness and injury dominated the first part of 2001 for DJ. In a report in the *Irish Independent* on 11 April, he explained that he expected to be sidelined for four to six weeks because of a dislocated rib sustained in a football match a couple of weeks previously. He said it was aggravated during training with Kilkenny, when he took a 'heavy shoulder and fell in a heap on the ground' but that fans need not fear for his availability for the Leinster Championship clash with Offaly on 10 June. 'This is the first time that I've had any problems with ribs since I played in the 1989 All-Ireland Colleges [for St Kieran's] against St Flannan's,' said Carey, who was ruled out of that Sunday's Allianz League clash with Derry.

At this stage, DJ was a regular at Alan Kelly's Old Bawn physiotherapy clinic in Tallaght, Dublin. Kelly, better known as 'AK', established himself as a physio to the stars, but Carey was one of those he saw most frequently in his practice. A sift through archival materials from the year 2001 shows that most of the headlines about DJ are dominated by illness and injury, and questions of whether he'd be fit to play or not. There's a lengthy list of different injuries mentioned in the reports, from mundane issues, such as flu, to torn ligaments, dislocated ribs and back and neck problems. It was May before he was back on the club scene – in a report published in the *Irish Examiner* on 11 May, he said, 'I have been back in training a week but, having been out for six weeks between flus and foot and mouth, I haven't really done much this year yet. I am a bit behind the other lads, I have been doing things with the cup too, which hasn't helped, at functions and things. It's good to be back in training, though.'

DJ's struggle to regain fitness was documented in the newspapers on 5 June, just ahead of the start of the championship. Reports stated that Kilkenny would have to make plans without their 'scoring ace' for the Leinster hurling semi-final against Offaly in Croke Park. 'Carey is struggling with an ankle injury and it will be much later in the week before his state of fitness can be established,' stated a report in the *Irish Examiner.* Yet DJ told journalists at a launch by Guinness promoting a 'summer of giants' ahead of the hurling championships that he was fit and raring to go for 10 June.

DJ and Kilkenny supporters knew that, after their success in 2000, they had a target on their backs. Although DJ had missed the league, he said he was still 'mad' for hurling. 'You don't get to live too long on the success you have in Kilkenny. It is all right to win one All-Ireland, but you have to move on from that. If the ambition is not high, you are going nowhere.' After intensive treatment, he did play a part in Kilkenny's Leinster

Championship victory over Offaly, but on 26 June Martin Breheny wrote on the front page of the *Irish Independent* sport section that Kilkenny had 'fresh worries' about his fitness after he limped out of a club match the previous weekend.

A month later, fans held their breath again when he received what appeared to be a serious head injury. Medical attention was sought from the sideline and a stretcher was brought onto the pitch. A newspaper report in the *Irish Examiner* on 17 July said that DJ lay on the ground for a 'full eight minutes and the greatest cheer of the evening was heard from supporters of both sides when he walked to the side-line after recovering'. He appeared heroic to the fans when he got to his feet and managed to walk off the pitch.

Despite having been dogged by niggling injuries for months, DJ lined out in the 2001 All-Ireland hurling semi-final against Galway. The Tribesmen dominated the game from start to finish, and even a late consolation goal by DJ couldn't make a difference on the day, with Galway sending Kilkenny out of the championship. DJ and his teammates felt deflated after that match, and they noticed how badly the loss was felt by Brian Cody. It was the 'best and the worst of years' for Kilkenny, as Barrie Henriques described it in the *Kilkenny GAA Yearbook*. Hurling fans had been left wondering if their season would ever get under way with the arrival of foot-and-mouth disease in the country. After a slow start, the defending All-Ireland champions had retained their Leinster title for a fourth consecutive season, but they didn't manage to get the one that mattered most. The 2001 silverware went to Kilkenny's arch-rivals and neighbours Tipperary, who beat Galway 2–18 to 2–15 in the final.

The following November, DJ revealed on Radio Kilkenny that he had suffered injuries in a car crash some months earlier. The time frame of the car accident is confusing, as a later report stated that it happened before the All-Ireland semi-final, while others say it happened 'in the autumn'. But the first mention of the incident in the public domain was in that November interview. Kilkenny supporters were shocked, particularly when, the next day, a newspaper reported that a cloud hung over the attacking ace's future hurling career. There had been very little talk of DJ since Kilkenny crashed out of the championship some months earlier, but now he was back in the headlines. Inconsistencies in DJ's accounts of what happened have led to doubts among some Kilkenny journalists as to how truthful DJ was about this collision in his radio interview, but several newspaper reports from the period refer to the injuries he sustained.

The Wednesday after the Radio Kilkenny exclusive, the *Irish Independent* ran a story entitled 'Carey squashes rumours', giving more information about the injuries he suffered. In the piece, Paddy Hickey reported that DJ hoped to play in some part of the 2002 National League but was suffering from a 'combination of a neck and back injury sustained in a car crash some months ago'. DJ told Hickey, 'I had an MRI scan which showed there was a prolapsed disc in my neck [one disc lying on another], and I'll be having a second scan in January to see if the discs have settled and gone back into place.' He elaborated on how he was experiencing 'a bit of discomfort when driving and sleeping but I can walk around without any problem'.

Hickey also reported that Carey had not 'picked up a hurl in anger' since Kilkenny were beaten by Galway in the All-Ireland semi-final. 'Obviously I'll have to wait until after Christmas to learn how the injury is improving, and that should give me an idea of when I'll be able to resume hurling. I'm quite optimistic about the situation, and perhaps too much has been made about the injury,' DJ continued. He went on to explain that the Radio Kilkenny interview had been to discuss the GPA AGM, and 'it just happened that my injury came up for discussion on the programme'.

At the time, Brian Cody seemed optimistic about DJ's health, saying the championship would not start until June and 'hopefully DJ will be fully back in harness well before then'. In January 2002 the Kilkenny boss held a team talk in the science lab of Kilkenny CBS after a training session, where he took most of the responsibility for the Galway defeat. DJ recalled how Cody's words made the hairs on the back of his neck stand up. As a leader who had publicly blamed himself for the Galway defeat, DJ knew the manager was now 'in a position to demand anything from us'. From the start of 2002, the training sessions intensified, with the players' performance in training determining who would make the starting fifteen.

Talk of how the injuries DJ sustained in the previous year's crash threatened his future was the focus of a *Sunday Independent* story by Dermot Crowe in late February. Crowe discussed how, if 2001 was a huge anti-climax, 'then his current concerns place it in softer focus. For weeks there has been growing, and not entirely wild speculation that his career may be under threat. An injury arising from a car accident last autumn could eventually force him to quit. The accident has caused Carey ongoing discomfort to his neck and back and he claims to experience frequent "pins and needles" sensations along his arm. Pain affects him most when in bed and driving and he hasn't trained since the diagnosis was made last October.'

There was talk of the prolapsed disc, which might need surgery, but that was the 'final option on his priority list as it will almost certainly end any hopes of him hurling for Kilkenny this season. Already, it seems he will miss the entire league.' According to Crowe, when contacted, Carey said he had visited a specialist at the Blackrock Clinic, who instructed him to begin light training over a period of eight weeks. 'If he comes through that unscathed, and without discomfort, then he may have a chance of making the championship squad.' Kilkenny's physical trainer, Mick O'Flynn, who had worked with DJ since 1991, said that his ability to come back from injury depended on his 'mental approach' and whether or not he was 'determined enough'. He said Carey was 'blessed' with the attributes of a top athlete.

Hints were dropped throughout the spring of 2002 about a DJ comeback, as he told reporters he was able for light jogging, 'a bit of golf' and could hit the sliotar without any problems. On 23 April, another story was published about his bid to return to intercounty hurling. This time, it was reported in the *Irish Examiner* that his return 'may be dependent on him gaining relief from a neck injury through occasional cortisone injections'. The report stated that he had been attending a specialist, who was encouraging him to 'go back and do as much as he could'. 'There is no question of him returning to training with Kilkenny, with manager Brian Cody having said he is not in their plans for the June 9 championship game with Offaly in Thurles. He hopes to train with Gowran and play a few club matches, but he says he can only be given a limited amount of cortisone. "If two a year allows me to play hurling, that will be super."'

DJ's recovery suffered a setback when, at the end of April, he was admitted to St Luke's Hospital in Kilkenny. It was reported at the time that he was suffering with stomach pains and was diagnosed with an inflamed appendix, which he had to have removed. In an interview with Vincent Hogan in the *Irish Independent* about his future with the Cats, DJ tried to explain his position, which was that he couldn't see himself returning, but he would 'never say never'.

By the end of June, DJ had publicly ruled himself out of the championship. The *Irish Independent* reported him saying, 'I'm not fit enough to play at intercounty level' and adding, 'I'm not hungry enough either.' He had played in two club championship matches but was unhappy with his performance. 'In fairness, I've missed seven months of training at this stage and so felt I was not in good enough shape to be part of a Kilkenny panel and give it what is required to win an All-Ireland title.'

Carey's absence was a huge talking point in Kilkenny, with hurling supporters fearing he might never play for the county again. Brian Cody, however, said DJ was still only thirty-one, and he saw no reason why he did not have another three or four years of top-class hurling in him. The report stated that 'Carey's woe [sic] began with a car collision last October which left him unable to do any winter training. Just when he was getting back in action he had to have his tonsils removed six weeks ago and that virtually killed off any chance he had of regaining match fitness.' It is interesting that this report claimed he had had his tonsils out, where others stated he had had his appendix removed.

The many different accounts of illness and injuries documented in the newspapers in 2002, with frequently conflicting details, make it hard to get an accurate picture of what exactly was happening with his health. At the time, most people didn't have any reason to doubt DJ's accounts of suffering various health issues and injuries, although there were some people who would raise eyebrows or scoff when they heard about his latest setback. A senior Kilkenny GAA source told this author that DJ was always 'prone to the dramatics', so it was sometimes hard to tell which parts of his stories were true and which were exaggerated. The source, however, pointed to the fact that some of the hurler's injuries were believable, given the amount of training and matches he took part in, and also how many miles he was driving weekly for work.

DJ's future with Kilkenny hurling may have looked bleak, but Brian Cody was undeterred. Six weeks before the All-Ireland semi-final, DJ's phone rang. It was Brian Cody asking if he would come back and train. When DJ reminded the manager that he hadn't trained since the county final the previous November, Cody replied, 'If it doesn't work out it doesn't work out, but if it does, we'd love to have you as some part of the panel or team if you're able to get that far.' Carey agreed and trained 'reasonably hard', but he was still surprised when he got a starting position for the clash with Tipperary. However, Cody must have known his presence on the Kilkenny team would have an important psychological impact on the opposition because he brought the 'DJ factor', which meant the crowds reacted differently when he was there. There was also the media interest it caused and talk of Carey's presence threatening to 'dethrone Tipp'. Despite this, it was a bold move for Cody; his reputation was at stake as he was parachuting Carey in ahead of other players who had trained hard all year, but he knew Kilkenny needed the win. He couldn't risk a repeat of what happened in the 2001 semi-final.

Writing in the *Irish Examiner* ahead of the 2002 match, Jim O'Sullivan said that 'without doubt, the inclusion of DJ Carey in Kilkenny's attack for the second of the Guinness Hurling Championship semi-finals in Croke Park on Sunday places their challenge in a very different light. There is no certainty that it will help guarantee them victory, but it promises to considerably enhance their chances of beating holders Tipperary.' However, O'Sullivan acknowledged that questions had been asked about DJ's match fitness and his physical fitness, given his 'much-publicised lay-off'. 'His selection may seem a gamble, and even possibly disruptive in the sense that he has leapfrogged over panel members who have been involved all year.'

Were there times when DJ's special treatment caused a

wedge between him and the rest of the team? While the other Kilkenny players had been training hard, DJ had spent much of the season doing media appearances, yet now he was able to take a starting position on the team with just six weeks' training behind him. If some of the players were more than aware that they needed DJ to score goals up front, especially if they were to win the All-Ireland, others were hurting because the usual rules didn't seem to apply to their famous teammate.

Carey's return not only divided opinion in the squad but among the Kilkenny public too. Contributors rang Radio Kilkenny comparing DJ to Roy Keane. In a subsequent interview in *The Sunday Times* in May 2003, DJ recalled how listening to the radio discussion made him feel: 'It wasn't nice what went on. "DJ Carey should be sitting in the stand with all the other oldies." DJ Carey is this, DJ Carey is that. Blah, blah, blah and blah, blah blah before we played Tipperary. And yet, after the All-Ireland, it was, "Jaysus, doesn't he have to put up with an awful lot." I was a great fella then you see. "Wow, doesn't he have to put up with an awful lot? Isn't he a great fella to be able to put up with it all and get on? Look at the amount of pressure he was under in an All-Ireland semi-final taking a 65." I've been taking 65s all my life. There's no pressure in that. That's not the pressure in my life.'

In an interview with Dermot Crowe in the *Sunday Independent* published on the day of the All-Ireland semi-final, 18 August 2002, Brian Cody addressed his decision to select Carey. 'Nobody is bigger than the team, especially myself. That's the most important thing. And, to me, the greatest strength that DJ

Carey has always had, in all of my dealings with him, is that in the team context he has never behaved like a superstar. And I didn't feel pressure. He never put demands on me. He never has.'

DJ's performance in the semi-final dismissed any questions about his fitness and justified Cody's faith in him. Kilkenny beat Tipperary 1–20 to 1–16. The win was only their second championship victory over their neighbours and hurling rivals in eighty years. It was their first since 1967 and their second since 1922, and now the Cats were celebrating. A typical headline encapsulating the coverage of the 2002 semi-final appeared in the *Evening Herald* on 19 August: 'Car crash and his appendix out, but it's the same old brilliant DJ'. There can be no doubt that DJ contributed in a significant way to his team's victory, with many observers saying he made the difference on the day. In just six weeks everything had changed, and now Kilkenny had booked their place in the All-Ireland hurling final against Clare.

Only four minutes were gone in that final when DJ Carey found the Clare net. It looked so effortless that he became the story of the championship. The Cats saw off the Banner by 2–20 to 0–19. DJ and Henry Shefflin scored an impressive 2–13 between them, but it was DJ's face on the front pages the day after the final. The front page of the *Irish Independent* pictured him being hugged by a smiling Brian Cody, and he featured on the front of the *Irish Examiner* alongside his two young sons.

In a year that had started with such uncertainty, DJ finished on a high when his club, Young Irelands, won the county final that October. He put in a man-of-the-match performance, scoring 2–7, 2–5 of that from play, all the while being marked by his formidable intercounty colleague Noel Hickey. He would also pick up another All-Star in December. Things were looking up in his hurling life once again, but his home life was not so simple. If DJ Carey's life in 2002 seemed dramatic, with his Lazarus-like recovery before the All-Ireland, in 2003 it was about to mirror a soap opera.

4

DJ THE VIDEO STAR

By late afternoon on Sunday, 12 January 2003, DJ Carey, his teammates, selectors, backroom team and a large group of their supporters were enjoying a welcome barbecue at the poolside in the luxury Cullinan Hotel in Cape Town, South Africa. Golfer and Kilkenny man Gary Murphy was the guest of honour, as he had been in action at the South African Airways Open that weekend. On his final round he was cheered on by DJ Carey. The atmosphere at the hotel was good, with the Dublin and Kerry teams also staying there. Golf was popular with the group, although not everybody played, but DJ, Charlie Carter, Brian McEvoy, Eddie Brennan, Andy Comerford and Henry Shefflin were among those who enjoyed the game. When the holiday came to an end, the players knew they had to brace themselves for their first training session a few nights later.

Since his dramatic return to Kilkenny after the string of injuries the previous season, DJ had played only three intercounty games before he was in bother again. 'The DJ Carey injury jinx has struck again' is how Brendan Larkin described the situation in the *Irish Examiner* on 4 March. He stated that the thirty-one-year-old had broken a finger in a weekend challenge match between his club, Young Irelands, and All-Ireland club finalists Birr. Brian Cody took it in his stride, saying, 'This is a setback for DJ, but this bad luck could be an opportunity for another member of the panel.' Carey's broken finger was supposed to rule him out of any hurling action for six weeks, but he was back by the end of the month, in time for Kilkenny's league match against Clare.

As it happens, the injury allowed him to spend twelve days on a promotional tour of Calcutta with charity organisation GOAL. His return to hurling was exciting, with newspapers reporting that he had only arrived back in the country 'hours' before throw-in at Nowlan Park. The *Kilkenny People* reported on 28 March that, 'After touching down in Dublin, Carey dashed to Nowlan Park and made himself available for the All-Ireland final repeat. He wasn't called into action but was togged out with the rest of the squad.'

DJ's life outside hurling had never been busier. By 2003 the Celtic Tiger was roaring and he was enjoying a whirlwind of trips abroad, launches, events and ribbon cuttings at new car showrooms. In February he lent his name and full backing to the 'DJ Carey School of Hurling' officially launched by Nickey Brennan, then chairman of the Leinster Council. A report in the *Offaly Independent* stated that the venture had been given a 'huge boost' by Carey's involvement: 'He intends to have a significant input into the School of Hurling during the two weeks. It will be run in St Kieran's College, Kilkenny, on a residential basis during July 15th–18th and July 22nd–25th.'

The idea behind the programme was to nurture the hurlers of the future, and DJ was instrumental in attracting interest in the school and getting it off the ground. He was a role model for thousands of up-and-coming hurlers around the country, and his name carried significant weight.

His star continued to climb. DJ's video/DVD was launched in May 2003 by none other than An Taoiseach Bertie Ahern. The event took place at Citywest Hotel in Dublin and *DJ: The Story and The Skills* was sponsored by the Irish Agricultural Wholesale Society (IAWS), whose chief executive, Philip Lynch, was a friend of the player's. An appearance on *The Late Late Show* and a visit to Aras an Uachtaráin followed.

While DJ was enjoying great success in early 2003, he was still obsessing over the rumours that continued to circulate about him and, at times, his paranoia came across in media interviews. In many of the interviews, his focus shifted to earnings or, more accurately, to the lack thereof, despite the huge sacrifices he had made for the sport he loved.

In 'The Big Interview' in *The Sunday Times* on 11 May 2003, Denis Walsh described these sacrifices, noting how most of DJ's days started closer to 6 a.m. than 7 a.m., with training nights detaining him until after dark. In an average week with DJ Carey Enterprises he drove 1,200 miles, but in a busy week it was over 1,500. While he 'would not like to see the games going professional', he noted how he could see himself 'giving up good time', and although he was happy to do that for the GAA, 'the few bob comes in handy if it's there. My kids don't see me. They might see me of a Saturday. I'll go from Dublin or somewhere to training and they're in bed when I get home. I'm gone most of the time before they get up the following morning. There has to be some reward.' So it was not surprising that when DJ talked about the GPA (of which he was president at the time), he mentioned how it had opened up opportunities for him and believed it could do so for others. 'I'd be hoping that down the road every intercounty player will have a sponsor. That they'll wear a logo for someone and they'll get a few bob. It won't be great, but it might be enough to lay a few bob down on a house. Whatever it is, it'll be something.'

Walsh asked Carey about what the 'knockers' thought of him getting rewarded for the game. 'I can sit back and smile about it. I exaggerate things. You really exaggerate. Exaggerate to the last and it makes it worse for them. Padraig Harrington always says, "If they say you make €100,000 from appearances, tell them, no, you make €200,000." It makes them worse. For me, time moves on. I'm still hurling okay. I'm still going okay, from a popularity point of view. I was never as popular – and I don't mean to be bragging about that. I wouldn't for one minute want to be bragging.'

Significantly, this interview seems to be the first time that DJ publicly addressed rumours that he was suffering from cancer. Walsh brought this up when addressing the whispers that 'persecuted' Carey and 'the epidemic of rumours': 'So many, so sinister, so false. A couple of years ago a story swept the southern half of the country that he was dying of cancer. He knows how it started. Suffering from stomach pains he was sent to hospital in Waterford for tests. The tests took place in the same area of the hospital that housed the oncology facilities. Sitting there he was seen and from such a sighting his cancer was born.' While DJ dismissed any suggestion that he was suffering from the illness, could it be that he fully appreciated the depth of the public's worry about his health and the power of his profile? He had, after all, been bombarded with questions about whether he had the illness, and it begs the question, is this where the idea to fake having cancer at a later date first came from?

Walsh also harked back to the stories that had started to circulate after the trip to Thailand. 'Every so often it is said that his business is in trouble and every so often it is said that his marriage is over. A couple of years ago Carey and his wife, Christine, brought home an au pair from Thailand, Jan, to mind their two children. Jan returned home nearly two years ago but in the lurid narrative of the rumour the marriage was over and Jan was the co-respondent in the split. The story last summer was that he was living in an apartment in Kilkenny. Untrue. All of it.'

DJ agreed with his assessment: 'You have no idea. You could go out there and say to somebody, "Carey is in here with a woman" and he'll go to the next lad and the next lad. And I won't know that's after happening and my immediate family won't know that's happened until somebody tells them. And who's going to stand up and explain what really happened? Do you understand what I'm saying? So much is happening around you. I've learnt that you're only letting yourself down by trying to deny it. It's as simple as that because you're only walking yourself into it. All you can do is smile and let it over your head.'

Why did people want to put him down? He told Walsh he thought the cause was rooted in jealousy, in his 'success and how visible it is. He was only twenty-three when he started DJ Carey Enterprises, doing a line in cleaning products. He was no fool. He knew he had a name and he had the neck to go it alone. At one time he had 15 people working for him but the operation had grown out of proportion to its prosperity and he was forced to pull back and restructure. Now he employs 9 people, selling nearly 500 different products and business is booming.'

Money came up again when DJ explained that the requests for him to give coaching sessions and present medals never stopped. 'He says he never asked for a fee and whatever he was given only amounted to his expenses: 30 quid, 40 quid, 50 quid in an envelope, or a piece of glass, lovingly presented. Beyond that, though, Carey knew the possibilities. The corporate sector had use for him and his name and his image. When Kevin Moran's sports agency ProActive organised an Irish launch in 1997 [sic] Carey was one of the GAA players to make an appearance. At the time GAA players weren't at liberty to accept payment for endorsements, but his presence was a clear statement of Carey's attitude. Since the GAA relaxed their rules nobody was in a better position than Carey to benefit. He was fielding so many enquiries from companies that six months ago he hired his own PR person, Barbara Galvin [sic]. Shortly, he will appear in a high-profile campaign for McCoy crisps but most of his personal appearances are outside of the public eye: corporate days, product launches, talks, golf events.'

On 23 May 2003, *Kilkenny People* columnist Gerry Moran wrote that he was half expecting to see DJ Carey's face on the back of his cornflakes box because, 'in fairness, DJ has been popping up everywhere of late'. He explained that one reason why DJ was being seen so much – apart from his 'wonderful work with Goal' – was the launch of his new video/DVD. In the same month, DJ also signed a personal deal with sports brand Puma. According to a report in the *Kilkenny People* on 30 May, DJ and Henry Shefflin were the only two hurlers to be part of this, but footballers who signed the same deal were Kieran McGeeney (Armagh), Michael Donnellan (Galway), Dara Ó Cinnéide (Kerry) and Trevor Giles (Meath). The report stated, 'While all sides remain tight-lipped about the terms of the agreement, it is believed the players will receive €2,000 for wearing Puma boots during the championship, and €500 for any personal appearance they might make on behalf of the company.' Carey defended his involvement, saying he had long advocated the need for players to be free to enter into arrangements such as this, and he commended Puma for giving something back to the players.

There were two Kilkenny captains in 2003. DJ's old classmate and fellow Gowran man Charlie Carter was the one who lifted the National League trophy on 5 May and made the presentation speech after a stunning performance. Kilkenny had beaten Tipperary by a point, in what was dubbed a 'smash and grab raid', on a scoreline of 5–14 to 5–13. The issue of the Kilkenny captaincy became a talking point afterwards because Carter wasn't chosen for the starting fifteen, so it was

DJ who led the team out on the field on the day. Charlie was brought on in the second half. In his book, DJ said the media became curious about the 'dynamic' between him and Charlie. 'There wasn't any issue whatsoever between us as far as I was concerned and I presume it was the same for Charlie. He was captain and would lead the team, provided, of course, that he was playing.'

A short time after the league final, both DJ and Charlie attended the launch of the All-Ireland Championship at Croke Park, hosted by Guinness. Captains from the competing counties were there for the photocall, so Charlie Carter was there as Kilkenny captain. DJ explained that he had been involved with Guinness and their sponsorship since 1995, 'so I was at all of their launches over the intervening years'. He said he didn't know if Charlie was surprised to see him at the launch, adding that he did some media interviews there but 'not as Kilkenny captain'. 'Charlie talked to the media as Kilkenny captain. We made no distinction, but I suppose it might have appeared a little odd to anyone who didn't know of my involvement with Guinness.'

DJ said he thought no more of the captaincy until early June, when Kilkenny were preparing to face off against Dublin in Nowlan Park. Carter was not picked for the team, so DJ was back as captain. 'We won easily [3–16 to 0–10] in a game that would be quickly forgotten except for the dramatic fall-out which followed,' said DJ. Carter was left on the bench all evening, and the following week he told the Kilkenny County Board he was leaving the panel. His departure cleared the way for DJ to take over as captain for the rest of the season. DJ claimed that this is when new rumours began. 'Apparently, I was happy to see Charlie go. It was even suggested to me that I should have either withdrawn from the panel as a mark of support to a Gowran teammate or else go to Brian and urge him to ask Charlie back. There was absolutely no way I was going to do either.'

After he lifted the cup following Kilkenny's Leinster final victory against Wexford in July 2003, DJ would apparently be targeted twice in the space of weeks by thieves. He was attending a celebrity golf challenge when his car was reportedly broken into while parked near a Dublin hotel. Valuables including two mobile phones, cash and his golf clubs, including a putter given to him by Tiger Woods at the 2002 AmEx World Golf Championship at Mount Juliet, were reported stolen by DJ. Woods had described how, at a private dinner hosted by renowned businessman JP McManus during the event at Mount Juliet, Carey had shown him how to hurl after presenting him with a hurl and sliotar. Reflecting on the meeting, Woods said, 'It was pretty neat to have DJ explain how he does it. His wrist movement is unbelievable – how fast he's able to move it, even with a hurl in his hand. He's a great guy, a really nice guy.'

On 10 July, Declan Fahy reported in *The Mirror* that Carey was appealing to thieves to return the putter. He wrote that, as well as the set of golf clubs, credit cards, two mobile phones and a 'substantial amount of cash' estimated at around €5,000 had been stolen. A friend of DJ's is quoted in the article, describing the putter as a treasured possession given to him by one of his heroes, and saying that DJ was 'very annoyed' and 'angry' and had 'an awful sore head about it'. The Citroën he had been driving was reportedly parked across the road from the Berkeley Court Hotel at the time of the incident. According to the friend, 'They smashed a passenger window and stole a lot of stuff. DJ [had been] playing golf that day at the Royal Dublin Golf Club and was due to attend a function at the hotel.'

The following month, on Friday 22 August, the newspapers carried a report about a 'Starsky and Hutch'-style car chase that had happened earlier that week, after DJ's 5-series BMW was stolen outside Crookstown service station in County Kildare. He had been on his way back from Dublin for hurling training in Kilkenny when he was targeted. After he filled his three-litre diesel car, he left the keys in the ignition and went into the shop to pay. When he came out, the car was gone. He looked left and spotted the dark-blue BMW speeding up the road. 'Speedy DJ turns the tables on car thief' was the front-page story of the *Irish Examiner*, as journalist Neans McSweeney reported on how the country's leading GAA star proved to be just as worthy an opponent off the pitch as on, when he jumped into an onlooker's car and pursued the thief in a chase that soon involved garda cars and a garda helicopter. She said the story ended with Carey catching up with the thief and pulling him from the BMW; however, the culprit eventually got away. 'The hurling star managed to recover his car but several mobile phones, as well as €2,500 in cash were taken. The culprit was still on the run last night.'

Colourful details soon emerged of how DJ jumped into the

car of a man waiting for his brother, and the good Samaritan followed the escaping BMW while DJ phoned gardaí. 'The Gardaí followed us for a while and then took over. But the thief put the boot to the floor and we lost him. The car was reported driving erratically around Clane a few minutes later and four or five garda cars joined in the chase. But he must have gone to ground because he escaped them,' Carey said. DJ phoned his sister Catriona, who picked him up after the initial car chase. However, instead of heading straight for home and leaving the investigation to the gardaí, they decided to try one last time to locate the car. 'We said we'd drive around for a while, to see if we could see the car. We went up around Celbridge and I spotted it. I saw a fella trying to get into my car. When he saw me, he made a run for it.

'He wasn't going to out-run me. I caught up with him and gave him a bit of a scare. I had him [pinned down] when another car pulled up beside us. I thought they were going to help me but it turned out to be an accomplice's car and he jumped in. I tried to get the keys out of their ignition, but they drove away. When you have a €50,000 car under you, you fight for it. Thankfully though, they didn't get a lot of valuables which were in the car.'

In a follow-up interview after the incident, McSweeney offered further details. Under the heading 'Top Cat DJ Carey is selling the car he risked his life to save after it was stolen from outside a garage in Kildare this week', she described how the car chase ended with DJ pinning the thief to the ground in Celbridge over three and a half hours after it all started. DJ recounted how he had left his Citroën in for a service, which was why he was driving the BMW. He mentioned how he had put the BMW up for sale, as there was no point in him having two cars. 'It's a fairly famous car now and if anyone wants to buy it, it is for sale. It would have been an absolute killer if it was burnt out somewhere. You don't know what will happen with insurance if you leave keys in it and it was robbed and burnt out. My insurance was on the other car and I had transferred it, but I didn't want to lose anything. At the end of the day, all these things can be replaced.'

In this interview, DJ made a reference to how a lot of people, including Brian Cody, were worried that 'if someone had pulled a knife or something, I'd be out of the All-Ireland'. DJ confessed that he had missed a training session on the Wednesday night because he had no car to get there. He described how his teammates reacted to the news. 'When I announced at training that my car had been stolen, there were a few sniggers. People didn't really believe it. I'm sure I'm in for a bit of sneering on Monday night.' Were DJ's teammates sniggering because they thought he was trying to get out of training and didn't believe his elaborate story? It seems that not everybody was prepared to take him at his word, even then.

Before the interview ended, DJ said, 'We all work hard enough to put things under us. Money doesn't grow on trees. My livelihood was invaded by this guy. I built up a bit of adrenaline and it would have been a different scenario if he stood up and fought. He ran. I don't think too many were going to outrun me in the situation. Even though I missed training, I got a bit of exercise in running after this guy.'

On Friday 22 August, the *Irish Independent* ran a front-page story about the car theft under the heading 'DJ the have-a-go hurler gives car thief some stick'. Sarah Murphy reported that the Kilkenny captain 'gave chase and recovered his BMW worth €50,000. The thief got away with €2,000 and two mobile phones that DJ had in the car. But the Cat got the cream. He had a €3,000 watch and €4,000 cash in the boot which the thief knew nothing about.' The good Samaritan who helped him chase the thief was named as Leonard Kinsella. 'They set off after the thief in Mr Kinsella's Jaguar. They kept the BMW in their sights as it manoeuvred in and out of lanes of traffic along the Naas dual carriageway at speed. The gardaí were alerted and they followed behind. A Garda helicopter was also involved in the chase but they lost the car thief after 20 miles at Kill, Co. Kildare.' In this story, DJ again explained how he resumed his hunt with Catriona, and how they spotted the BMW in Celbridge, but there was no mention of him running after or pinning down the thief. The report simply stated that 'the thief sped off with accomplices in another car'.

There are a number of discrepancies in the different accounts DJ gave to reporters after the theft, and there was no explanation offered as to why he left the keys in the ignition of a €50,000 car, or why he was keeping valuables in the boot. Rumours circulated in Kilkenny that he had cash in the boot from the sale of All-Ireland tickets, but this was never confirmed by Carey.

Three months after the high-speed chase, on 27 November 2003, a twenty-one-year-old man was jailed for five months and banned from driving for five years in Waterford District Court over the incident. The *Irish Independent* reported that cocaine and heroin abuser John McGrath, a father of one from Birch Drive, Birchwood in Waterford, pleaded guilty to stealing the car and cash from outside the Crookstown Motors service station on 20 August. Initially, he pleaded not guilty to the offences but later changed his plea. On Friday 28 November, the *Evening Herald* reported the sentencing of McGrath. It stated that the man had 'hopped into the Kilkenny hurler's five series BMW, containing €20,000 cash, and raced it around the midland counties while chased after by the star'.

Interestingly, this court report shows that, once again, there were discrepancies in how much money was supposed to have been in the car. Earlier reports stated that Carey had €4,000 cash in the boot, but now the court was told there was €20,000 in the car when the thief 'raced it around the midlands'. The facts surrounding what had happened with the car theft are difficult to substantiate when there are so many conflicting accounts and rumours, and the interviews that add to this confusion came from DJ himself. Was he exaggerating the story about running after the car thief and pinning him down to appear more heroic? It seems odd that, if he did pin him down as he claimed, the assailant still got away.

DJ always gave the impression he was a 'salt of the earth' type of guy, but sometimes the details of his stories simply did not add up. He clearly embellished stories about his life, something that people who knew him well often joked about. Perhaps this explains why so many sources for this book described him as a 'Walter Mitty', the kind of man who escapes his ordinary life through fantasies. People who regularly came into contact with DJ knew he didn't always tell the truth.

The car chase was not the only drama in DJ's life that summer. He and his wife had separated, and the press were hungry to confirm the story. The split was old news in Gowran, but locals were tight-lipped and wouldn't comment on what was happening, despite some journalists being dispatched from Dublin to substantiate the news. There was a flurry of interest in DJ's private life because he was a commodity – his name or photograph on the front pages could sell newspapers. Speculation was rife that, come the day of the All-Ireland hurling final between Kilkenny and Cork, a national newspaper would run a story about the break-up of DJ's marriage.

It was actually on Friday, 12 September 2003, two days before the big match, that the *Irish Mirror* ran with the headline 'Broken Hearts; Hurling Star DJ and Wife Christine Split Up'. The *Evening Herald* published a story on the same day covering the backlash in Kilkenny against 'prying media reports'. It stated that furious local GAA officials were slamming stories that Carey was living apart from his wife and were seething over what they called 'dirty tricks', just forty-eight hours before the All-Ireland showdown. Journalist Ralph Riegel wrote: 'The Cats – who are bidding to equal Cork's record number of All-Ireland wins on Sunday – are now deeply concerned of the impact the story will have on their star player and on team preparations.' There was no official comment by the Kilkenny County Board, but one of the members stated, 'We're having our final workout today and we're due to travel with the panel to Dublin tomorrow. This is an appalling thing to do to DJ, his family and all of Kilkenny.'

One of the most impactful stories was published in the *Sunday Independent* on the day of the final, 14 September. Every detail had been carefully verified by the journalists, Jerome Reilly, Jimmy Guerin and Liam Collins, who had spent a lot of time fact-checking. Nonetheless, there was still a major discussion in the newsroom before the story went to print, and the newspaper was braced for a hostile response from Kilkenny if things didn't go the Cats' way in Croke Park. There was some concern over the front-page photograph accompanying the story, which showed a devoted Christine hunkered down in their family home in Gowran reading to the couple's two boys, Michael (4) and Seán (6), who were in their hurling gear. A separate image of Carey on his own featured on the left-hand side of the front page with the main story. Many thought this was a step too far, and the intrusion into DJ's private life and the photograph of his children would anger readers. It was a risky call by the then editor, the late Aengus Fanning, given the stature of Carey at the time.

The strapline of the story gave away the main source: '"Everybody knew about the break-up," says his sister'. DJ's sister Catriona was handling his media affairs by then, and she had spoken to the *Sunday Independent* about the break-up. In response to a question asking whether DJ was thinking of pulling out of the match, she said, 'I have no idea where all these stories are coming from. He is grand. I don't want to talk about it anymore.' But she continued, 'If he's there, he's there. There have been so many stories, even I don't know what to believe,' she said. 'Everybody knew about the break-up.'

In the newspaper's comment and analysis pages, journalist Jerome Reilly gave more details about the end of DJ and Christine's 'seven-year marriage'. The story stated that around the time Carey had prematurely retired in 1998, before changing his mind, there had already been talk of marriage difficulties. 'At that time there were rumours that the Careys were working hard at overcoming difficulties and this may have had something to do with his initial decision to quit.' According to Reilly, the marriage had actually broken down eighteen months before the 2003 final but the couple did not want it aired in public. 'It is a fact the dogs on the street knew that there had been a breakdown in the couple's relationship for a very long time. It's sad but it happens to thousands of couples every year.'

Reilly also said that DJ's captaincy of Kilkenny, his standing as one of the greatest players of all time, and the high profile that he had 'fostered and encouraged and benefitted from financially' had made him a public figure, open to scrutiny. He pointed out that it was unprecedented for a GAA player to get the same treatment as a multimillionaire premiership footballer. 'But Carey is the David Beckham of Gaelic games, albeit with neither an army of agents and PR people spinning on his behalf, nor any multimillion euro deals to soften the intrusion into his private life.'

The journalist went on to note that if hurling was DJ's life – and it was – he had a canny ability to make it pay, and pay lucratively. He described how DJ's image was emblazoned on hundreds of bus stops in Dublin that week as part of an advertising campaign for McCoy's crisps costing tens of thousands of euro. DJ was being promoted as 'The Real McCoy'. To be fair to the hurler, though, while he made some money from commercial sponsorship deals, the sums were not remotely comparable to what English footballers were getting from global brands. At the time, top GAA stars were likely to get around €500 from a company for a public appearance, not the thousands of euro people might assume they got.

Also discussed in this article was the fact that DJ Carey had been the subject of vicious rumours in the past, 'including a story that swept the country that he was terminally ill with cancer'. People had heard or had been told he had a terminal illness, but it was not clear where those stories came from. Who would say somebody had cancer, when they were fit enough to play in an All-Ireland final? While people were talking about DJ going for tests and battling cancer, the source of the rumours was unknown.

The *Sunday Independent* piece stated that officials in Kilkenny had been 'incensed' by the media coverage in the forty-eight hours before the final, with some going as far as to imply it was 'blatant sabotage' of Kilkenny's campaign to equal Cork's record. Reilly rubbished these claims, calling them nonsense. 'The truth is that today's All-Ireland final was just the catalyst. The story [about the separation] has been around for months, years actually. It became public when media organisations finally decided to cover it. Journalists have been scouring Kilkenny for at least two weeks now, talking to people willing to talk, talking to those who have been whispering behind the player's back for ages now.'

Despite these protestations, there was a sense of relief in the *Sunday Independent* newsroom when Kilkenny beat Cork by three points on a scoreline of 1–14 to 1–11. There was also relief that DJ played that day, as otherwise fingers may have been pointed at journalists for everything going wrong. For DJ, it was a moment he had always dreamt of – accepting the Liam MacCarthy Cup as captain of Kilkenny in Croke Park. It was his second time as captain, but the previous time, 1997, had been an unsuccessful year for Kilkenny. So, as he accepted the honour, he should have been feeling on top of the world, but instead he was bothered by thoughts of those who believed he should not have been captain. In his book, he wrote, 'I knew there were those … who felt I should have refused the greatest honour that can be bestowed on a county player.'

DJ liked to control things, on and off the field, and he didn't like the media intrusion into his private life in 2003. Relations had, up until that point, been mostly cordial, with DJ answering journalists' calls regularly and rarely saying no to an interview request. In his book, he stated that 'courting publicity was never my thing', but he was 'always co-operative with sports journalists as I felt I had a responsibility to promote hurling'. Carey made his feelings known about the media coverage of his marital breakdown in an article by Tom Humphries in *The Guardian* on 4 October. 'The whole business,' he said, 'was coming down to what they would write if I didn't tell my side of the story. What they could threaten me with. What came out eventually wasn't what I was being threatened with. Things are going through a legal phase at the moment so I can't go into too much detail.' He said he diverted his phone to his office so he could stay focused on his hurling in the run-up to the final.

Humphries reported that DJ's sister took calls and was 'widely misquoted'. 'In the end, I looked at it all in terms of if somebody went with a story and they had one fact wrong, they were going to pay.' DJ sent legal letters to newspapers, and 'there was widespread talk of boycotts of the newspaper most commonly mentioned in connection with the business. On the Sunday morning they backed off. Carey had sent a hurling ball down the wolf's neck.' DJ continued, 'You sit and wonder is this what people are paid to do? Going after as much dirt as they can, no matter who it hurts or what it hurts. I have two children. Adults will get over this in time; it's my kids who are going to be hit with stuff. It's not right.'

After the break-up, and even after their divorce in 2004, DJ remained friends with Christine as they co-parented their boys together. But people who know DJ well pause whenever they're asked about his friendships. Apart from Christine, who were his closest friends? The answer is usually the same. He spent a lot of time on his own. He had a wide circle of associates – hurling people, handballing friends, people he played golf with, businesspeople – acquaintances you might call them, but not lifelong friends. As a non-drinker, he rarely went to the pub, and this put some distance between him and some of the other players at times. He preferred to hang out with older, retired hurlers, rather than his own teammates. On a rare occasion when the Kilkenny hurlers hit the town, there was no shortage of glamorous women vying for their attention, but DJ was sensible. The only time he ever drank was once, when he had a temperature and he wolfed down a hot whiskey. He said drink played no part in his upbringing, which is probably why he never liked pubs. A brandy was once kindly offered to him when he was sick, and his response, which seemed uncharacteristically mean, was, 'If I wanted piss, I'd drink my own.'

He clearly did have some close friends, however, as in his book DJ described why these friendships mattered to him: 'I have good friends, people who I trust and who I know are there because they are genuine. I regard friends as people who are always there for you and who don't judge you. They understand what you're about and accept you for what you are. They tell you if they have heard rumours about you because they care. Otherwise, you wouldn't hear what's being said and lies can go unchecked. It's the same with me. I would go to a friend and tell them if rumours were flying around about them. I would ask them did they need anything and what I could do to help.'

His best friendship, according to him, was still with his ex-wife. He noted that the separation had been as amicable as possible. 'We arranged our financial affairs without solicitors because we were able to sit down and work through it. We got it legally formalised when we were finished, but it was our agreement, not one drawn up by someone else.'

After his marriage ended, DJ would enter a different world away from the simple pleasures of Gowran, a village where he was protected by the people who loved him.

5

ENTER THE DRAGON

The same year that DJ Carey established his cleaning supplies business, 1994, his future girlfriend had just set up a venture of her own. Sarah Newman, later of *Dragons' Den* fame, was twenty-five years old and had not completed a secondary school education, but she had a computer and an idea to sell hotel nights to travel agents. Four years later, when Ryanair was selling flights largely by phone from a call centre near Heuston Station in Dublin, Newman claimed she pestered the company to give her a desk at the centre so she could talk to passengers in need of a hotel. Her company, Needahotel.com, was born before Ryanair's own online booking service came on stream, so she was doing something innovative, matching budget passengers with hotel rooms ahead of the posse. Her clients were travel agents and airlines. She operated an online business and also employed around eighty people at the firm's base and call centre in Glenageary, County Dublin. Previously, Newman had worked for GTA, a UK company which sold hotel rooms at wholesale level.

Little was publicly known about Essex-born Newman

before she clapped eyes on DJ Carey. Afterwards, a picture of her emerged as she began to give interviews describing how she had started her travel empire from her bedroom as a single mother picking up the pieces after a divorce. She had two small children, aged three and four, and she was living in a country where she didn't have family nearby and knew just a handful of people. Sarah revealed in media interviews that she met DJ through Barbara Galavan, who had produced the documentary about DJ's life. Former friends of the couple tell stories of how they met, with one saying Barbara introduced the pair while Sarah was viewing a property in Mount Juliet, the golf and hotel resort in County Kilkenny. The exact date they first encountered each other is not known by this author, but it was reported that Carey had hired Galavan as his 'manager' by the end of 2002, so it seems likely that DJ and Sarah began their relationship soon after this.

The couple quickly became known for attending social events and supporting charity fundraisers. In the early days of the relationship, they split their time between Sarah's houses in Dublin, where they mostly lived with her children, and a luxury property in the grounds of Mount Juliet. DJ enjoyed a period of anonymity in Dublin that he hadn't experienced when permanently based in Kilkenny, where everybody noticed his comings and goings.

Even before the media ran the story about DJ's marital breakdown, he was living with Sarah, and they hired security guards for the week of the All-Ireland to deal with possible trespassers. 'We had security guards with us the whole time that week because the threat was we were being followed and we were being photographed and all sorts of stuff was going on,' DJ explained in Denis Walsh's book, *Hurling: The Revolution Years*. 'At the end of the day my marriage had broken up. Whatever they were going to write other than that was libel, and that would be proven down the road,' he continued.

Less than six months after his marital breakdown had been publicised everywhere, a photograph of a smiling DJ and his new millionaire girlfriend was circulated to newspapers showing a sparkling ring on Newman's ring finger. A photographic agency distributed the image of the couple taking part in the launch of the Cappagh Hospital St Valentine's Ball fundraiser at the Portmarnock Links Golf Club. In it, they posed to promote the charity event, but it was obvious the photograph would spark more questions about DJ's private life. Yet he was unimpressed with the media queries that followed about a possible engagement. On 8 February 2004, the *Sunday Independent* ran the picture with a story on how the hurling maestro was maintaining his silence amid reports that he and his new love were engaged. 'I am a public figure on the hurling field. Off the pitch I am a private figure,' he said.

DJ was adamant he did not want to answer questions from journalists on his private life. While appearing as a guest speaker at a 'success and life balance' seminar organised by Motivation for Life in Castletroy, Limerick, in February 2004, he even took the opportunity to lash out at the media coverage. At the event, he angrily criticised the methods of some media who, he said, 'don't give a shit' about getting their stories correct.

A report by Colm Ward about the event appeared in the *Limerick Leader* on 28 February stating, 'In one instance, he said, a Sunday newspaper called him up for a comment and threatened to run a story alleging that he was a wife-beater. On another occasion, an incorrect report that Mr Carey's wife [sic] was worth €30m led to her having to hire personal security.' Carey made these comments to a group of some 150 people. At the time, there was a discussion going on in the public domain about whether the GAA should allow other sports to be played at Croke Park, and DJ also gave his opinion on this when he said, 'I think the GAA should remain in charge of Croke Park, but I think it should be opened up to other sports.'

In March 2004 DJ and Sarah were on the front of the *RTÉ Guide* to promote a new episode of RTÉ's *No Frontiers* programme, which they had co-hosted. This was part of a PR blitz for the programme, and DJ shared details of his living arrangements in the magazine, saying he had set up home with Newman in Mount Juliet. He revealed that he and Sarah were 'very happy' and that relations with his ex-wife were still good. The new couple didn't comment on rumours of an engagement, but on presenting the show in South Africa he said, 'I was delighted to do it and, certainly, this was an opportunity of a lifetime. It was enjoyable, very enjoyable, and it's something I'd like to do again in the future.' DJ certainly didn't need to boost his profile, yet he was now broadcasting details of his new relationship to the nation after his highly publicised marital breakdown.

Soon after Sarah and DJ's relationship came into the

spotlight, stories emerged of how Newman was in the process of selling her company. On Saturday 13 March, social diarist Angela Phelan wrote about how the GAA All-Star and his 'stunning partner' had attended her book launch. In her column, she said that Sarah was 'in the process of selling her IT company for more than €90m'.

While the couple were being snapped at charity and golf events, DJ was conscious of his commitment to Kilkenny hurling. At the start of the season, he had vowed to go 'hell for leather' in the chase for an All-Ireland three-in-a-row. In an interview with John Knox in the *Kilkenny People* in January 2004, DJ said, 'Winning means a lot more to me now than it did years ago.' Despite his stated intentions, he was dropped from the Kilkenny team after missing training the week before the Leinster semi-final against Wexford on 13 June.

In his book, he admitted that he had let the side down 'by putting around greens of the K Club rather than putting in some hard work in Nowlan Park. There had to be consequences.' He was playing at a Pro-Am golf event in the K Club on the day he was due to train with the Kilkenny team. Bad weather had delayed his tee time, so he felt he had no choice but to skip training. 'I phoned Brian Cody and told him I wouldn't be able to make it down that night. Typical of him, he made no fuss. "Right so, DJ." I felt bad about it but what could I do? Besides, it wasn't as if I had a history of dodging training. In fact, I fairly rarely missed a session over all the years.'

On Sunday 13 June, Kilkenny lost in the Leinster Championship for the first time since the 1997 final, with a score of Wexford 2–15, Kilkenny 1–16. 'It was my own fault,' said DJ. 'I had broken the discipline code and, by doing that, may well have cost Kilkenny a place in the Leinster final. Now, instead of preparing for the final and staying on the direct route in pursuit of the All-Ireland three-in-a-row, we were headed for the "back door".' Despite the challenges, Kilkenny managed to reach the All-Ireland final in 2004, where they met Cork. DJ described the second half of that game as a 'total nightmare'. 'The idea that Kilkenny would score only two points in 35 minutes in any game, let alone an All-Ireland final, might look bizarre but that's exactly what happened.' Cork beat Kilkenny by 0–17 to 0–9 in what DJ did not yet realise would be his last All-Ireland final. 'It meant I lost my first [1991] and last [2004] All-Ireland finals – still, I was lucky enough to win five in between.'

While his on-field life may not have been going so well, off-field things were looking rosy. By the time he met Sarah, DJ was an established figure on the corporate circuit. He had played golf with international celebrities and had enjoyed trips abroad. People said his mother, Maura, was happy about his new love match. Locals in Gowran remember when not one but two new Range Rovers would arrive in the village at the weekends, so DJ could spend time with his family. He would drive around in one with his children, and Sarah would arrive in another. However, observers of his relationship thought he sometimes looked out of place next to Newman. Sarah confessed in a radio interview with Ryan Tubridy that she loved 'oil and airplanes and big houses and swimming pools, big hair, big shoulder pads', and she cut a glamorous figure. She had grown up watching *Dallas*, and she liked the comforts that her new wealth brought with it.

In addition to her homes in Dublin and Kilkenny, Carey and Newman purchased two properties in the luxury golf resort, the K Club in Straffan, County Kildare, in 2005, when it was the place to be seen. They moved there and started to spend a lot of time playing golf and socialising. Jonathan [not his real name] remembers the couple living at the K Club in the mid-noughties. He said DJ was courteous and always sober as a judge, describing him as a 'choirboy type'. Sarah, on the other hand, loved a few glasses of wine, and her presence made up for DJ's dullness, in this man's opinion. She appeared to relish networking, socialising and being in the limelight. Jonathan described how Sarah had the money, DJ 'the notoriety' – but the hurler seemed to enjoy his new lifestyle.

Jonathan firmly believed it was Sarah's money that allowed the couple to buy into the K Club, and that DJ was 'just along for the ride'. He knew DJ before and after his relationship with Newman and said DJ's appearance transformed after he met Sarah. Jonathan recalled seeing Carey in the bar in the K Club after playing golf, where he was wearing a belt 'you wouldn't tie your dog up with' – then, all of a sudden, he turned up in the 'very finest Gucci belts and designer shoes'. Before he met Sarah, his shoes always looked odd, his dinner jacket was too big for him, and his trousers didn't appear well-tailored, but afterwards, he was immaculate. Jonathan also described how DJ was recognisable by his gestures, how he'd tell a story and throw his head back, smiling from 'ear to ear'. He recalled that DJ was 'good at getting people on board' and getting the financial support of businessmen, citing the example of Philip Lynch of IAWS who had sponsored DJ's video/DVD.

'God love her, she [Sarah] loved the exposure, she loved the idea at the time. The K Club was very fashionable, the Ryder Cup was coming up [it was held there in 2006], there were a lot of the right people buying properties there. She wanted to be rubbing shoulders with them. She wanted to buy into Irish high society. She came from a poor background, Essex, and with DJ, it was all about the money as far as he was concerned, for sure, and she gave him a taste of a lifestyle that he couldn't afford. She said to me one day, "He's in very bad form." I asked, "Why?", and she said, "He won't fly commercial … I'm going to have to book NetJets or fly privately." He didn't want to be queuing up at a Ryanair desk.' NetJets, an executive jet company, charged up to €15,000 a trip.

Jonathan, who regularly talked to the couple, was convinced that Sarah had her work cut out trying to appease Carey, although outsiders thought it was the other way around. He said Sarah looked smitten, or as he put it, she had fallen for the hurler 'hook, line and sinker'. She confessed to Jonathan that she had never seen anybody else walk into a room like DJ – he could light it up and 'command such attention'. Jonathan remembers playing golf with DJ, whom he described as a 'good golfer' with a low handicap but one who often exaggerated his scores. 'We'd go in for a tea [after the game], and he was Walter Mitty. He'd tell you about scores he had, "Oh Jaysus, I was out last night on my own and I had three eagles or four birdies" … he'd talk like this.' Jonathan couldn't understand why he exaggerated, as his game was already good.

Jonathan's suspicions about Carey telling lies were confirmed by a high-profile businessman who had many dealings with Carey. He swore Jonathan to secrecy before confiding in him that Carey was not to be trusted. The businessman believed DJ was a scammer, up to no good, and wanted to make sure that Jonathan would not lend the hurler any money or get caught out by him. The businessman who flagged concerns about Carey did it carefully, trusting Jonathan not to repeat what he said. But why would someone be so secretive about his concerns about DJ? And if he suspected DJ was a conman, then surely he should have warned others? Jonathan kept these concerns to himself because this was DJ Carey, the great Kilkenny hurler who was constantly in the newspapers, while Sarah was the 'girl with the Midas touch'.

It was during his time in the K Club that DJ started telling people that he had cancer, confiding in some of the people with whom he played golf. At times he seemed to do this for the sympathy and attention it would garner, but there were other instances when he did it so that people offered him money for tests and treatment abroad. He did not talk openly about his health problems in front of Newman, and he told people he wanted to keep these matters private from her. Jonathan said DJ never discussed 'sickness or his cancer' with him, but 'he did with loads of others', friends of his. 'He never cried on my shoulder; probably because of the fact that I saw through him or knew about him, that I didn't listen to him. He discussed it with anybody who'd listen. It was widely known that he had cancer here.' While Jonathan was sceptical, he thought other people bought the idea that DJ was ill. While in the bar, after a round of golf, DJ would regularly point to scars on the back of his head, and Jonathan remembers how he'd often wear small plasters on his head.

The story that he had cancer was not the only one DJ Carey was telling people at the K Club. He told several members there about making 'ten fortunes' from land in 'Africa or somewhere like that'. 'He had to fly out the next day to sign documents,' said Jonathan, who added that he was 'very plausible'. 'He got away with this for a long time, and the reason he got away with it, with businessmen and everyone else, is he told a great story.'

DJ had long been known for helping to promote charities, and after he met Sarah, the couple supported many events together. Cancer charities were some of the causes that DJ promoted most of all. There are photographs taken at a star-studded event at St Margaret's Golf Club in May 2005, where celebrities from the world of sport, TV and music teed off for the third annual Ronnie Whelan Golf Classic in aid of two Irish charities: the Marie Keating Foundation and the Grace Nolan Foundation. The Marie Keating Foundation was set up by singer Ronan Keating and his family after their mother's death from breast cancer. The Grace Nolan Foundation charity was formed by Michael and June Nolan in 1999 after the death of their nine-year-old daughter, Grace, from hereditary haemorrhagic telangiectasia (HHT). Liverpool football legends Alan Hansen and Phil Neal attended alongside Niall Quinn and Steve Staunton. Westlife's Nicky Byrne was among the guests, and each paid €1,000 to play on the championship course in Fingal, County Dublin, that day. Irish website Showbiz.ie published a photograph of a smiling DJ wearing a cream polo neck and Sarah Newman in her golf gear, alongside a gallery of other celebrities at the event, with this caption: 'Hurling legend DJ Carey was also at the event with his partner Sarah Newman, some days later it was reported that he was rushed to hospital with health problems – apparently he is back on the mend this week …'

A story on page one of the *Irish Independent* on 21 May tells us more about what happened to Carey. Paul Melia reported that 'Kilkenny hurling star DJ Carey was rushed to hospital last night after he collapsed following a game in the Kilkenny Senior Hurling League. Although the 33-year-old finished the game for his club, Young Irelands Gowran, shortly after returning to the dressing room he collapsed and fell to the floor. An ambulance was called and, after receiving treatment at the scene, he was taken to St Luke's Hospital in Kilkenny.' A spokesperson for his club, Beatrice Treacy, was quoted as saying they were unsure as to what had happened. The hurler had complained of pain in his neck and right shoulder after receiving a knock early in the second half. He received treatment and played on but was 'visibly in some distress'. His condition was later described as 'comfortable'.

Another report on the incident, by Michael Lavery in the

Evening Herald, appeared the same day and gave more details. In the article, Young Irelands' club secretary John Comerford said DJ got a 'bad bang' during the game, with the other player involved sent off. DJ was brought by ambulance to St Luke's, where he was assessed and X-rayed. Lavery wrote that a spokesperson from the HSE in the South East Area said the star 'wasn't admitted to hospital'.

After DJ's recovery from this incident, it was not long before he was out injured again, just ahead of Kilkenny's Leinster final clash with Wexford. On the morning of the final, 3 July, Dermot Crowe wrote in the *Sunday Independent* about Carey's omission from the team. DJ insisted he was unfit for selection, 'claiming an ongoing neck and back injury' was behind his omission. Crowe reported, 'County board chairman Ned Quinn said Carey wasn't injured when contacted yesterday. Carey, however, refuted this. "I definitely knew I would not be playing, I knew that for a good while. I trained last Monday night and that has been it for five weeks," he said. "I played against Offaly but it was a struggle and I played two local matches but the injury hasn't settled down." He said the injuries needed time to heal and ruled out an appearance as a substitute in today's Leinster final. Manager Brian Cody, who chose Conor Phelan at full forward instead, has a history of dropping big names.' It's unclear why Ned Quinn told a newspaper that Carey wasn't injured, when the player was claiming the opposite.

Kilkenny won the Leinster final that day without DJ, beating Wexford by three points, on a score of Kilkenny 0–22 to Wexford 1–16. DJ returned to action for the All-Ireland quarter-final against Limerick. Newman was in Croke Park for the game with Andrew Collins, managing director of Needahotel.com, as the pair were taking part in a short film to give a flavour of their personalities after being shortlisted in the international category for the 2005 Ernst & Young Entrepreneur of the Year award. In the film, Newman is heard saying, 'No. 14 down there, that's my boyfriend. That why I'm interested.' She also compared her business to a hurling team, saying forwards were like sales staff 'shooting for goal', midfield was her call centre doing all the 'donkey work', and defence was her finance department, who let 'nothing through the net'. She compared herself and Collins to Kilkenny boss Brian Cody, before saying, 'You know the best team will always win.'

Newman and Collins didn't win the award as it happens, but Kilkenny won the match. The Cats managed to clinch it by four points, although they didn't score any goals. Speaking afterwards to the *Kilkenny People*, Cody praised DJ for a 'terrific point', as he explained how Kilkenny had slowly worked their way back into the game. Kilkenny had survived everything Limerick had thrown their way, but now it was time to prepare for Galway in the semi-final.

When Galway and Kilkenny met on Sunday 21 August, it was an epic battle that produced huge scores. Reflecting on the game in his book, DJ said, 'The 2005 semi-final has gone down as one of the great classics which I suppose it was if lots of scores is the yardstick used to measure the quality. In all, it produced 9–36 with Galway winning by 5–18 to 4–18.' What he didn't realise was that this would be the last time he would

ENTER THE DRAGON

play in Croke Park and the last time he would wear the black and amber jersey.

Things had changed for him. He was spending more time in Dublin and enjoying his relationship with Newman. He admitted the 'relentless obsession' that had fuelled his hurling success and kept him going just wasn't there any more. In his book, he described how he started thinking, 'I have to go training tonight', instead of doing it automatically. 'Training was a huge part of my life, even if I didn't enjoy it a whole lot. Still, I loved the competitive element, trying to be first in the runs, trying to out-wit lads and always looking for new ways of doing things.' After the 2005 Championship finished, DJ thought mentally he was 'a bit softer' and physically his speed was dropping. 'Once my speed had dipped, one of the main anchors of my game was gone. I could have hung around in 2006, probably got a few runs as a sub and picked up a sixth All-Ireland medal, but it would have meant absolutely nothing to me. As far as I was concerned, I would be there as a player challenging for a starting place all the time or not at all. That super-sub stuff wasn't for me.'

There was much speculation about DJ's future after Kilkenny bowed out of the 2005 Championship, but he postponed any decision on retirement until the new year. On Sunday 28 August, DJ and Sarah appeared in Barry Egan's column in the *Sunday Independent*. Egan reported that while DJ had 'put off the decision' about his retirement, his 'pretty partner Sarah Newman' seemed 'to have her future mapped out'. He said, 'Sarah and DJ recently moved into Sarah's plush pad in leafy

Blackrock in Dublin. (Sarah also has a home in Mount Juliet.) It is not too difficult to tell when the sporting legend is at home. There is a van in the driveway with DJ Carey Enterprises printed in bold letters on the side. Some neighbours think it's funny to see Sarah's big car alongside DJ Carey's rather less posh form of transport. But I don't doubt he'll be going places in it once he retires.'

While DJ was keeping quiet about his future with Kilkenny, Sarah Newman was in the middle of negotiating the sale of her online hotel bookings business. Confirmation hit the newspapers in February 2006 that the deal was done, and a photograph of Sarah and DJ dressed for a black-tie event appeared alongside a story by Tom McEnaney in the *Irish Independent* under the headline 'Celtic tigress nets €60m after selling company'. The report stated that the entrepreneur and 'highly successful partner of DJ Carey, has just sold the hotel booking business she founded, for about €60m'. It stated that the company had annual sales of more than €100m, booking more than one million hotel beds every year.

The actual amount Newman got after the sale of her company was significantly lower than reported. Several sources, including a member of DJ's family, said they believed the figure to be closer to €12.5m. DJ also addressed the worth of his partner's business and mentioned in Denis Walsh's *Hurling: The Revolution Years* that he and Sarah had been targeted by thieves because of the exaggerations: 'They put my partner Sarah in a very vulnerable position by quoting the worth of her business that was way off the mark. The angle they're trying to get at is, "Well, the reason he left (his wife) is because she had so much money." The consequence they actually don't care about. Like, we've had a number of break-ins at the house. Not here, where we were before. They had photographs of the house we have in Mount Juliet (golf course) published in the paper and all that. Unfortunately the law doesn't protect the individual; these people can do what they like. So they'll print when we are in Mount Juliet, or where we were on one of those occasions when our house was broken into – and there was €30,000 worth of stuff taken out of it. And then the amount of nasty letters that would come about God wouldn't do this for profit. God is this and God is that and God is your only judge. The amount of those sick letters that you'd actually get because of what people print.'

Four months after the sale of Newman's business, DJ contacted a number of people, including Brian Cody and Kilkenny County Board Chairman Ned Quinn, to tell them he was retiring from hurling. The formal announcement came in his weekly column in the *Kilkenny Voice* newspaper, which was ghostwritten by journalist Charlie Keegan, who said he found DJ 'very easy to deal with' and always 'good for a quote'. At the age of thirty-five, DJ said he was not 'jumping out of his skin to play for Kilkenny' any more. 'If I had any regret, it would be that I am retiring under the management of Brian Cody, but on the other hand I had to do it some time. And I felt now it was the right time, particularly with Kilkenny winning the National League, things going well and hurling is in very safe hands (with Cody) at the moment.' Responding to DJ's retirement, Cody told the media: 'Hurling is losing an idol to all young players and hurling is losing the person who has been the top player over the past 20 years.' Eddie Keher praised DJ as the 'most complete hurler' he had ever seen: 'He mastered every skill in the game and contributed enormously to hurling since he first came on the scene.'

During his reign on the Kilkenny Senior team, DJ racked up 34 goals and 195 points in 57 Senior championship games. His medal haul included five All-Ireland Senior hurling medals for Kilkenny in 1992, 1993, 2000, 2002 and 2003. He won ten Leinster titles and four National League medals. He was named Hurler of the Year in 1993, and again in 2000. He helped Young Irelands win their first-ever Kilkenny Senior hurling title in 1996 and their second in 2002. He won nine All-Stars. He had great success as a schoolboy with St Kieran's College, winning two All-Ireland Colleges Senior hurling titles. He won an All-Ireland Minor hurling title in 1988. He didn't play dirty and was never sent off – there's a small dispute about whether he was given even one yellow card in his long sporting career.

DJ was not just an outstanding hurler. In one month alone in 1988, while at St Kieran's, he won four All-Ireland handball titles. He also has two world champion handball titles for under-23 singles and doubles (with Ciaran Curran of Tyrone) in 1994. He won Senior All-Ireland handball doubles 40x20 with Michael 'Ducksie' Walsh in 1994, 1995 and 1998. He went on to win Masters titles with Ducksie in 2012, 2014, 2015 and 2016. He was also an impressive golfer.

DJ and Sarah were flying high after his retirement from

Kilkenny hurling. They were enjoying the profits from the sale of her business and the economic boom. Life in the K Club was good. However, they would soon come crashing back to earth.

6

HIGH-FLIERS

When DJ Carey was a young hurler, his little sister Catriona would stand at the back of the goal and puck the ball back to him during practice sessions. There are seven years between the brother and sister, and for three decades the pair were described as 'very close'. After his marriage to Christine broke down, Catriona took a far greater role in DJ Carey Enterprises – the pair were co-directors of this company from 2001 to 2009.

Catriona trained as an accountant in a firm in Kilkenny city from August 1999 to August 2003, but never actually completed her final accountancy exams. After she left the accountancy firm, she worked for clients as a bookkeeper. People who observed her work during this period said she had the ability to do book work but would leave accounts in an 'absolute mess' because she would neglect the basics. She did not spend enough time balancing the books and ensuring the paperwork was in order, so it is not really clear why so many local businesses in Kilkenny put their faith in her.

At the time, she had a good reputation because she was DJ Carey's sister, as well as having her own sporting accolades, both locally and internationally. Catriona played camogie for Kilkenny and international field hockey with the Irish women's national team, earning an impressive seventy-two caps. She retired from international competition in 2006 but continued to play club hockey for the Hermes Ladies' Hockey Club based in St Andrew's College in Dublin, of which she had been a member since she was a teenager. At the time of her retirement, she said it was a very hard personal decision, made due to 'work pressures' and living so far from the regional and national training sessions.

By 2006 Catriona was devoting a huge amount of time to the day-to-day running of her brother's business from its base in the grounds of her family's farm in Gowran. It was at this time that she fell foul of Revenue rules, when she produced an incorrect invoice in relation to VAT for DJ Carey Enterprises. She also claimed a repayment of VAT to which she was not entitled. The matter ended up in Kilkenny District Court in 2008, and Carey was fined €1,500. This didn't appear to be picked up by the media until three years later.

While Catriona was busy running DJ Carey Enterprises in the autumn of 2006, DJ and Sarah were attending gala dinners and charity lunches, and mingling with businesspeople and celebrities. After the sale of Newman's company, they were enjoying the good times and had become a poster couple for the Celtic Tiger. Sarah was generous and loved to treat family and friends. Catriona told this author that she remembered going on a 'few ski trips' that Sarah paid for, as well as attending dinners in upmarket restaurants, all things she greatly enjoyed.

The couple's names appeared regularly in Angela Phelan's social diary in the *Irish Independent*. In October 2006 she wrote that 'Sarah Newman and DJ Carey cut a dash on the dance floor' at the ISPCC Dove Ball. A month later, Newman and Carey were guests of Norma Smurfit at the annual First Step Business Awards lunch in the Four Seasons Hotel in Dublin. On 16 December, DJ and Sarah were mentioned again by Phelan, this time at the 19th annual Renault Sports Celebrity Awards at the Burlington Hotel. JP McManus attended the event, and Phelan noted that there was a 'great cheer for Ian Woosnam and an even bigger one for Woosie's special guest – the Ryder Cup'.

In 2007 the black-tie, red-carpet events and charity fundraisers continued. In February DJ called on walkers throughout Ireland to join him for the Irish Heart Foundation's Overseas Walk in India. In April he was pictured in the *Irish Examiner* launching a skipathon at Scoil Bhríde in Dublin, as 50,000 children from around the country were said to be 'skipping for a healthier heart'. In October Angela Phelan wrote about a 'much talked about gala ball', all proceeds of which were going to Childline and the Rape Crisis Centre. She reported that the 320 guests 'had forked out €10k per table'. The guests included Neil Jordan and 'music maestro' Louis Walsh, 'about to go live with *The X Factor* next week', and was 'topped off' with an appearance by Tom Jones. DJ and Sarah were among the big names mentioned attending the ball.

While the good times rolled in his personal life, the company accounts for DJ Carey Enterprises showed that liabilities for the hurler's cleaning company had been increasing from 2006 onwards. The company losses were €81,911 in 2006, and they had increased to €144,186 in 2007 and €207,189 in 2008. Such amounts, however, were small change compared to the multimillion-euro sums he had borrowed with Newman from AIB to purchase their properties at the K Club and Mount Juliet golf resorts. Land Registry records show that in April 2006, DJ Carey was registered as the owner of 908 Ladycastle at the K Club, and two years later, in May 2008, he was registered as the owner of a second property, at 5 The Inch, Mount Juliet. He also signed a personal guarantee agreeing to repay AIB €1.5m borrowed by Sarah Newman on another K Club property, at 821 Ladycastle. These properties were in addition to the couple's family home on Alma Road in Monkstown, County Dublin, where they spent much of their time, and a chalet in the Swiss Alps.

In October 2008 RTÉ announced details of its own version of the popular TV show *Dragons' Den*. 'It will be the dragons' own hard-earned cash on the table,' a spokeswoman for the show said, as reported in the *Irish Independent* on 9 October. 'These are shrewd businesspeople who have heard it all before and who are not afraid to say "no" in the harshest terms,' she added. Among the 'dragons' announced in the line-up for the first series of the show was Sarah Newman. She took her place alongside founder of LMFM radio and 'property millionaire' Gavin Duffy, 'coffee bean baron' of the Insomnia chain Bobby Kerr, entrepreneur Sean Gallagher, and Niall O'Farrell, 'the man behind the Black Tie chain of menswear'.

After the first season aired, one of the talking points was

how Sarah had failed to invest a cent in any of the contestants' business ideas. In the final episode of the first season, she offered chef Tim Rooney €100,000 to invest in his idea for a healthy snack firm, but the chef turned her down. On 9 April 2009, Conor Feehan reported in the *Evening Herald* that Patricia Callan of the Small Firms Association had commented on Newman's lack of spend in the series, saying 'it was probably "symptomatic of the climate" and that the dragons have probably taken a hit'.

Serious problems were now emerging in DJ's business that were not yet in the public domain. Catriona had stepped down as director in 2009, and Newman had stepped into the role, but this caused division in the family. On 9 May 2009, Catriona, DJ's mother Maura and another sister, Liz, set up a rival cleaning company, Carey Cleaning. Meanwhile, auditors were poring over the accounts of DJ Carey Enterprises, trying to establish why losses had been increasing in recent years. There was a family falling out, which was not unusual for the Careys, but this time DJ's parents took Catriona's side.

Newman, meanwhile, was trying to sell her most expensive purchase. On 25 November 2009, an article by Anna Tyzack in *The Telegraph*, under the heading 'Sky property: Buy into the high life', described how Newman had bought Chalet Grace in Zermatt in 2007, and in 2009 was charging up to €40,000 per week to rent out the property, which included food and wine for fourteen people and 'a professional chef and staff'. 'I fell in love with Zermatt – it's such a charming village with no cars and amazing restaurants. It's the only place where my children can go off for a hot chocolate on their own and I know they are safe,' Newman said, indicating that the couple used the luxury property when it wasn't rented out. The report stated that the chalet, named after Newman's daughter, had panoramic views, a cinema, gym, spa and open-plan reception room with sun terrace. 'It was such a fun project and it's always going to wash it's [sic] face – we've already sold 60 per cent of the weeks for next year, and it will rent as a bed and breakfast in summer,' Newman added. The report, however, then explained that, due to 'commitments with *Dragons' Den* and several new business ventures, she [Newman] has put the chalet on the market for CHF17–20 million (£10–£12 million)'.

By the time she started on *Dragons' Den*, Newman's wealth had dwindled, after the value of her properties dropped to a fraction of what she and DJ had borrowed for them. On 29 November 2009, she told Niamh Horan in the *Sunday Independent* that she and DJ were going into business with healer Michael O'Doherty – the man who 'cured dancer Michael Flatley from a mystery illness'. This interview was the first time Newman laid bare how the couple were suffering financially. She talked about being in contact with other businesspeople who were finding it hard to cope, and how their 'problems are almost coming at them like a hail of machine-gun bullets which they're not able to dodge anymore'. She explained that O'Doherty could apply the process of 'moving energy through the body to make people feel better, more relaxed and better able to cope', and that she and DJ had personally sought the healer's help 'after coming under pressure from the downturn themselves'. 'I want to dispel a myth right now – just because you've been successful in business, doesn't mean you don't have the same difficulties as everyone else. I have been under tremendous stress over the past 18 months. The general rule is the more you have, the more you've borrowed basically,' she said.

Newman explained that she had 'not been able to sell certain assets, they are no longer worth as much as they were'. This would appear to be a reference to Newman and Carey's properties, bought at the height of the boom, which diminished in value as the country went into recession. There were things which she wanted to offload 'which are now a burden and I have to carry the cost of that. I'm also heavily involved in business enterprises where I have yet to get paid by clients, so cash flow is also a problem. Everyone is in the same boat. I now work more hours than I ever did in my life. But we all need to be strong to get through this difficult time.'

She revealed that Carey had sought help from O'Doherty, as he was suffering from stress. 'DJ has found that he is a lot more positive now, he feels stronger and he has far more energy than before. If you're under a huge amount of pressure it is like someone switches off a light and for DJ it was like someone unplugged his power support. But ever since he visited Michael, it's like a cloud has been lifted.' While the business with O'Doherty never got off the ground, what Newman said in relation to DJ seeking help from the healer was true.

With his financial problems mounting, DJ went to a businessman, Declan (not his real name), for a loan, explaining that he needed treatment abroad for 'health issues'. Declan said he knew DJ and Sarah as a couple, but he believed that Sarah, whom he described as 'salt of the earth', did not know about the loan request. 'DJ was doing his own thing, separate from Sarah. It's like his own life was parallel to his life with Sarah,' the businessman explained. Declan arranged to meet Carey in a Dublin hotel in early 2010, where the hurler asked him for €10,000 to fund tests in the US to find out what was wrong with him. 'Look, he came to me, and he needed help. He was going through health stuff and asked for a loan ... I assumed I was giving the guy a few quid to help him out,' Declan told this author. Carey never mentioned the word cancer, but he promised Declan he'd pay him back within three months. He also said he wanted to deal with his health matters 'privately'. 'I believe he definitely kept Sarah in the dark; she never discussed DJ's health issues with me,' said Declan.

Time went by and there was no sign of the loan being repaid. While Declan never forgot that DJ owed him €10,000, he was busy and didn't call in the loan until five years later. In the meantime, the pair remained on good terms, talking occasionally about hurling matches on the phone.

In 2010 Newman, as the new lady captain of the K Club, became an ambassador for Firstlight The K Club – a venture to offer timeshare or co-ownership of K Club properties, to encourage people from Ireland and abroad to visit the five-star resort. In promotional material posted on their website on 4 January, Newman gave some details about her private life with DJ and their four children, who were then aged between eleven and fifteen. 'I play golf here twice a week and while others have bought property at The K Club for an investment to let out, we're a family who've bought a home here at Ladycastle and we use it.' The website stated that Newman 'also lets out her designer chalet in the top Swiss ski resort of Zermatt all year' and 'employs another 33 people at DJ Direct, the consumable distribution firm that she jointly owns with partner DJ Carey'.

Newman wrote a 'celebrity diary' in the *Evening Herald* on 26 February, where she gave another glimpse into her and DJ's home life. She explained how one of her children had been sick, but she was lucky enough to have a 'full-time housekeeper' to help out. She mentioned the excitement of seeing the debut episode of the second series of *Dragons' Den* in one of her co-star's homes. 'Niall O'Farrell, held an exclusive gathering at his house on Shrewsbury Road so myself and my partner DJ Carey had a wonderful evening catching up with everyone from the sound crew to the make-up artists to the gang from Shinawil [the production company behind the series].'

In the same issue another story about Newman and DJ appeared on page 5 – this time journalist Lorna Nolan reported that the couple hoped to hold a 'low-key wedding ceremony in the mountains' later that year. Presumably, this refers to the mountains where Newman's Swiss chalet was located. 'The RTÉ star and renowned businesswoman, who is a self-confessed fan of the outdoors, says she has no interest in having a big celebrity wedding with the Kilkenny hurler. Instead, Sarah plans to tie the knot with her other half in front of just a handful of close friends and family.' The report then stated that Newman said, 'We have no definite plans yet but I have strong suspicions that we might just run off and get married in the mountains.' Despite these hints from Newman that she would marry Carey in 2010, this didn't come to fruition, and it would be some time before the wedding plans progressed further.

Ireland's Rich List was published in the *Sunday Independent* in March 2010, and Newman featured at number 222, with €35m 'IT' beside her name. The report stated: 'The best-looking Dragon in the den and probably the richest too. Newman, whose partner is Kilkenny hurling god DJ Carey is thought to have netted €40m from the sale of her hotel booking firm Needahotel.com in 2006. She's the lady's captain at the K Club too.' The list's estimate of Newman's wealth was based on publicly reported information in 2010, and her debts may not have been considered, as her financial difficulties were not fully known at this time.

On 9 January 2011, the mounting problems at DJ Carey Enterprises were finally made public when Larissa Nolan broke the story for *The Mail on Sunday*. It was some weeks before other newspapers could pick up the story because, without DJ or his family commenting on it initially, it could not be covered for legal reasons. Nolan had a good source and substantiated what was being talked about in Kilkenny – that DJ had made a complaint to the Garda Bureau of Fraud Investigation about his own sister 'after funds of up to €1m could not be accounted for in the firm they ran together'. The article stated that the complaint had been made in 2010, and Revenue had also been asked to look into the matter 'by Carey'. 'Gardaí are now investigating the finances of his sister, Catríona, 32, who is herself an elite camogie star and multicapped hockey international.'

Nolan's report confirmed that Catriona had stood down from the firm in March 2009, and the 'company's auditors were unable to affirm the accuracy of its most recent accounts, "whether caused by fraud or other irregularity"'. It continued, 'This weekend, Miss Carey was not at the family home in Gowran where she lives with her parents. Her father, John Carey, said he would pass on a message to call. Asked about the fraud complaint and the apparent split between his son and daughter, he said: "I think that's all been sorted out. I don't think she'll comment but I'll let her know." Further requests for comment received no response.'

A source is quoted as telling Nolan that there were details of how DJ made the complaint and provided gardaí with 'relevant documents and bank records and details of money transfers and cheques. There are cheques there that the bank accepted but that DJ denies he ever signed. There are a lot of questions over vehicles and monies being transferred into other individuals' accounts.' It was described as a 'very complex case' in which the Revenue Commissioners were involved, since, 'if a person allegedly takes money out of a company, then they should pay tax on that money'. A source stated that while DJ was willing to accept that there could be some explanation for the missing money, 'he has not found one so far and so has had to go to the Fraud Squad'.

The auditors, Brophy Gillespie, said they could not obtain all the necessary information from the 2009 accounts of DJ Carey Enterprises 'to provide [as required by law] "reasonable assurance that the financial statements were free from material misstatement, whether caused by fraud or other irregularity or error". The evidence available to us was limited because we were unable to obtain sufficient and appropriate explanations and evidence from a former employee in respect of a number of transactions recorded in the books of account of the company.'

DJ's business had recorded losses of €497,801 for the year ending March 2009. Nolan reported that the accounts also showed '"unvouched-for expenses" of €164,344, which means this money cannot be accounted for by the company by receipts or payments out ... The auditor notes that the "directors intend to recover this amount" but have written it off for the time being as an "exceptional item". In excess of €300,000 was spent over the years on vehicles, which business insiders say is far above the normal spend on transport.'

The article detailed how sources close to the Careys said, 'the bitter row has torn them apart. It is understood that personal attempts were made to resolve the issue but a total breakdown in communication between brother and sister meant this was not possible.' Nolan quoted a source saying it was a 'typical family feud over money', that had 'driven a wedge' between the brother and sister who were once 'very close'. She went on to note how Catriona had started a new business apparently in direct competition with DJ's firm and had registered an accountancy practice, Catriona Carey & Co. In the end, nobody was ever charged in relation to the alleged fraud at DJ Carey Enterprises.

In early February 2011 businesses in Ireland were struggling, with figures showing company closures soaring, leaving millions in unpaid debt behind each day. DJ's businesses were no exception, with Donal O'Donovan of the *Irish Independent* reporting on 9 February that creditors' meetings had been called for three of his companies 'which supply cleaning and sanitation products to pubs and businesses'. 'It comes after the business [DJ Carey Enterprises] had to write off €200,000 of "unauthorised transactions" which were uncovered by auditors.' O'Donovan recorded that DJ's business had 'racked up combined losses of close to €2m by 2009'. According to him, 'after discovering a series of unexplained and "unauthorised transactions"' at DJ Carey Enterprises, 'Mr Carey and Sarah Newman vowed to "pursue the recovery of this expenditure in full"'.

O'Donovan also stated that DJ had moved to recover some 'value from the company' and sold most of the operations to 'Tuam-based company Western Hygiene last Friday'. He noted: 'It is common practice for a company in trouble to sell off the best parts of the business to raise cash to pay off debts. The phones are now being answered under the name of Western Hygiene.' It was also reported that DJ himself had previously lent more than €600,000 of his own money to the company to 'keep the business afloat'. 'Because Mr Carey has lent this money in loans to the company, he will be the largest creditor when a statement of affairs is presented at the meeting next week.' Ulster Bank was reportedly owed 'around €170,000, [and] a portion of this is covered by a personal guarantee from Mr Carey'.

On Sunday 13 February, following on from Larissa Nolan's original story, Mark Tighe reported in *The Sunday Times* that Catriona had three convictions for tax irregularities and was a director of her brother's cleaning companies at the time of those convictions. 'In 2008 Carey was fined €1,500 by Kilkenny District Court after she pleaded guilty to knowingly or wilfully producing an incorrect invoice to Revenue in connection with VAT in 2006. She was also found guilty of furnishing incorrect information to Revenue and, also in 2006, claiming a repayment of VAT to which she was not entitled. She resigned within six months of the court hearing.'

It was around this time that Sarah Newman was replaced by Norah Casey for the third season of *Dragons' Den*. On 17 February, a story by Allison Bray appeared in the *Irish Independent* Business Week section, stating that insiders of the show 'knew for years a business owned by former hurling star DJ Carey and partner Sarah Newman was floundering ... Executive producer Larry Bass said it came as no surprise to him or the "Dragons" when it was revealed last week that DJ Carey Enterprises is €1.7m in debt and facing possible collapse ... "For us it's an old story. We were aware there were problems for a number of years. Business is business and we all have our ups and our downs," he told the *Irish Independent*.' However, Bass also said that this was not the only reason Newman didn't return for the third series of the show: 'Other business commitments in Canada and Switzerland also resulted in scheduling problems, leading her to forgo taking part in this series.'

On 19 February, following the creditors' meeting mentioned by O'Donovan, there were reports in the newspapers involving DJ Carey's former companies: Dublin Janitorial Centre, DJ Carey Enterprises, and Alton Limited. DJ had set up his first company, Dublin Janitorial Centre Limited, in 1988, when he was just seventeen years old. The business, which later used the name Omni Hygiene & Catering Supplies, continued to trade until 2009. Company records show the firm incurred a net loss of €893,397 in the year ending 31 March 2009, and that it was dissolved in September 2016. DJ's main company, DJ Carey Enterprises (also called DJ Direct), was incorporated on 21 June 1994. Its final accounts were also filed on 31 March 2009, with a loss of €704,989. The third company mentioned, Alton Limited, was founded in May 1992 and had recorded losses of €232,767 by March 2009. An article in the *Irish Independent* stated the creditors' meeting 'wasn't the usual faceless encounter that generally signifies the winding up of a company'. DJ stopped and made small talk with everybody, and there were 'smiles exchanged all round'. The creditors who showed up, including a supplier of bleach to DJ's business and a 'former employee', were 'highly embarrassed to be there'.

The report described how, when DJ went into business at twenty-three, he was still the 'brightest jewel in Kilkenny's hurling riches', calling him a 'true aristocrat of the ash'. 'He rubbed shoulders with Tiger Woods, played golf with Colin Montgomerie and demonstrated hurling in African villages.' It stated that his contacts book had come 'ready made', so his move from Croke Park to the business stage was an 'easy' one. 'DJ later teamed up with the multi-millionaire businesswoman Sarah Newman of *Dragons' Den*. Then emerged the shock of financial irregularities that DJ uncovered within the company, with €200,000 written off as "missing". That's why, when it all came tumbling down in a bleak boardroom of a suburban hotel, it seemed like an embarrassing twist to the DJ legend.'

Around twenty people attended that final meeting when his business affairs were wound down. O'Donovan reported that there were tensions in the room as attempts were made to appoint a different liquidator, but those efforts were 'doomed' because Carey and Newman were 'owed more than 50pc of debts run up by the business. This gave them final say.' In the same newspaper, O'Donovan reported DJ's loans to his business, totalling around €600,000, to 'help it trade through its difficulties'. Yet, 'Much of that loan was used to pay rent on premises at Grant's Road Business Park in Dublin, which he owned himself.' It was also stated that 'unauthorised financial dealings at the group running to hundreds of thousands of euro are the subject of an ongoing garda investigation'.

Only a month later, on 29 March, the *Evening Herald* reported, 'Star DJ fights back with new sales job'. The story confirmed that Carey and eight of his staff had joined the Galway company that had acquired his cleaning supplies business a month earlier. The managing director of Western Hygiene, Kevin Collins, reportedly said, 'We are delighted to welcome him [Carey] and his team on board – it's a very positive step for our business.'

On 10 May, the full extent of DJ and Sarah's debts made the papers, as media outlets reported on how a 'Celtic Tiger dream turned into a nightmare'. It emerged that, while DJ was battling to keep his cleaning business afloat, himself and Newman were already being chased by AIB for large property loans that had been the subject of a hearing before the Commercial Court a day earlier. The front-page headline of the *Irish Independent* read, 'Bank targets Sarah's €10.5m Swiss chalet'. The story stated that Newman faced losing her 'trophy' Swiss chalet, and the couple also risked losing their Monkstown home, after they were ordered to repay a €9.5m bank loan. AIB stated in court that the bank wanted to move against the Swiss property, which would be enough to pay off the couple's debts, but was 'worried it would not be able to take ownership of the property – solely owned by Ms Newman – because it was outside the State.' The report stated that this latest crisis came as Carey and Newman fell behind on 'massive mortgages on investment properties they bought' at the K Club and Mount Juliet.

In the Commercial Court, Mr Justice Peter Kelly granted a judgment to AIB for more than €9.5m against the couple, and, although not present, the couple consented to the judgment. The *Independent* report gave details of the mortgages Carey and Newman had on their three properties at the K Club and Mount Juliet: 'In order to borrow such huge sums, the couple entered into a complicated loan arrangement with AIB. Mr Carey borrowed €7.85m against two of the properties and signed a personal guarantee agreeing to pay back €1.5m borrowed by Ms Newman against a third property. Ms Newman borrowed the €1.5m in her own name and signed personal guarantees for Mr Carey's €7.85m loan.' The report then stated that the arrears owed to AIB were 'modest', but the bank 'had got no response from Mr Carey after the loans fell into arrears'.

DJ was given four weeks to come up with a solution, after

which time the bank would be allowed to move against him. 'However, Mr Justice Kelly refused to allow similar breathing space for Ms Newman after being told by AIB it may be able to recover some of the money owed if it successfully moved against the Swiss property.' This report also mentions Newman's worth, stating that 'Needahotel was reportedly sold for €30m in cash with the rest only to be paid if targets were met after the deal closed. US documents show the buyers believed as early as June 2006 that the targets would never be met.'

Inside the *Irish Independent*, also on 10 May, Donal O'Donovan wrote that in the same week that DJ Carey had called a creditors' meeting to tell lenders and suppliers to his cleaning business that it would have to be put into liquidation, AIB had written to Newman (on 10 February) calling for repayments of arrears of €7,349 on her mortgage account. 'On February 18 Noel Murphy was appointed as liquidator to the Kilkenny legend's loss-making business. By then AIB was seriously concerned about its €9.5m exposure to the couple.' Journalist Laura Noonan also carried out an analysis of the couple's debts, saying that AIB's decision to advance a €7.85m mortgage on two golf resort properties looked like 'absolute madness' when viewed through the 'prism of crisis-riddled 2011'. 'The really curious thing about the deal was how Sarah Newman and DJ Carey convinced the banks that they were going to be able to pay back such a staggering loan.' Noonan pointed out that even on a 3 per cent interest rate – the lowest the duo was likely to have gotten – the monthly repayments on the twenty-year mortgage would have to come to about €43,000. Surely the banks had asked Carey and Newman to produce evidence of substantial income and to demonstrate their ability to make these payments? The bank had also put in another protection in this case, 'a personal guarantee from both of them for the sums owed, so the pair would be personally liable'.

On 11 May, Carey and Newman issued a statement rejecting suggestions that they had failed to engage with AIB over the loans, saying that 'detailed and comprehensive financial proposals, prepared by their financial advisers, were submitted to the bank on a number of occasions'. They also stated that they had dealt proactively and professionally with the bank. AIB pursued the sale of Carey and Newman's properties to recover some of the debt, but there was still a significant shortfall, as the market value of the houses had plummeted. Newman sold Monkstown and moved into rented accommodation, while a report in *The Irish Times* by Suzanne Lynch on 12 December 2011 stated that there were no details of how much AIB accepted for Chalet Grace in the end.

By late 2011 the cracks were starting to appear in DJ and Sarah's relationship. Their finances were under severe strain, and the people around them in the K Club could tell they were in a desperate situation, frantically asking other residents to invest in some business or another. On one occasion Sarah called to a resident's house to tell him about a new venture and to look for an investment, while DJ sat outside in the car.

Then came the incident that would turn those cracks into an unbridgeable fissure. On 6 July 2025, Sarah Newman spoke to Niamh Horan in an 'exclusive interview' for the *Sunday*

Independent in which she described how her world imploded on a sunny day in the K Club. Newman told Horan how a mutual friend of the couple, 'a wealthy businessman who has since died, gave Carey a brand-new Range Rover, with Carey promising he would pay [for it] in instalments'. When the cheques bounced, the businessman called DJ looking for the money, but the hurler claimed he was in the Mayo Clinic in the United States having treatment for an 'incurable brain tumour'. Newman knew nothing about this, but when she returned home from a trip to Switzerland, the vehicle had vanished from the driveway. When she asked DJ about it, he claimed it was in the garage with an electrical fault.

Horan continued the story: 'Some time later, Ms Newman was driving down the avenue of the K Club when she passed the businessman in his car. Moments later, he telephoned her and said: "You're unbelievable, you know that? You and him, you're unbelievable." Ms Newman was left speechless and asked him what on earth he was talking about.' Newman asked him to pull over so they could talk 'face to face'. During this conversation the man told her that 'Carey had confided in him that he had been diagnosed with incurable brain cancer. For Ms Newman, that was the moment her world began to fall apart.' She had been completely unaware that DJ was telling people at the K Club he was ill.

Newman told Horan that when she confronted DJ he 'gaslighted her', saying 'the businessman was mad and lying to her'. However, she didn't believe him and asked him to leave. It was only after this that she discovered the 'lie about the brain tumour ... was only the start of it. After the couple split, others began to tell her the stories Carey had been spreading in order to get money, including that he had to get his spleen out – when he was seen playing golf a few days later.' Horan wrote that some weeks after Sarah and DJ split, Newman sat down with the journalist and 'confided – off the record – that she was horrified to learn Carey had been compulsively lying about health and money issues'. Newman further claimed that she had reported Carey to Blackrock Garda Station in Dublin in 2012 for stealing from her but said her complaints were not followed up.

The 2025 interview gave a very different story to a piece that appeared in the *Sunday Independent* on 22 April 2012. In another 'exclusive' with Niamh Horan, Newman had announced the end of her nine-year relationship with DJ Carey, admitting that she had been fitted for her wedding dress, the bridesmaids were picked and the date had been set for 4 July 2012. When asked who made the final decision to call time on the relationship, she told Horan, 'There is always somebody I suppose who makes that final call and I think in this case it was DJ. It was over Easter. So then I had to go through the very humiliating and humbling experience of cancelling everything that was booked.' Newman said she had been looking forward to her 'dream day' when DJ announced that he didn't want to go through with the wedding. 'I guess I thought getting married was going to be my happy ever after and that's why I get so upset because at the end of the day, and I know it sounds so corny, but I am just a girl who really really loved DJ Carey.'

She described being 'heartbroken', but said she thought DJ was 'heartbroken equally'. 'The difference between him and me is that I'm much more of a social animal – there is never a night that goes by where I'm not out for supper with friends or cooking or entertaining – and I've got brilliant girlfriends and I love to chat and share my feelings and emotions. DJ, on the other hand, is intensely private and I know he is very hurt and I know he is very lonely. But we made a decision and we have to stick to that.'

Newman explained how the couple had broken up a number of times in the past, but one of the benefits of owning several properties was that if they had a row, he could 'bugger off to the K Club'. This time, however, the separation was final. 'We're not talking at the moment, we have to give each other some space and give each other some distance. Whether we will ever be friends again or not I just don't know.' She said that DJ was still living in the K Club. 'I don't know what he's going to do with his life, that is something he has to figure out.' Had being a woman who was also the breadwinner had an effect on their relationship, particularly as she had invested in DJ's business? 'I think that's a really interesting question ... but part of the reason why I fell in love with DJ was because he wasn't interested in the material things.' Before finishing the interview, Newman said there was no one else involved in the break-up.

It's impossible to know why Sarah Newman said that DJ was the one to call time on the relationship in 2012, and only thirteen years later, in an interview with the same journalist, felt able to detail her 'horror' over the lies he was telling about having an incurable brain tumour to get money. Perhaps she feared a public backlash in 2012, because of Carey's huge popularity in Ireland at the time, and it was only in 2025, after the truth about DJ had become public knowledge, that she felt strong enough to give the complete story. What is clear is that when Newman's complaints to the gardaí were 'not followed up', it left Carey, as Horan says, 'free to embark on a trail of deception'.

Three days after Newman gave the 2012 interview about the end of her relationship, journalists started to get phone calls about DJ collapsing in the public waiting room of Kilkenny Garda Station. He was at the station to get a form signed when he took ill. Details were sketchy, but there were concerns that he may have suffered a heart attack. The front-page story of the *Irish Independent* on 25 April was, 'Stressed DJ to face series of heart tests', while the *Irish Examiner* reported, 'DJ Carey in hospital after heart attack'. His mother told the media, 'He's comfortable, that's all that we know.' Denis Quinlan, chairman of the Young Irelands club in Gowran, told the *Irish Examiner*, 'He had some sort of a turn as far as we can gather. But he's seemingly comfortable in hospital. Whatever happened, we wish him a quick recovery.'

On the same date, the *Herald* reported that DJ's brother Martin said DJ had been rushed to hospital after suffering a panic attack due to stress. He reportedly said, 'DJ's very much on the mend. We believe he suffered a panic attack. It was an awful shock but thank God he's grand.' The following day, there were more reports on DJ's condition – this time his ex-wife Christine told the *Irish Daily Star* that an ECG had confirmed there was nothing wrong with his heart. 'It's been an upsetting day because of all the stories going round, but DJ is not at death's door or anything like that,' she said. 'He had chest pains and he collapsed but his heart is fine. Our sons Seán and Mike have been seeing this stuff on Facebook and on the radio about their father but his heart is fine. And to be honest, DJ doesn't need the added pressure of that right now ... he's going through a hard enough time as it is. This was stress more than likely and that's all there is to it.'

Just over a week later, on 3 May, *The Sun* ran a story on how DJ 'nearly died from a heart infection' when he collapsed the previous week. The newspaper reported that Carey had been diagnosed with 'myocarditis, a viral infection of the heart', and his father, John, told the newspaper: 'He was struck down with a viral infection of the heart. It was very serious. He is out of hospital now, but he is on medication and he is not in the best of shape. He's had a tough time of it.' He added, 'I heard talk that he had a panic attack – but that was rubbish. It was a heart infection.' He concluded, 'We're family. We're here for him. He's had a very tough time recently – and none of it was DJ's fault.'

The different accounts given by various members of DJ's family puzzled reporters as they tried to establish what actually happened. Was it a heart attack? Or was he under severe stress and did he suffer a panic attack? Or was it a viral infection of the heart as his father suggested? In his book, DJ addressed the health problems he experienced in April 2012, saying he had been getting bad headaches for a while but put them down to stress 'related to business and personal matters'. He had 'also been experiencing chest pains but attributed them to the same thing'. DJ said he was diagnosed with a condition called 'pericarditis, a virus that attacks tissue around the heart wall'. On its website, the British Heart Foundation says pericarditis is not usually a serious condition, although it can be difficult to diagnose.

DJ recalled, 'I spent a week in hospital and when I was being discharged I was told I would need a brain scan to check why I had collapsed. It seems the pericarditis wouldn't cause that to happen on its own. The scans delivered some chilling results. Seven clots and two aneurisms showed up. Whatever about the clots, the aneurisms could have been dangerous. I underwent an operation straightaway and, thank God, all went to plan. I'm fine now.' He said he was lucky to have contracted the heart virus as it led to the discovery of the clots and aneurysms, which were dealt with 'by the medical experts'. He then stated that the medical view was that 'most likely' his condition was caused by 'taking knocks to the head'. 'In the long term, it could have been fatal if I hadn't had the operation. That's the stark reality, one that all hurlers should reflect on.'

In August 2012, just a few months after his health scare and the operation he claimed he had for blood clots and brain aneurysms, DJ togged out as a referee for the first ever Hurling For Cancer Research charity match, held in St Conleth's Park in Newbridge, County Kildare. He was one of the sports personalities who had supported the event since its establishment in 2011, when leading flat trainer and hurling fan Jim Bolger challenged champion jockey Davy Russell and his weight-room colleagues to a game of hurling against him and his staff to raise money and awareness for cancer research. That August DJ joined Bolger, Russell and other well-known personalities, including Michael O'Leary, Gráinne Seoige and Niall Quinn, to take part in the event, which raised around €123,000 for the Irish Cancer Society. This may have opened DJ's eyes to just how generous the Irish public were when it came to supporting cancer causes.

His own finances were not looking so positive. Once Sarah had moved out of the K Club, it was clear to other residents who knew the couple that DJ was struggling. While he had remained in one of the couple's K Club properties immediately after the break-up, a businessman who owned a home there and was friends with DJ recalls how he was after the relationship ended. The man remembers giving DJ fills of diesel for his car 'four or five times' and he also bought him dinner. Once, DJ asked him for a loan of a car, a BMW, and the man had to pressure DJ to give it back after three or four months. 'I got on great with him, but there was something there. He was complaining and telling me stories about going to America. He had cancer of the head, a tumour or something he told me.' This man regularly met DJ and he'd talk about his 'head thing'. He said the ex-hurler got 'mad into juices and health foods' and constantly talked about his 'illness'. He knew DJ was looking for sympathy but said he was never directly asked for money. This man said an acquaintance of his also loaned DJ a car, a Volkswagen, but he never got it back.

Despite the rumours having started as early as 2003, and DJ himself having told people in 2005 that he had the disease, it was from 2013 on, after his financial setbacks, that DJ began to share the story that he had cancer in much greater detail with the people around him and that he became increasingly proactive in asking them for money to fund his treatment abroad.

7

'IT'S ALL IN HIS HEAD'

In August 2012, soon after his relationship with Sarah Newman broke down, DJ had started seeing a woman after meeting her on dating website Plenty of Fish. When DJ revealed to Jane (not her real name) that he had been diagnosed with multiple myeloma and regularly travelled to Seattle for treatments, she was devastated. Multiple myeloma is a type of bone marrow cancer that can affect areas of the body such as the spine, skull, pelvis and ribs.

The relationship soon became serious, and, from January 2013, Jane started to spend a lot of time with DJ at his K Club home – she stayed there for around five months. Unlike the impression others had of DJ, Jane said that he seemed to have plenty of money for holidays, meals and living expenses. She didn't question where this came from, thinking 'this is DJ Carey' – she believed he had business interests, as he had mentioned commercial property and start-ups like Go2 Communications, where he worked as managing director. He also told Jane about a 'land deal' somewhere between Thailand and Cambodia, and that, when he travelled there, he needed bodyguards who stayed outside his door at night. Bizarrely, he even gave names for the bodyguards, telling her they were called 'Hans' and 'Suk'. He presented Jane with a printed email purporting to be from his accountant in Hong Kong – a man called 'David James'. 'He'd gotten a deal for €500 million to sell land in Asia.' He sent emails from this accountant to Jane, but when she looked at the source address it was DJ's own regular Gmail account.

While she was living with DJ in the luxury four-bedroom, five-bathroom property, Jane started to probe more about his cancer treatment, as he was spending long periods away from home. She had no idea where DJ was when he claimed to be abroad, but she suspected something was off from the start. Looking back now, she believes he was likely staying close to home all along. She explained that she never called him when he was away, supposedly for treatment, as the couple usually texted or else DJ called her. When she asked him about the large scar on the back of his head – 'Is that scar from the brain surgery the papers said you had?' – Jane said DJ got irate, and he never gave her a straight answer about it, no matter how many times she quizzed him. She also questioned him about his visits to Seattle, so, one day, when he was supposed to be there, he sent her an image of the view from his hospital window. She quickly realised this was a satellite view image from Google that anybody could download from anywhere in the world – so she didn't believe DJ was in Seattle.

There were times when Jane felt put down by DJ, who often made remarks about her weight and told her she 'should run around the golf course to tone up'. He'd make comments on make-up not being washed off her face properly and how her hair wasn't nice or she wasn't 'pretty enough'. His mood could change rapidly, as she found out one day when he turned on her for chewing her food too loudly. DJ was also sensitive about his height, and she claimed he sometimes stood on his 'tippy toes' for photographs to appear taller.

During the relationship, DJ introduced Jane to his ex-wife, Christine, and her husband, Gary Preston (who sadly passed away suddenly in November 2023), and he also brought her to medal presentations around the country, where they received rapturous receptions on arrival, like a celebrity couple. She also met a friend of DJ's on 'numerous occasions', 'an elderly lady who owned a big estate in Kildare', and they visited a dying priest (believed to be the late Fr Joe Gough – a missionary priest and teacher from Gowran). DJ's girlfriend noticed the strong interest he took in both and wondered why he would want to spend so much time in their company when he was a busy dad of two with other places to be. She didn't understand the visits at the time. 'I thought it was strange; why would you be visiting and interacting with these people? Now I think he was trying to sell them a story, but at the time it was as if they were a relative or a friend. He didn't discuss money or illness with them in front of me.'

Despite the fact that he didn't seem to be lacking funds, Jane noticed some odd behaviour from DJ, such as the fact that he used to 'borrow' cars from dealerships. 'They'd be hounding him to get them back.' She also noticed how his home was being 'depleted' of furniture, which DJ claimed

Sarah Newman was taking back. 'I saw him with dodgy men on one occasion taking stuff away'. DJ borrowed over €17,000 from Jane herself during the relationship, claiming he needed it to pay 'outstanding bills in relation to property'. It was only through 'sheer pressure' that she got it all back, but some of the cheques DJ used to pay Jane back with were from third parties in Kilkenny. 'My sense is that he was probably borrowing from others to pay me back. They weren't cheques from employers, they were normal cheques written to him by individuals, I'm fairly sure.' This stacks up with what many sources believe DJ was doing, such as Declan, who told this author he was 'robbing Peter to pay Paul'.

Once Jane started to really question some of the claims DJ was making about his health and having to travel abroad, the relationship changed. 'I pushed and pushed and pushed and he knew the game was up, so he started treating me badly and left.' By May 2013 the relationship was over, but DJ's weird behaviour played on Jane's mind for many years to come.

After his retirement from intercounty hurling, DJ had devoted a lot of time to talking about his health, worrying about being healthy, visiting hospitals, dropping into support groups, asking people about their own symptoms, and gathering up literature and information. He spent time observing people undergoing treatment. He talked to many people about their own or their loved one's cancer and asked probing questions. At the time, people saw his actions as sincere and thoughtful. Health concerns had dominated DJ's life from the very start of his hurling career – he always seemed to be injured, regularly appearing with a bandage or needing a scan of some sort, but that was not unusual for somebody hurling at his level.

However, there were occasions when people who trained with him thought it was odd, as they knew his skill at staying away from tackles and avoiding potentially harmful situations. There are those who doubted DJ's injury claims and wondered if he was faking it to appear more heroic when he played a match. Others thought this was DJ's way of handling situations. Their view was that DJ would use injury as an excuse to get out of an obligation or to renege on a commitment. DJ's own take was that he was lucky with injuries. He had taken blows to the hand – one finger was fractured seven times – and he picked up hamstring, shoulder and collarbone injuries but 'nothing major with knees or ankles'.

To the outside world, DJ seemed to be relatively fit and healthy, and his public persona in 2013 would reflect no signs of any dire health issue, despite a short stint in hospital in January with pneumonia. On 31 July, a wet Wednesday evening in Gowran three days after Kilkenny had crashed out of the All-Ireland Senior Hurling Championship the previous Sunday, DJ lined out in a Junior game between Young Irelands and Lisdowney alongside his teenage son Seán. DJ had taken the job of team trainer in 2012, but just when it seemed his playing days were long behind him, here he was, at forty-two years old, making up the numbers for Young Irelands.

In the *Sunday Independent* on 4 August, Marie Crowe documented the father and son outing: 'Watching Carey on the pitch it is clear he still has the skills of the game: he can slot the ball over the bar from tight angles, pluck it out of the air and pick a player out with a perfect pass. He's in good shape too; daily cycles and a healthy diet mean he is still the same weight he was back in 1992. And although the burst of speed over ten yards – one of his most outstanding attributes when in his prime – is still decent, problems arise if he has to go much further than that. It's then the injury worries set in, the fear of a pulled muscle or a groin tear, injuries which will take longer to heal at this stage in his life.'

Crowe related how after the game, DJ had an ice-bath and then dropped Seán home to his ex-wife Christine, and from the interaction among the family, it was evident to Crowe they were 'all on great terms despite what the perception is in the outside world'. DJ, who was still living in Kildare at this time, mentioned to Crowe that if he was not around Kilkenny, 'there is something being said and if I am around there is something being said ... Most of it is not true, it's just people guessing things about me for their own benefit. Whatever happens in my private life stays there, because I keep it that way, and whatever people are saying they are guessing, nothing will come out from me.' He was not explicit about the rumours he was referencing, so it's not clear if these were about his finances, his love life, his health or all of the above.

Crowe detailed how Carey was feeling fit and well but had suffered a 'difficult few months' since his health problems of 2012. He said the blood clots 'came as a massive shock'. Carey told Crowe, 'You take it for granted when you wear a helmet that you are safe, but people don't realise the amount of hits you get on the head while wearing one. I've been hospitalised with concussion seven times in my career and had to replace my face guard on my helmet four times because it was damaged.'

DJ's focus on helmets in this and subsequent interviews around this period, reflects the fact that concussion had become a hot topic. He told Crowe that 'getting another belt on the head is a big fear I have now, just because you can't see the damage doesn't mean there isn't some internally'. Crowe stated that overall, 'Carey has a positive attitude and outlook' – even when his world 'seemed to be crumbling', he held his head up high, consistently doing media work and training teams. 'And while out and about he's been met with a phenomenal amount of support. Of course there will always be begrudgers and those who are happy to see him struggling but they are outnumbered by people who have told him they are saying prayers and lighting candles for him, by those who care.' DJ also told the sports reporter before she signed off, 'You can make a million in business and you can lose it, so therefore it can be taken away but you can never take away what someone achieves on the sports field.'

A month later, DJ lined out again for Gowran when Lisdowney met Young Irelands in the North Kilkenny Junior A final, with the game eventually finishing in a draw after extra time. A report appeared on Balls.ie the next day, 26 August, which stated: 'Young Irelands managed that draw largely in part [due] to their super sub, a 42-year-old named DJ Carey, who scored two goals from two chances.' So, during the late summer of 2013, DJ Carey appeared to be in the best of health, even making appearances as a 'super sub'.

While DJ was getting back in the game, his sister Catriona became the focus of a newspaper investigation. Since leaving her brother's business, she had become involved in a 'shadowy property trust', the Rodolphus Allen Family Private Trust. Throughout the summer of 2013, the trust attracted around 2,000 people who wanted to remain in control of their properties but were saddled with debt. It claimed to have discovered a way to split mortgages from properties. As Conor Ryan reported in the *Irish Examiner* on Monday, 14 October 2013, many of the people who signed up to the trust were involved in business during the boom and put their faith in the 'mysterious property trust'. 'The trust, which ascribed to a quest for divine consciousness, said its secret would remain on a need-to-know basis and said those with doubts should stay out. Even on those terms people paid up, signed in, and were told that when the time was right, the Rodolphus Allen Trust would unveil its secret in court and strike down the mortgages.'

Liz Allen, in a *Mail on Sunday* investigation published on 15 September, reported that Catriona was a 'key participant in a trust' that had been reported to gardaí. Allen said the Trust stood to take 'at least a €100m ownership stake in the properties of its members, if its campaign against financial institutions is successful. Catriona Carey, 35, is one of three main players – alongside the figurehead Charlie Allen and a David Walshe – who are associated with the administration of the Rodolphus Allen Family Trust, which claims it already has well in excess of €1bn in distressed property on its books since its formation in July.' The *Mail*'s investigation uncovered a number of findings in relation to the 'mysterious trust', including that it had been referred to gardaí by 'Fianna Fáil senator Thomas Byrne after he became concerned about its activities following a meeting with the three main protagonists in June'.

According to Liz Allen, the Trust operated on a cash-only basis, with a minimum €525 fee charged to prospective members with one property to register. The members signed over their properties to the trust 'without being told about the secret legal strategy the trust claims it will employ against banks – or who their legal team will be'. Senator Byrne confirmed to the *Mail* that he had complained to gardaí following a meeting with Charlie Allen in Leinster House in July 2013. 'I took the meeting because a constituent was in mortgage distress and said he had heard about this organisation that could help. I met Mr Allen and another man and a woman. Mr Allen told me: "We've found a flaw in mortgage deeds". I told him I was a solicitor and I asked if he had a website. He said: "It's word of mouth only." Mr Byrne said that when he mentioned New Beginning (which assists distressed property owners) the meeting ended.' Byrne described the whole meeting as 'bizarre' and went on to report his concerns to gardaí and to raise the matter in the Seanad. He was concerned that those joining the trust were 'already in dire straits … I am also asking what is happening to the monies being paid into the trust,' he said. One property developer who attended a meeting of the trust with two colleagues said, 'it just didn't feel right'. Catriona's activities with the property trust were thoroughly documented in this article, but no charges were ever brought against her or any of the others involved in the trust. It's thought she had little interaction with her brother during this time, after their falling out in 2009.

Just days after this investigation was published, DJ Carey was the personality behind the media launch of the 2013 Pfizer Health Index, which had tracked people's health and well-being over the previous eight years. His smiling photograph appeared in media coverage of the launch, which showed that 90 per cent of people believed that depression, anxiety and mental health problems had increased since the recession. Speaking at the event, DJ said, 'I can't emphasise enough how important it is to look after your health, and in particular your mental health. Thankfully, I have no lasting effects [from his earlier health issues] and my underlying level of fitness helped me out of it. I played some hurling with my club this year and all is good.'

A report on the Pfizer launch appeared in the *Irish Independent* on 18 September. In it, Eilish O'Regan stated that Carey had 'reinvented his lifestyle after ending up in intensive care more than two years ago, when a virus attacked his heart at a time he was feeling low over personal and financial problems'. She said that DJ's breakfast was now 'wheatgrass juice instead of his favourite fry, and he is back on his bike cycling as well as training with his old hurling club in Gowran, Kilkenny.' He emphasised that he had 'no lasting effects' from his health issues, and 'all is good'. According to O'Regan, 'He has not found a new relationship but is making a business comeback with a company called Go-To Communications [*sic*], which installs credit card machines. And he has a book "DJ" due for launch next month.'

'IT'S ALL IN HIS HEAD'

Four days after these announcements about his health in public, DJ would give some contrasting and devastating news to a small number of officials involved in organising the Asian Games. On 22 September 2013, prior to Mayo being defeated by Dublin by a single point in the All-Ireland football final, officials from the Asian Games were in the Croke Park Hotel with their sponsors. The Asian GAA County Board holds an annual two-day tournament, bringing together clubs from all over Asia. The games have men's, ladies and youth competitions in hurling, camogie and Gaelic football, with up to 180 matches played.

The event has been building since it started in 1996, and to make it more attractive for sponsors and to garner publicity, organisers go to great lengths to entice high-profile people to attend. Well-known sports journalists and sporting legends, such as Mícheál Ó Muircheartaigh, Brian Mullins, Cora Staunton, Bríd Stack and Jack McCaffrey, have attended over the years, and although there was no appearance fee, flights and expenses were taken care of by the board. The plan that year was to attract a huge name to the games – officials had set their sights on DJ Carey. He had never attended before, but there was massive reverence and respect for him at home and abroad.

Páraic McGrath, who was then chairman of the Asian Games, was one of those who met DJ Carey in the Croke Park Hotel. McGrath was excited at the prospect of meeting DJ, saying he had long harboured ambitions of attracting Carey to the games. But just as he started explaining the event and the fact that he would be honoured if DJ would travel as their guest to the games, Carey turned to Páraic and said in hushed tones, 'I've a bit of cancer; I've to go to America for treatment.' Páraic was floored at what he had just been told.

DJ went on to explain that he had a rare form of brain cancer and the only treatment available was in America. 'I'm putting efforts into getting the money together; you know the costs are horrendous,' he said. Páraic was unsure if this meant DJ would be unable to travel, or what exactly his circumstances were. When asked questions, DJ explained that he was trying to get the treatment out of the way, but if he got that done, he'd be able to travel to the Asian Games. Then he turned to those present saying, 'I'd want money for this, maybe about ten thousand to go out.' He made it clear that, unless there was a fee paid, he wouldn't be going. For a moment the officials were stunned into silence. Páraic explained to DJ that there weren't any funds in place to pay appearance fees, but that they covered the cost of what would be a once-in-a-lifetime experience. 'Right, sure, I'll see ... okay, well, good luck to you anyway,' DJ said before walking off.

The men were shocked at DJ's revelation of brain cancer. They didn't discuss the matter with others at the time, as it seemed to be a private health issue, and they didn't wish to break any confidences. However, Páraic said later that he couldn't understand how somebody of DJ's stature was fighting brain cancer, yet there was nothing about it in the public domain – his thoughts were, surely the public would be glad to help? DJ was a hurling hero, and adoring fans would gladly get involved if he was looking for help. Thinking back, one of those present said DJ's tone was 'different' when he talked about his cancer, and the way he delivered the message 'felt off'. A decade later, when word started to filter out about a GAA star involved in a cancer scam, Páraic remembered the conversation at the Croke Park Hotel on the day of the 2013 All-Ireland football final. 'I was talking to people [in 2023] who were saying, "DJ's going around everybody saying he has cancer. There's nothing wrong with him but he owes money."' Páraic had assumed DJ had made a recovery in the intervening years, but when he heard the rumours about a cancer scam, he clearly recalled his interaction with the hurling star.

There are some who never believed that DJ Carey was telling the truth and were aware of the 'tall tales' he liked to tell; they discussed with others how they thought he faked and exaggerated injuries over the years. DJ's old teammates told others that he courted attention, one calling him a 'strange man', while some had heard stories of him borrowing money for treatment abroad. Not everybody knew that DJ was faking cancer, but many close to him thought he had credibility issues and weren't sure about his health claims. It may seem strange, but some GAA people who knew DJ never took what he said seriously, and they would laugh and joke about some of the claims he made, without realising the damage he was doing.

Shortly after the Asian Games event, there was some good news for DJ Carey. IT Carlow announced him as its new Ambassador for Hurling, and staff and students there were delighted to welcome him into the role. He joined the then Kilkenny Senior hurling trainer and selector Mick Dempsey, who was IT Carlow's course tutor for the BA in Sport and Exercise (GAA), to promote and enhance hurling in the college. On 1 October, Independent.ie reported that, in reaction to his new role, DJ said, 'I'm absolutely delighted to be the Ambassador for Hurling at IT Carlow. With the top-class facilities that IT Carlow has developed, it is now the prime location for developing hurling skills and playing at the highest level – the Fitzgibbon Cup. It's an exciting time for the development of hurling and I'm really looking forward to getting involved with the club here at IT Carlow.'

The going rate for a third-level college hurling coach would be somewhere between €200–€250 per session, but if you were DJ Carey you could name your price. However, a source said that he didn't seem interested in money when it came to deciding his rate, and, in the early days of his involvement with college hurling, DJ 'didn't want any money for it'. In fact, there was a point in time when he was being chased to put in his expenses claim for mileage. This changed over time, and the position later provided him with a welcome regular income.

Soon after his new role with IT Carlow was announced, DJ issued an appeal for the return of some of his All-Ireland jerseys, claiming they had been stolen from his Monkstown home two years earlier. In an interview with Nicola Anderson for the *Irish Independent*, he said it had come to his attention that one of the jerseys was for sale on eBay with an asking price of '€400 or €500'. The *Independent* reported that an online search revealed the item was no longer available. DJ issued this appeal: 'I just say to anyone that if they come across my All-Ireland jerseys, just to know that they were stolen and I emphatically say they were stolen from my house.' Carey said he had already tried to get the black-and-amber jerseys back with an appeal on Facebook and by email, but without success. '"If you do come across them, I'm not difficult to contact; I'm on Twitter," he said.' Like other stories DJ has given to the media over the years, which often involve dramatic thefts and events that grab attention, the main source of this story is DJ himself, so it is difficult to substantiate or disprove what he is claiming.

Just three days after the story about the jerseys was in the *Irish Independent*, DJ Carey's autobiography was ready to officially launch. Written in conjunction with Martin Breheny, the book was launched by Brian Cody on 28 October in Kilkenny's Langtons Hotel. Cody told the room that Carey might have been the finest tackler he ever saw play hurling. On 2 November 2013, Vincent Hogan wrote that 'Old gods of the game like "Babs" Keating and Eddie Keher were in attendance, as was racehorse trainer Jim Bolger, looking a good two decades younger than someone whose 72nd birthday will fall on Christmas Day. Modern greats attended too, men like Brian Whelahan, Tipperary's Eoin Kelly, Eddie Brennan, John Power, Ollie Baker, Charlie Carter and James McGarry.' DJ's beloved aunt, Peggy Carey Muldowney, and his uncle, Martin Carey (who died in 2024), were also there. DJ then went on a book tour for the next number of months, signing copies of the book in towns all over the country. There are photographs in local newspapers showing crowds of people queuing to get their book signed. It was a remarkable testament to DJ's enduring legacy that, seven years after his retirement from intercounty hurling, there was still such interest in his autobiography – it even landed him a prime-time television slot on *The Late Late Show*.

While DJ was millions of euro in debt to AIB, some of his new colleagues in IT Carlow observed strange contradictions in his life. In early 2014, around the time he started asking Denis O'Brien for financial assistance, he came into the college and announced he was 'off to the Super Bowl', posting on Facebook on 2 February 2014: 'Thrilled to be in New York for the Super Bowl. Great atmosphere. Nearly as good as all-Ireland weekend lol [laugh out loud].' Comments underneath this post show how wide his network of contacts was in the United States from his many trips there over the years. A man called Pat Fitzpatrick told him, 'swing by Dallas again DJ!' and he replied, 'Hopefully may Pat'. Colleagues wondered where he got the money for the trip.

DJ seemed in good form when he returned home from his trip. Retired detective garda Shem Brophy was organising a dinner dance for members of Carlow Hurling Club to honour the Senior, Junior and Intermediate teams for their contributions on the hurling field, and he decided to ask DJ to be the special guest. Brophy planned a four-course meal with live music and some awards for Saturday 8 March. It had been twenty-five years since Carlow had won a Senior Championship, and Shem, as chairman of the club at the time, thought it would be fitting to bring people together to mark the occasion. He was thrilled when DJ agreed to come along to present awards on the night. 'I played with St Patrick's Ballyragget [Kilkenny club] and I knew him to say hello. I'd met him at Nowlan Park a good few times over the years through the hurling,' explained Shem. When he phoned DJ to invite him to the event, the hurler accepted and asked if he could bring one of his sons with him. 'I said, "Bring him on, we've a bit of dinner for everyone" ... On the night I addressed the club, I intro'd DJ and he said a few words – he spoke very well, and I can tell you he was in no rush going home. He arrived early, he spoke to everyone and left at maybe 1.30 a.m.'

Shem conveyed how DJ took time with everybody who wanted to talk to him and, when it came to paying him at the end of the evening, DJ waved his hand and said he wouldn't take the money. 'He just said, "The club needs it." He didn't want to take a shilling.' Shem said that he gave DJ a small amount of money – 'you wouldn't give it to a child for their confirmation' – to cover his expenses and that he 'shoved it into his pocket'. At the time, Shem said he was 'aware' DJ was having 'health problems', and he was led to believe the cost of his treatment was covered by the fact that he had played world handball in the US – 'somebody told me that'. However, DJ didn't explicitly tell Shem he had cancer.

Around the same time, the GAA was targeted in a spate of speed 'smash and grabs'. On 30 March, Jerome Reilly wrote in the *Sunday Independent* that DJ Carey had lashed out at 'scumbags and arseholes on free legal aid' after his 'family became the latest victims of a spate of robberies around the country at GAA grounds'. The article noted that one of Carey's brothers had his white BMW stolen 'when thieves targeted the dressing room of the Young Irelands GAA club from Gowran as they played a challenge match with O'Loughlin Gaels at Tinryland in Carlow'. As well as the car, 'the thieves also took 8 iPhones, cash and other valuables from the dressing room including a phone owned by the All-Star hurler's son, Seán.' On the same night as the Tinryland incidents, DJ stated that 'Carlow IT was also robbed' and claimed, 'The thieves are getting dressed up in tracksuits so they blend in. It's very professional. There are not enough gardaí because of cutbacks and at the same time if they do get caught these arseholes and scumbags get free legal aid and a slap on the wrist from the courts.' DJ did not realise, when he was lambasting the legal aid system, that a decade later he would be relying on the same system to fund his defence.

Throughout 2014 DJ lent his support to good causes. In May a committee was established to financially support former Waterford hurler and All-Star Ken McGrath in his recovery from open heart surgery. A benefit match was held in Walsh Park on Friday 27 June with Noel Skehan, Eddie Keher and DJ on the line for Leinster against Munster. Later that summer, in August, DJ signed autographs for children as he once again turned out at the Hurling For Cancer fundraising match in aid of the Irish Cancer Society at Saint Conleth's Park, Newbridge. He didn't appear to be in poor health at any of these events, nor did he look like a man who had a serious form of cancer and was undergoing specialist treatment for it. Notably, when supporters would later suggest holding a similar event for DJ, he would refuse on the grounds of privacy. Perhaps he was worried that such a public event might expose his lies.

8

FALLING FOR DJ

When Alison (not her real name) started seeing DJ Carey in December 2014, it was casual; she didn't for a moment think she was falling in love, nor did she picture herself getting into a serious relationship with the hurler. Saying that, her friends thought she was intrigued by him, and they could see she had struck up a friendship before the relationship became intimate. Alison is eleven years younger than DJ, and while they shared a love of GAA and grew up in villages not too far apart, they did not announce their relationship to their families. Carey introduced her to very few friends or family members during their five-year relationship, and they attended very few events together.

When the couple first met, DJ was still living in the K Club and driving a BMW, and he occasionally frequented Carton House pool and leisure centre, where Alison was also a member. A short time later, DJ had to leave his K Club home after it was seized by AIB, although his financial difficulties with the banks were far from over, and it would be three more years before he would secure a debt settlement with AIB. DJ didn't take his new girlfriend to fine restaurants or whisk her away on expensive weekend breaks, nor did he appear to lead an extravagant life when they were together. In fact, there were times when he was doing the opposite and appeared to be struggling financially. He often relied on her for money. On one of their first dates he claimed he had left his wallet in a hotel in Dublin after a business meeting. He also regularly asked her for loans, claiming he needed to pay taxes.

Friends said Alison was surprised at how open DJ was with her about his money worries when they met. She was aware that the bank was trying to take back his K Club home and she knew his finances were in a bad way. DJ also revealed the worst possible news to Alison soon after they started seeing each other: he told her he had a terminal illness, explaining that he had a diagnosis of multiple myeloma. That very first Christmas they were together, DJ explained to Alison that he had to go to Seattle for cancer treatment. After he returned, Alison noticed he had no hair or eyebrows and wore blister patches on his neck.

It was this story about his illness that made Alison reluctant to challenge DJ on the obvious contradictions in his behaviour. Despite his claims of being broke and his regular borrowing of money from her, DJ went on a number of expensive trips abroad while they were together. While she was troubled by this, she seemed afraid to go against DJ, and she told her closest friends that she didn't want to be mean to somebody who was 'terminally ill with cancer'.

On one of the rare times DJ and Alison were seen at a

public event together in the early stages of their relationship, DJ brought her to Croke Park. While they were sitting in a hospitality lounge having dinner with a group of others, DJ leaned in close to the man next to him and talked in hushed tones. An observer at the table heard DJ mentioning 'stem cell treatment', but when Alison asked DJ, 'What's that you're talking about?', he stopped the conversation, and the man next to him joked, 'Marry them young and tell them nothing.'

DJ's new relationship continued after he lost his K Club home, and he moved to an apartment in Wellington House in Ballsbridge, where he stayed for almost fifteen months. This apartment was loaned to him by Denis O'Brien, although he initially told Alison he owned it. She never cohabited with DJ, as she did not want to uproot her daughter, but DJ's son, Seán, who was studying commerce in UCD at this time, stayed with him during term time. DJ told neighbours that he was travelling over and back to Seattle for cancer treatment, and he mentioned in casual conversation that a businessman was covering the cost of his flights. He said he just needed to contact this man's secretary to ensure flights were booked. It's not clear if this actually happened, but that's what he told people. Whether the generous businessman he was referring to here was Denis O'Brien or someone else is not known, but DJ would drop this information into chats he shared with punters and businesspeople he met during regular visits to Searson's pub on Baggot Street.

Another link to O'Brien came in February 2015, when there was an official announcement that DJ Carey had signed an exclusive deal as a GAA analyst with Newstalk 106–108 FM, then owned by O'Brien's Communicorp. He signed with the *Off The Ball* team to contribute to the station throughout the GAA season; he also took part in outside broadcasts. DJ Carey's new gig was widely publicised, with the *Irish Independent* reporting that he was 'delighted' to be joining the team: 'The station's coverage of all sports is second to none, and I'm hoping that my experience both on and off the field will provide a new dimension to the GAA coverage. It will be a great challenge, but one which I'm relishing, and I'm sure we will also have some fun along the way.' This author contacted Ger Gilroy, managing director at *Off The Ball*, about DJ's stint at the station, but he declined to comment. DJ's commitment to the Newstalk deal seemed to fizzle out quickly, or at least he didn't get huge airtime at the station that anybody can recall.

On 8 April, two months after the Newstalk announcement, DJ was letting the world know, through his Facebook page, that he was in Augusta for the US Masters with his son Mikey. He got lots of comments and 'likes' on the post he shared, which said, 'Great day at the par 3. Irish guys in great form.' The comments underneath were almost all positive, though there was one that had a strange tone. It was from Declan, the man who had loaned DJ money five years previously, and he asked DJ to make contact. 'Hi DJ great to see you are enjoying urself in Augusta.???? Can you contact me ASAP Much appreciated. You have my number. Enjoy.'

This was the second message the man had left publicly on DJ's Facebook page trying to get in contact with the former hurler. Declan was frantically trying to make contact as he wanted his €10,000 back. He had not initially chased DJ for the money because his own business had been doing well, but times had changed and now he needed it. Declan could see that DJ had the money to attend the Masters and was well enough to go on a golfing jaunt with a group of golfers, so why hadn't he returned his ten grand? A passionate GAA man, Declan started to phone around his contacts and people who knew DJ, and was told that the hurler had 'borrowed a lot of money', but most people 'didn't know the size of it'. He said it quickly became 'obvious' to him in 2015 that everything from DJ 'was lies'.

Thinking back, Declan recalled an elaborate story that DJ told him several times about owning land in Vietnam. It was similar to a story that DJ had told to another man in the K Club around 2010 and to a business associate in Northern Ireland some years later. Declan said that Carey compared the worth of the site to owning the most valuable seats in Croke Park, telling him the land was rich with minerals and he was going to make a fortune. 'He was saying it was all in the process; he was telling me this during phone calls, and I believed him. That's the thing, you'd believe DJ. He also had evidence – it wasn't just me he showed this to, he had an email with details of the deal. There were others giving him money too; he said the land was worth €300m and he'd be paying us all back.' It's not known how many others DJ sold this line to, or if any of those who gave him money as a result ever got it back.

On 8 May 2015, Declan texted DJ: 'We will be in dublin in a while DJ were can u meet [sic].' DJ replied that day: 'I ordered

€10k cash in this morning but they said it won't be ready till Monday morn. I can DD this into ur Accor [*sic*] I'll have to wait till Monday morn. I thought I sent u text this morn but just realised it didn't go. I will be in Dublin about 7ish. Are u free for a call?'

Despite Declan sending him several texts about meeting up to collect his money, DJ did not meet him that day. In one message sent by Declan to the former hurler a few days later, on 13 May, his impatience was clear: 'Ur making a cunt of me DJ'. There was no response. While he didn't respond to Declan, two days later he did share photographs of himself, his son Mikey and others on a trip to Dallas, Texas. In one of the snaps, DJ is visiting the AT&T Stadium.

Declan sent another message on 29 May: 'DJ call me I will meet u in Kilkenny or where suits. I am in ur area.' Again, no response. Despite this, Declan never reported DJ to the gardaí, as he didn't think there was any reason to do so. 'I was an adult in that I gave him the money, I gave him it in good faith. I was never going to get my money back, why would I waste my time going to the gardaí?'

Declan finally gave up chasing DJ for his money, and five years later, in 2020, he got a call out of the blue from Carey, asking to meet up and saying, 'I'm after having a tough time, I'm after overcoming multiple myeloma.' Declan said this time DJ didn't sound credible to him, as he was well aware of the serious implications of that type of cancer. 'I was resigned to the fact, look, I'm not getting my money back, and I'm not falling out with him … But I knew what he was saying about the multiple myeloma just wasn't right.' While he didn't believe what DJ was saying, he continued to take calls from him occasionally and they talked about matches and 'GAA stuff'. Declan is one of several people who describe DJ as a 'Walter Mitty'.

There are many others like Declan who loaned money to DJ from 2010 to 2020, but they are not willing to talk to this author out of loyalty to the former hurler. Not everybody gave DJ money for 'cancer treatment' – there were various reasons given, including to 'help a guy out'. People have given this author the names of wealthy individuals in the United States and Australia who also loaned DJ significant sums of money, but when contacted, the individuals declined to comment on the matter.

While living in the affluent area of Ballsbridge in 2015, DJ became friendly with a convicted fraudster. Thomas McLoughlin, better known as 'Tom the Con', was one of DJ's neighbours in Dublin 4. Regular listeners to RTÉ's *Liveline* may remember a lengthy campaign to find 'Tom the Con' in the year 2000, after he scammed people by paying for stays in guesthouses and hotels using false bank drafts. On 16 February that year, Fergus Black reported in the *Irish Independent* that McLoughlin was a 'real life Del Boy', who went under several names to 'charm' people out of their cash. Eventually, in July 2009, the law caught up with McLoughlin, a former prison officer, but he escaped with a three-year suspended sentence at Dublin Circuit Criminal Court. The court heard how McLoughlin had forty-one previous convictions, all relating to fraud. Most of the money was eventually paid back to his victims, but Judge Frank

O'Donnell noted there was a 'consistent pattern of offending that falls under the umbrella of deception, theft and fraud'. McLoughlin's crimes were not violent, but he showed no regard for his victims.

DJ and Tom were often seen together, such as eating in Searson's pub, and Tom regularly dropped into DJ's apartment for a chat. By that time, Tom's crimes were well documented and DJ would have been well aware of who he was. A source said they were 'bosom buddies' at one stage. As with many things in the former hurler's life, there was a lack of clarity about what happened between the two men, and also about what they discussed during their visits and what they had in common with each other. DJ was usually secretive about his business with Tom. We don't know if they shared secrets or swapped stories about how they conned people during their interactions, but a neighbour who observed the two men said that at some stage 'Tom the Con' and DJ fell out – they stopped visiting each other's apartments and DJ told a friend that the two of them had had a row, but he refused to elaborate.

On 31 August 2015, DJ Carey appeared on the *Ray D'Arcy Show* on RTÉ Radio 1 ahead of that weekend's All-Ireland Senior hurling final clash in Croke Park between Kilkenny and Galway. Carey used this interview as an opportunity to address rumours that his health problems were all 'in his head' – and to continue to lie. At the time, listeners were left believing that DJ had cancer – without ever explicitly telling D'Arcy about a cancer diagnosis, he certainly hinted at it and mentioned getting treatment abroad.

Years later, when the full picture of Carey's fraud was uncovered, many people would listen anew to Carey's responses to D'Arcy's questions given what they then knew. The public were intrigued about whether D'Arcy knew of DJ's false cancer claims, as his line of questioning on DJ's health seemed to be rather pointed. D'Arcy asked how DJ was, after he told his radio listeners there were 'health things' the hurler did not want to discuss, and then remarked on how 'healthy' DJ looked. DJ replied that he was doing okay but had had to travel to the United States 'for the guts of a year' for treatment. He then chuckled that he had hurled at a game the other night. He mentioned Tipperary hurler Noel McGrath, who had testicular cancer four months earlier but after an operation came on in an All-Ireland semi-final. DJ said 'lifestyle' could help – he said he didn't eat sugar any more and had changed a 'huge amount'. One of the biggest things DJ said had changed was that he was 'reasonably anonymous' living in Dublin. He explained that he was not well known in Dublin and needed peace and quiet 'when going through stuff'. When he was living in Kilkenny, people noticed his comings and goings a lot more.

When Ray mentioned 'terrible stories' about DJ over the years, Carey inhaled deeply before giving his response, which ended with, 'I've often heard stories about myself … "Oh there's nothing wrong with yer man, oh it's all in his head" … I wouldn't have met that person in ten years, but it's a presumption that they know something.' Before the interview wrapped, Ray asked DJ, 'When all of this thing that we haven't talked about … is over, will you come in and talk to us about it?' 'I will certainly,' DJ said, 'it's something that I have to keep as private as possible.'

This 2015 interview highlighted just how audacious DJ Carey was when it came to fabricating his cancer story. His behaviour had escalated from lying to individuals to convincing a national radio audience that he had undergone treatment abroad for a year. Another thing that DJ did cleverly was to use this interview as an opportunity to praise Irish businessman Denis O'Brien. He emphasised that he was a 'great admirer' of O'Brien and stated that the businessman got a lot of 'bad flack' but was 'a very generous man' with Ireland's best interests at heart. This does not come as a surprise, considering that O'Brien was already supporting DJ in a number of ways. Not only was he living in an apartment owned by O'Brien, but he was also working for businesses where O'Brien had huge interests, namely Newstalk and Topaz, for which he was a brand ambassador.

It is not known how DJ initially approached O'Brien, or if somebody opened the door to give him access to the billionaire, but a former close friend of DJ's said that after he got money from O'Brien there was no going back. 'He saw how easy it was to get money once he mentioned cancer. He just seemed to get worse after that.' A spokesperson for O'Brien told this author that the businessman was not in a position to comment. It would be some years before O'Brien would spend hours in a garda station speaking to detectives from the National Economic Crime Bureau about how DJ Carey had conned him.

He was not the only one being conned. As Alison's relationship with DJ continued, her closest friends became wary of her new boyfriend and cautioned her that the relationship was not good for her. They had a sense that she wasn't truly in love but was being manipulated by Carey – and much of the time she was being asked for money. Over the five years they were together, DJ often gave Alison excuses about not having money. He claimed that his insurance covered his cancer treatment in the US, but any money he had was needed for the trip and for his expenses while he was there. Another common explanation he gave for not having money was that his card had been compromised or was frozen because of fraudulent or suspicious transactions. He frequently changed vehicles and from 2014 on didn't appear to own a car, instead hiring one occasionally or driving a company car during his brief stints as a sales representative with various firms. DJ also behaved in a strange way in the run up to one trip abroad, acting quite 'hyper' and claiming to his partner that 'nobody' would help him. He behaved coldly towards her if she refused him a loan.

Alison's friends were aware that her relationship with DJ was low-key, but they often invited DJ to events and were frustrated when he never showed up. He was usually at a meeting, at training or at a match. They wanted to meet the hurler in person, and it was becoming embarrassing for Alison that he never came along. It became a running joke that they'd ask, 'Where's DJ?', knowing he would not be around. The couple's only outings seemed to be on the sidelines of GAA matches at weekends. When Alison's friends would ask, 'How's DJ?', she wouldn't say much in response, other than, 'He's grand.' Those close to her noticed that the normally bright and bubbly young woman was becoming withdrawn and losing her sparkle.

While he wouldn't appear for Alison's friends, DJ was happy to play his part in more prestigious events. In the run-up to the All-Ireland hurling final in September 2015, he participated in a photoshoot to promote the Topaz Quality Fuels campaign alongside Ireland rugby star Alan Quinlan; both were ambassadors for Topaz. In November that year, he opened the Éigse Sliabh Rua festival in the Rhu Glenn Country Club Hotel, and he was on hand for the forty-five-year celebration of Éire Óg An Charraig Mhór in County Monaghan alongside Jarlath Burns and Brian Cody.

In January 2016 DJ Carey was the guest speaker for the WLR/Granville Hotel GAA Awards. Phil Fanning, reporting in the *Waterford News & Star*, stated that DJ came across as a 'very down to earth man who loved his hurling and was well grounded throughout a sparkling career'. He said he had some 'good advice for the Waterford players and management going forward and his anecdotes about Babs Keating and Joe Hayes went down a treat'. DJ was also starting to get attention for his work with the IT Carlow (now SETU) hurlers around this time, and on 9 February the *Laois Nationalist* reported: 'Carlow IT have turned a few heads with two fine scorelines under former Kilkenny star forward DJ Carey.' There were other reports of the team being 'on fire' under DJ as they advanced to the quarter-finals of the Fitzgibbon Cup. In March DJ joined a host of Kilkenny hurling greats as one of the guests of honour for a Kilkenny GAA Race Day at Gowran Park. Kilkenny's All-Ireland winning captains from 1963 onwards were present.

In June 2016 Seamus O'Hanlon penned a column in *The Argus* in which he mentioned Clan na Gael's annual golf classic held in the Ballymascanlon Hotel and Golf Resort in Dundalk. There, he 'had the pleasure of golfing with hurling legend DJ Carey'. O'Hanlon did not mention the word cancer but stated, 'The last few years have been difficult for DJ as he fought battles on several fronts including his health, finances and personal life, but I found the Kilkenny man a warm, genuine and engaging individual who was accommodating to everyone who attended both before, during and after the event.' During this time, DJ appeared to be attending fundraisers and playing golf regularly, but in an *Irish Independent* report published on 13 October, he seemed keen to tell a different story. In the 'Tee to Green' supplement, in response to the question 'How's your golf?', DJ answered, 'Well, my golf is very limited now. I'm kept going, trying to keep my head above water, but I haven't played that much for a while. I think the lowest handicap I had was 1.7 and I'm a 2.0 now.'

In the piece, he was also asked about meeting Tiger Woods at Mount Juliet in 2002. What was it like? 'Through a request from JP McManus, we had dinner and he wasn't interested in talking golf. He wanted to talk about amateur sport and hurling and the banter was good between JP and himself! JP is a passionate hurling and GAA man and he's very big on the importance of the GAA remaining amateur. And coming from the professional ethos, Tiger said he wouldn't do what we did as amateurs.'

He also mentioned in the interview that he had been to the US Masters (held in Augusta, Georgia) four times 'and played the course as well'. 'John Carr is a member and he brought me. You arrive in the evening, go for dinner and then the following morning you go out and play it twice, go for dinner and then go back and play another 18 in the morning and maybe the par-threes.' DJ also revealed he'd been to another famous US golf club, Pebble Beach, 'three times and never played it because my timing was wrong'. Finally, when asked what his idea of 'perfect happiness' was, DJ replied: 'Is there any such thing as perfect happiness? Sport is enjoyment – win, lose or draw … For me, happiness is sport.'

DJ and Mick Dempsey had a slice of happiness when they led their IT Carlow hurlers to victory in the Higher Education Senior Hurling League final in November 2016. 'IT Carlow make history with three-in-a-row' was the headline in the sports section of the *Nationalist* on 29 November, after the Barrowside beat Limerick IT by four points in Thurles.

In late 2016 or early 2017 DJ had to move back to Kilkenny when he had to leave the Ballsbridge apartment. He told some family members and friends that the apartment was being renovated, but whether that was the real reason for him leaving is unknown. For a short period before finding somewhere to rent, he relied on family and friends, and he confided in at least one person that the 'well had run dry' with Denis O'Brien. This source believed he stayed in Christine's home for a time, as the two of them remained on good terms. There were odd Saturday nights when the family shared takeaways together, and they regularly attended matches together to watch their sons playing. On one occasion Kilkenny fans noticed them all eating sandwiches and drinking tea from the boot of the car on the day of a big match at Croke Park, when Christine was parked on Clonliffe Road.

In 2017 DJ started renting Apartment 54, Station House, New Quarter at MacDonagh Junction in Kilkenny city. The two-bedroom apartment was a massive comedown from the Dublin 4 quarters. Alison visited him frequently for overnight stays and weekends. Friends believed that she was sticking with DJ out of loyalty because she thought he was dying. Alison, who had lost her own mother to cancer when she was just sixteen, told them that he had nobody else and she couldn't abandon him. Her friends knew that Carey gave Alison the cold shoulder when she refused to give him cash. She had told them that he threatened, more than once, to pack up and go to Australia, where he said he had a good friend who could help him start a new life, as he had nothing left in Kilkenny. Carey had previously been to Australia, where he had enjoyed the hospitality of Kilkenny GAA fans for the entire trip, had been given the use of a car and provided with accommodation, and had generally been treated like royalty. Once during a trip there, while on his way back to the airport, he asked a man for a loan of €50,000. His request was declined.

Alison's friends believe she was being used by Carey to help him pay his rent and bills. She confided in her closest friend that she also gave him lump sums over the years, including €6,000 around the time of his mother's funeral. On 24 September 2018,

Maura Carey died at the family home at the Demesne, Gowran. People remember how she had not looked well but wouldn't admit that she was sick. She suffered from cancer and had a difficult death in the end. DJ never thanked Alison for the loan, seeming interested only in how quickly he would get it, asking, 'Is that AIB to AIB?' If money was transferred directly from one AIB account to another, it would be immediately accessible, but, if not, he would have to wait for it to clear. It's not known if the money Alison gave him went towards funeral expenses or into his pocket. That year, while he appeared to spend thousands on gifts for his family at Christmas time, he didn't buy Alison so much as a card. This was one of the times when he claimed to her that he was broke and going for treatment.

At an unknown date, sometime between 2017 and 2019, while living in the apartment at MacDonagh Junction, DJ reported a burglary to the gardaí and complained that an expensive set of golf clubs had been taken. However, the apartment is in a highly secure location with CCTV, and it would not have been easy to get in or out without being seen or picked up on nearby cameras. It's understood the incident was thoroughly checked out by detectives in Kilkenny, but DJ's story simply didn't add up. Gardaí could not find any evidence of a break-in at the property, and they subsequently flagged the report for their own internal records as suspicious. Detectives had doubts about whether the burglary ever happened, although it's not clear if they ever considered charging DJ in relation to making a false report.

While Alison and DJ were together, he would regularly

disappear for weeks at a time, explaining to her that he needed to go to the US for treatment and to completely 'switch off'. However, on one occasion, her friends were convinced they saw him in Carton House when he was supposed to be in Seattle. Another time, he was spotted in Maynooth. On both occasions, when confronted, DJ swore to Alison that it wasn't him, saying her friends were probably 'seeing things'. When questioned, he'd put up his finger with a calm demeanour and say, 'incorrect' or 'not true'. Alison believed DJ because the alternative was unthinkable – why would he lie about having cancer? He'd also return from his purported treatment abroad with no eyebrows or hair on his chest, yet there was hair elsewhere on his body, such as his legs. He regularly wore women's heel protectors on his neck. He told Alison they were plasters applied after treatment in Seattle. Then, on finding just such a packet of heel protectors in his bathroom, when she questioned him as to why they were there, DJ tried to convince her they belonged to her.

Dramatic events always seemed to happen right before DJ asked Alison for money. He regularly said he was attending St James's Hospital having 'his blood washed', but then things would get 'really bad' and suddenly he'd need a transfusion, or he would have to go to Seattle for treatment again. Alison noticed, like Jane before her, that DJ had a 'morbid fascination with people sick or dying'. When she quizzed DJ on this, he replied, as she had suspected, that it was about money.

One day, three of Alison's female friends arrived at her home to have a serious discussion with her – an intervention of sorts. They suspected DJ did not have cancer and wanted his partner to face reality, pleading with her to leave him. She admitted she was not in love with Carey but vowed to stay with him because she was still convinced he was sick. However, her friends suspected that even Alison, at this stage, was starting to feel unsure about whether DJ actually had cancer. 'She was afraid to leave him in case he had cancer. She couldn't imagine the guilt of leaving him if he did turn out to have cancer and ended up dying on his own. He had a power over her, so that she stayed as long as she did,' said one friend. Alison told her friends that she pitied DJ, who once said to her, 'Every woman has screwed me over in my life including my mother and my sisters.' Alison's friends asked her to get proof of DJ's cancer, but this demand upset her. She didn't want to question DJ over his illness, as it seemed heartless, and any time she asked if his sons knew he was ill, DJ would get annoyed and tell her they were 'getting on with it', that they knew their dad had cancer but would not 'wallow' in it like her.

In the weeks leading up to the end of the relationship, DJ seemed to be constantly stressed, and his phone was always ringing. Alison mentioned to friends that she thought he was under pressure and was acting paranoid. DJ complained that somebody had tried to hack his phone and, as a result, he had silenced his notifications. He also had a second phone, a 'burner', which he guarded closely. He claimed that he needed it when he was travelling abroad for treatment.

Alison told friends that she felt 'gaslit' by DJ – she was constantly worried he was going to die from cancer but was also frustrated at how he disappeared for long periods at a time for his cancer treatment, and how he would switch off his main phone while he was away and not resurface for weeks at a time. He would sometimes cut off all contact – the relationship was on his terms only. There were times when he was effectively in hiding, as Revenue were pursuing him for tax liabilities. On 20 July 2018, a judgment was registered against DJ Carey by the Collector General for a sum of €27,938.62.

While DJ appeared to be under stress during this time and afraid to answer his door, contradictions in his behaviour remained. Just a month before the judgment was registered against him, he very publicly took part in the filming of a programme for Sky. On 9 June 2018, there was great excitement in Nowlan Park as Jamie Redknapp, Freddie Flintoff and Rob Beckett from the show *A League of Their Own* appeared at half-time for a special hurling challenge with DJ. The spectacle came during Kilkenny and Wexford's clash in front of a crowd of over 20,000. The action aired on 18 October as part of the series finale of *A League of Their Own*. In the episode, DJ prepares the trio before the big match day by testing their skills. Redknapp complains that Flintoff had 'definitely done this [hurling] before' but DJ points out that 'Jamie was a bit moany.' 'I think as a coach you need to put a guy in his place,' he tells the camera. While Redknapp struggles with the hurl, comedian Beckett turns to DJ to see if they can find something Redknapp is 'good at', to which DJ quips, 'Like what? Sunbathing is it?' The producers used this line to promote the episode on Sky.

Around this time, another company, Bunzl McLaughlin, a supplier of hygiene, catering and personal protective gear, employed DJ. As a sales representative, he spent a lot of time on the road travelling the country and visiting business premises like hotels. Sources said that, while working for Bunzl McLaughlin, he availed of a corporate membership in Mount Juliet and spent a lot of time there.

Meanwhile, his relationship with Alison continued, despite her friends' worries. Then, one weekend in November 2019, Alison was attending the wake of a lifelong friend who had died of cancer. Mary Smyth, a hugely popular figure because of her work as a founder member of the Éist Cancer Support Centre in Carlow, died on 16 November. A man approached Alison at the wake and was overheard asking her, 'Where is DJ? Is he not with you?' Alison was heard replying that he was out of the country getting treatment. 'He's out of the country?' The man laughed loudly as he repeated the phrase, looking at Alison incredulously. Alison looked shaken as the man continued, 'He's no more out of the country – sure he was having food with a brunette in Mount Juliet when I saw him today.'

Friends of Alison's remember how she retreated to her car and burst into tears. She had been so afraid that DJ would die from cancer, but now she had to face the truth. He had been lying to her. The next day, as Alison parked outside St Lazerian's Church in Leighlinbridge, where she was due to attend the celebration Mass of Mary's life, her phone pinged. A friend hugged her tightly as she read the message. It was from DJ, letting her know he was ending the relationship. Alison sat outside the church and wept. She didn't go inside.

While his personal life was in flux, Carey was enjoying a

renewed prominence in the GAA. In October 2019 Michael Dempsey, who had been part of Brian Cody's set-up since 2005, stepped down as selector for Kilkenny, and he left big boots to fill. Dempsey not only interacted with Carey through their work together at IT Carlow but also lived in the same apartment complex in Kilkenny city. They were often seen dining together in Langtons, deep in conversation. When asked by this author if he knew about Carey's bogus cancer claims, Dempsey refused to talk about the situation. He offered no insight and no comment into his friend's predicament, but sources close to Michael and DJ thought Dempsey had serious doubts about DJ's cancer, and by 2020 he had figured out that Carey was lying.

After a meeting of the Kilkenny County Board, DJ Carey was confirmed as taking over Dempsey's recently vacated job in Brian Cody's management team. He took the position, having been Kilkenny's Under-20 hurling and Minor football manager since September 2018. It seems strange that felt able to take on this role, having spoken to many people about his cancer treatment and needing to travel abroad regularly for treatment. Speaking to RTÉ 2FM's *Game On*, he said: 'I stepped down from the under-20s to take a break from it. All of a sudden, I get a call a couple of days later to see would I meet Brian. I didn't realise what it was. He didn't give much away on the phone. I had some reservations. One of my sons [Michael] is on the extended Senior panel for 2019. Obviously he would be looking to step up next year, and I'd have reservations on that myself. He [Cody] didn't accept it as an excuse, so here we are.'

On 2 December, Cian O'Connell reported on GAA.ie that

DJ was looking forward to being involved with Kilkenny in 2020. The report stated that in recent years Carey had been enjoying managing IT Carlow in the Fitzgibbon Cup, 'while also taking charge of the Kilkenny under-20 outfit'. 'My role is slightly different, I have been manager with most of the teams I have been involved with,' Carey said of his role as selector. 'In terms of hands-on coaching I haven't been doing an awful lot, so this will be a bit different. I would envisage that I will be doing more coaching, [but] Brian is obviously the boss. Martin Comerford, James McGarry and I will be in there coaching and hopefully making a bit of a difference. I'm looking forward to getting stuck into it, to see where it will take us. It is a new adventure for me. I played the game, I'm not any sort of a qualified coach or anything, I'm just bringing my own experience and thoughts to it more than anything else. We will see where that leads us.'

Carey was given this role despite the fact that some Kilkenny GAA officials were clearly aware of the credibility issues around his cancer claims and borrowing of money, two issues which were being discussed in Kilkenny at this time. An incident in early 2020 gives some insight into how suspicions were growing about Carey's behaviour within GAA circles. Around January 2020 DJ approached a Leinster GAA source looking for help from a benevolent fund. He explained that he was suffering from multiple myeloma and needed to travel to the US for treatment. The man remembers DJ showing him marks on his head. He felt sorry for him but knew due diligence was needed before he could agree to offer any financial help. The Leinster source contacted Kilkenny GAA, and word came back that DJ should not be given any money. The Kilkenny GAA person who rang the Leinster source did not explicitly say DJ was lying about his illness but agreed it would be unwise to hand over funds, so DJ's appeal for financial help was turned down.

However, Leinster did not give him a straightforward no. As DJ had said he was in a hurry, claiming he had to travel for treatment the following week, he was told their accountant was away, so there was nobody there to sign off on releasing any funds. The Leinster source said, 'I told him he could ring Leinster himself, but he rang me again the following week when he was supposed to be in America getting treatment.' When the man said, 'I thought you were to be in America this week', DJ replied that his treatment had been cancelled or postponed. But this didn't ring true. The Leinster source described DJ as a 'confident trickster' who told a good story with heartbreaking details.

So why was he given a role in Brian Cody's set-up for the 2020 season? When asked, another GAA source suggested it was a 'legitimate way of giving him a small few bob. Maybe they [Kilkenny County Board] hoped it would get him on the straight and narrow.' This source also said it was a 'natural progression' from his role with the under-20s, and the situation was further complicated by the fact that some would have known 'more than others'. 'Not everybody knew,' the GAA official insisted. 'Also, there was a little bit of illness early, so people were unsure if it was a total scam or not. If you didn't have your facts, how could you say?' There was no indication that Brian Cody was aware of what DJ was doing. The source said that Kilkenny people saw DJ as a hero and were defensive of him. 'It was very difficult for people who didn't want to believe what was happening.' Another hurling source expressed surprise to this author about DJ getting the role as selector in Cody's backroom team. 'Once DJ went in, it was never going to work,' he said of the decision. 'He had a weird way of thinking about hurling, and he'd clash with fellas.' Carey lasted just one year in the position, leaving the role in January 2021.

After DJ ended his relationship with Alison, despite his various jobs, he struggled to make his apartment rent payments on time and fell into arrears. During this period he spent a lot of time with Nicci St George Smith. While still seeing Alison, DJ had struck up a friendship with Nicci when she was volunteering with Community Radio Kilkenny City. She told people that she was working on making a documentary with DJ. While Nicci told friends she was not romantically involved with him, DJ appeared to quickly become infatuated with her. In 2020 she spent a lot of time with him in his apartment, with one man who knew the pair saying she played a 'Florence Nightingale' role, believing that she was looking after a sick man. She would cook healthy, organic food for DJ, although a friend said she discovered takeaway paper bags in his bins on more than one occasion. Other visitors to the MacDonagh Junction apartment saw 'medical garb' in his apartment and leaflets about cancer treatment.

Eventually, DJ had to leave the apartment at MacDonagh Junction when he could no longer pay his rent, and around spring 2021, he moved into 10 The Avenue on Granges Road in Kilkenny, a property belonging to the McCarthy Brothers Building Contractors that had been vacant for some time. DJ had asked this local builder for a favour, telling them that he needed somewhere to stay for 'three or four weeks' until the sale of another house came through. He had a connection to this company through an uncle who had worked for the McCarthy Brothers. It's understood DJ was given temporary access to the house as a favour and was not paying rent.

Three or four weeks turned into many months, and there was no sign of DJ moving on from the property. The owner, who was keen to prepare the house for rental on the open market and to start earning an income from it, didn't fall out with DJ but eventually told him: 'It's time to go.' DJ thanked the man for his patience. He didn't mention cancer or look for a loan from the builder, but he had made it known to him that he was going away for treatment. Residents in the houses around him were aware that DJ spent long periods away from the property while he was living there, as there were often times when there were no signs of life in the house. What is unclear is where DJ actually was during these periods, as he was not abroad getting treatment for an illness he did not have.

Strangely, after DJ was asked to leave the house on Granges Road, his belongings were simply left behind, so the landlord gathered them up and put them in storage at a facility on the Hebron Road in Kilkenny. These items included his All-Star awards, precious sports memorabilia, framed photographs with Tiger Woods and clothing. Also among the items were boxes of paperwork, letters from banks, letters relating to a previous garda investigation into DJ Carey Enterprises, and medical letters. DJ was asked many times to collect the items, which were all packed into black refuse sacks and boxes waiting for him, but in the end it was Nicci who made contact with the landlord. She approached cautiously, as she was unsure what kind of reception awaited her. 'She [Nicci] sorted it, she took all of it,' said a source, after explaining that calls to DJ and his family members had gone unanswered.

A number of people had access to where DJ's personal belongings were being stored, and one told this author about a strange letter they had seen lying on some furniture. It was a medical letter about John Carey, DJ's father, and his cancer diagnosis. However, the name 'John' had been blacked out. It looked like a crude job, as if done with a black marker, and the original name could be seen when held to a light. The person who found the letter said, '100 per cent, I could see his dad's name,' and he described how the scene inside the storage facility painted the picture of a man in 'serious trouble with banks and maybe the gardaí'. The source told this author that their hunch was the letter was being used by DJ for nefarious reasons. Otherwise, why would his dad's first name be blacked out? It stopped this man in his tracks at the time.

Throughout 2021, DJ was regularly seen with Nicci St George Smith in Kilkenny. They spent special occasions together, such as New Year's Eve, when they went to a small venue in the city centre called The Hole in the Wall. They were seen dining in upmarket restaurants, such as Zuni in Kilkenny, and they went on trips around Ireland together. DJ introduced

Nicci to his friends and associates, including Declan, who had loaned him €10,000 in 2015.

Joan (not her real name) noticed how DJ started asking her for loans from 2021 onwards. She had been a long-time admirer of DJ as a hurler, and the two were friends for many years. DJ had mentioned to her that he was going for medical treatment abroad. However, when he asked her for money, it was never on that basis. Instead, Joan said, he occasionally rang her looking for personal loans – for instance, in 2021 she loaned him money three times after he claimed he had lost his credit card. He usually asked for €2,000 or €3,000 to tide him 'over the weekend'. This seemed like a lot for a weekend in Joan's eyes; she added that he never asked for less than €2,000.

Did Joan not think it was strange that DJ kept losing his credit card? 'He told me he'd searched his bins and looked everywhere and couldn't understand where his credit card went. He said it would be sorted within four days, but it would usually take three to four weeks to get repaid – it was always cash. I'd give him cash, and he'd give me back cash.' She insisted that she always got her money back, but not before asking for it several times. Of course, she thought it was odd, but she didn't question him about his reasons for needing the money. Then, on one occasion, when he'd supposedly lost his card again, he was seen dining out in an Italian restaurant in Kilkenny city with Nicci and a friend. He was sitting just inside the front door, so people were stopping to say hello to him as they were passing. After that, Joan vowed not to give him any more money.

Christmas was usually a time when DJ would tell people

he was going abroad for treatment. In his previous relationship with Alison, it was usually in December or early in the new year that he would disappear for weeks on end. A Kilkenny businessman, Colin (not his real name), got a call around Christmas 2021. DJ had played golf with Colin in the past and had business dealings with him through his cleaning supplies company, so they knew each other well. Colin was naturally concerned after DJ confided that he needed to travel to the United States for treatment for cancer. DJ then asked him for a loan of €20,000. Colin remembered how he had taken a similar call around five years earlier. DJ had also asked for money back then, but not with the same urgency. Colin had not entertained the first request, but during the 2021 phone call he became convinced DJ's cancer was much more serious this time. Still, there was something about the way the message was delivered that made the businessman pause before agreeing to hand over such a large amount of money. He told DJ to give him forty-eight hours to think about it and he'd call him back.

In the meantime, the man made a phone call to a mutual acquaintance: DJ's old physiotherapist, Alan Kelly, who had known DJ since he was a young hurler in the 1990s. Kelly warned Colin not to give the hurler any money. 'Don't touch him with a barge pole,' was the gist of the message. DJ did not wait for the forty-eight hours as requested before he got back in touch with Colin, but he didn't get the positive response he wanted. This was not the first time that Alan Kelly had warned somebody about DJ and prevented them from getting swindled, but when contacted by this author he did not wish to comment.

Sadly, he was diagnosed with three different cancers himself over the years, as well as having suffered from a stroke, and he told *The Echo* newspaper in 2023 that he felt 'lucky to be alive'. There were others like Kelly who knew that whatever DJ was suffering from, it was not cancer, and they too tried to prevent people from falling victim to him, but not everyone was as lucky as Colin, and many took DJ at his word.

9

HURLER ON THE RICH

DJ had a different playbook depending on how much money you had in your bank account. He had a detailed story he pitched to his wealthier victims about compensation pending from a medical negligence case, as he claimed an Irish hospital had given him too much radium. He told people he would get from €1.5m to €1.8m from this HSE settlement, and explained that he needed a loan to settle his debt with AIB first, to ensure the bank didn't get access to the medical negligence compensation he was due. The amount he sought by way of loan varied from €60,000 to €120,000, depending on who he was talking to. He explained how he'd pay them back as soon as his compensation came through from the HSE in a matter of weeks.

If he perceived you to be of middle income, he told you he had multiple myeloma. He said that it was serious and that he was travelling over and back to Seattle for specialised treatment. He claimed that most of the cost of the stem cell treatment was covered by the elite sporting status conferred on him by his world handball titles, but he desperately needed to come up with the rest, as well as some money to cover the cost of his flights.

If you could just spare him €10,000 or €5,000 or €3,000 (again depending on who he was talking to) he'd be so grateful, and he'd pay you back. After a long-term friend of his agreed to help him once, he texted him back saying, 'You're a lifesaver.'

There were times when he looked for cash on the spot, such as while ordering a cup of tea at the bar of a golf club, and ran with a simpler story. 'I'm fundraising for my cancer treatment, if you can spare anything', he'd tell his victim, before he'd pocket as little as €100. Other days, he 'forgot' his wallet or 'lost' his credit card. Carey pitched these stories up and down the country, north and south, for over a decade. Whether he was sitting at a table in the lobby of a busy hotel with his pot of tea and a scone, or playing nine holes (with cancer he claimed he didn't have the energy for eighteen), he rehearsed his story constantly. He didn't always ask for money. Sometimes, he was putting in the groundwork for another day. He was dedicated to the scam and turned up in various business premises from early in the morning to late in the evening, always on the prowl.

When he told the cancer lie, he made his victims feel like they were the only ones in the world who were helping him in his battle against the illness. He kept in regular contact with people about his treatment and made sure they knew how grateful he was for their support. He told them graphic details of fictitious treatments he was having, such as full-body blood transfusions. Sometimes he'd say he couldn't talk on the phone because he had tubes down his throat. Some people think that he only targeted the super wealthy, but this is not the case. Whether you were rich or poor, a millionaire or an ordinary Joe

Soap, you were targeted if you showed empathy for his plight. He also targeted friends who'd known him for many years through hurling and handball. He regularly scrolled through his phonebook and bulk messaged his contacts. Sometimes he only changed the name at the top and copied the same urgent text message to several people simultaneously. Other days he made phone calls. His contacts always found the calls came 'out of the blue' and 'sounded urgent'.

One of DJ's perceived middle-income targets was a businessman he became friends with over the years through business and sport. Although he can't be sure of the exact date, around 2019 Seán (not his real name) went to meet DJ at Cork Airport at his request. He told this author that DJ described to him how he had multiple myeloma and needed 'specialised treatment' in Seattle. He asked Seán to help him, as he had a shortfall in funds to travel.

Seán confided to DJ that his relative was sick, coincidentally with the same cancer as DJ claimed to have – multiple myeloma. During a visit to his area some months later, DJ insisted on going to see Seán's relative and sat in the house with her for an hour drinking tea. 'He was basically talking about how they had the same cancer.' The man's relative listened intently and empathetically with other family members present, as DJ told them how he dealt with 'oxygen chambers' and 'quarantining' over in the United States. Seán said the details DJ gave were hard to listen to for all present – it was harrowing. Seán's relative constantly asked afterwards, 'Any word of DJ?' 'In fairness, he knew what he was talking about,' said Seán.

DJ continued to keep in touch with Seán and sent him the occasional text message, like one from 30 June 2020, which he also sent to other contacts in his phone around the same time. He just changed the name at the top of the message, but the rest was, word for word the same message others got. In it, he asked Seán how he was doing, and said, 'Could you give me a call?' Seán ignored the request because he thought DJ would be looking to borrow money again. Another text came from DJ on 27 July 2022, letting Seán know that he was on 'pain management but doing OK'. He also explained that he wouldn't be letting his name go forward for the Kilkenny hurling manager job, which was being talked about at the time. 'Other priorities,' explained DJ in his message.

Seán thinks it was sometime in that year when he got a call from a mutual friend of his and DJ's warning him not 'to entertain' requests for money from Carey. This gave Seán time to think of an excuse to give DJ, as he didn't like refusing the hurler. When DJ rang him in 2022, the conversation soon turned to money, and DJ once again asked him for a loan. 'He was giving out about his brother [Jack] spreading rumours about him, but, you see, I'd already got a heads up. I was told not to entertain any calls from DJ looking for money, he was on the hunt.' DJ was annoyed, as it seemed Jack had cautioned people not to give him money. When the ask came from DJ, Seán quickly told him, 'Listen, I'm tortured with this massive business project.' Straight away DJ's tone changed, and that was the last time he phoned Seán.

Seán told this author that he personally knows people who

loaned DJ cash but did not complain to gardaí when they never got any of it back. Seán said he met another man recently who handed DJ €15,000, and he described what DJ was doing as 'emotional blackmail'. 'What's worse than taking money from people is that he sat there and lied to my family [the time he sat with his sick relative]. If my [relative] was alive to hear what he's done, she would be devastated,' he added. When asked why people he knows did not report DJ's fraud, Seán said they were too embarrassed to report what had happened.

There are many men who have been long acquainted with Carey who feel deeply torn over his cancer lie. Thomas Butler, better known to his friends as 'Tommy', idolised 'DJ the hurler', but he told this author that 'DJ the conman' is the person who deceived him. 'He was bigger to me than any other sports person in the world,' said Tommy, who displayed a framed photograph of his hurling hero inside his home for many years. Visitors often commented on it, and Tommy would take pride in explaining his connection to DJ. In the picture the hurler is grinning widely, suited and booted – it was taken in the Burlington Hotel after Kilkenny won an All-Ireland final. Tommy would have done anything to help DJ when his hurling hero first told him he had cancer. A member of Mount Juliet golf club since 1989, he has known DJ since the days of DJ Carey Enterprises. At one stage Tommy was employed by a large firm in a similar business to DJ's, so their paths crossed in their working lives.

Occasionally, Tommy and DJ bumped into each other in the clubhouse in Mount Juliet. On one occasion in 2019, when Tommy approached him to see how things were, the pair had a quiet conversation about DJ's cancer in a dark corner of the clubhouse. They were alone when DJ opened up and gave Tommy a stark account of his illness. He explained he couldn't golf as much as he used to because he was 'too exhausted', but he'd manage nine holes now and then. DJ went into graphic details about his treatment, so much so that Tommy remembered feeling 'uncomfortable'. DJ talked about travelling over and back to Seattle and having to have his body 'flushed out' – before confessing that he was in dire financial straits. 'It wasn't nice, I can tell you, how he described it [the treatment], it was horrible.' DJ explained how he had money problems and was unable to afford the lifesaving treatment he needed. Tommy was shocked and wanted to help in any way he could.

One day in October 2019, Tommy's phone rang – it was DJ and he urgently wanted to meet up. The purpose of the meeting was not abundantly clear, but they met in a hotel in the southeast, with Tommy thinking maybe he just needed a friend or some advice. Tommy does not usually carry large amounts of cash on him, but that day he had withdrawn €700 or €800 from an ATM and the money was in his pocket. He had planned to buy new golf clubs later that day. When he got to the hotel, DJ was waiting, and he told him a gut-wrenching story about his cancer treatment and how he didn't have the money to go back to Seattle. Tommy felt very sorry for DJ and privileged that he had chosen to confide in him. It made him feel like a special person, like the only friend DJ could turn to in his hour of need. DJ told him just how bad things were – he said he didn't even have the price of the fuel to make the journey home to Kilkenny. The fact that DJ had driven 90km to the meeting without ensuring he had enough fuel to get home didn't arouse Tommy's suspicions. In fact, it was the opposite – Tommy's heart went out to DJ, who was in a desperate situation. Tommy wanted to help his hurling hero immediately, so he put his hand in his pocket, took out the cash he had with him and gave it to DJ. DJ told Tommy, 'I don't know what I'd do without you. You're the only one helping me.'

That was just the start. In the following years, this man, who is not of substantial means, took money from his pension fund to help his hurling idol. It was hard to turn DJ down, especially when Tommy thought they shared a special friendship. The only person he told about meeting DJ at the time was his wife, but they vowed not to tell anybody else out of respect to the sportsman; as they saw it, it was a private health matter. Text exchanges offer a glimpse into how a canny DJ coaxed Tommy over a period of time to help him, while also keeping up the pleasantries about golf and GAA. On 20 May 2020, Tommy said, 'Hi DJ, Just a thank you for a very enjoyable round of golf with both you and Ritchie. U make the game of golf look so simple. Take care and enjoy the long weekend.' DJ replied, 'Really enjoyed. Thank you. We'll do it again soon DJ'.

Less than a fortnight later, DJ was in contact after another round of golf, but his message had a more serious tone: 'As I said too [sic] you the other day I'm nearly there with AIB. I have a deal done with HSE for €1.5m compensation. I have to pay bank €100k as full and final settlement but do not want to let them know about this deal. I'm €15k short presently to finalise this deal as it's not easy to raise presently. I'll keep you informed, DJ'.

Tommy replied, 'Hi DJ ... On the issue with AIB I would appreciate u keeping me in the picture & it goes without saying no one is aware of our conversations to date (only my wife). There has to be a way to sort the €15k as you cannot lose €1.5M over €15k. U probably have another 3 months extended time from June from AIB. If u like we can chat further over the phone to ensure u have explored all options on raising the €15k. Kind regards'.

DJ responded, 'Yeah I've exhausted most with financial institutions. I do not want AIB to know anything beforehand and I'm afraid if application was made it could be exposed. I've tried a couple of people and they haven't the cash presently. I believe if I totalled the €100k I could have it all wrapped up in 6 to 8 weeks.'

Tommy agreed to call DJ at 9 p.m. the following evening to discuss his dilemma. He got a thank you from DJ on 4 June: 'Tommy great to talk too [sic] you last night. Thank you for that. I got €7k in this morning from my salary and IT Carlow so I'm heading in the right direction. I have a few bits and pieces that I can sell so I'm going to put them on eBay or done deal and see what happens. I'll chat too [sic] you soon, Thanks again, DJ'.

Eight days later, on Friday 12 June, DJ was texting again: 'Just to fill you in. I got €4k there for some personal stuff I had for sale. So I'm only €3k short now. Just said I'd keep you updated. DJ'. Tommy agreed to give DJ the €3,000 shortfall, and on 15 June DJ got in touch to tell the man, 'just in case you might be making a transfer to me today, I'd say my account number has changed'. Tommy responded, 'Hi DJ, That's fine. I will make the transfer today into the new account when you forward it.' DJ sent on his new bank details.

The trail of messages between the two make it clear that DJ was using this kind-hearted man as a source of funds. He knew Tommy held him in high esteem and enjoyed his company. There were messages about a fourball that Tommy had booked at Mount Juliet for 2 p.m. on 2 July 2021, where they were joined by Eddie Keher, who was unaware of Carey's fraud. After the game, Tommy sent on a photograph of DJ and Keher with a message stating: 'Thanks for a very enjoyable afternoon of golf, I will treasure the photo of playing with 2 legends of Kilkenny hurling.'

In all, Tommy gave DJ around €17,000. Some of it was in cash, but there were also several bank transfers. The biggest loan came shortly after their encounter in Mount Juliet in October 2019 and the first conversation about cancer, when Tommy transferred €10,000 to DJ. His bank statements show he also transferred the following amounts: €3,000 in June 2020, €1,000 in June 2022, and €900 in November 2022. The final transfer was sent reluctantly. 'I was trying to give him the hint that I'm not an unlimited source of funds. I hadn't that money to spare as such. I took that out of my pension fund. That's why I feel annoyed. What will the kids think? Will I have to explain?'

He had a straight talk with DJ. 'So anyhow, I said to him, "Look, I can't do any more for you financially DJ, I've done as much as I can. But what I will do is I guarantee I'll help you as much as I can."' Tommy came up with an idea – he wrote up a list of businesspeople with whom DJ had some association or who had supported him in the past. He drafted a letter explaining the situation that DJ was in with his health. Tommy offered to contact the people on DJ's behalf, to ask them if they could help fund his cancer treatment. His idea was that, if DJ got €1,000 from 500 people, he would have no more issues with paying for his treatment as over €500,000 would be raised. He showed DJ the letter he had drafted, together with the list of names with their contact details. DJ told Tommy to 'leave it with me'. A few days later, DJ called to explain how he'd prefer to keep things quiet. 'I'll tell you, I'd prefer not to, I'd prefer to keep things private to be honest with you,' he said. Tommy was taken aback, as he thought this was a life-or-death matter that needed urgent attention.

'DJ put me under a lot of pressure to sign off on a letter he wanted as verification of his illness and financial predicament to the GPA. I got persistent calls when I was out of the country in September 2022 to sign off on the letter and to forward it to Ciarán Barr, CFO of the GPA.' Tommy's phone was ringing constantly while he was away, and he felt coerced into sending an email that confirmed that he knew DJ well and that he had a life-threatening condition that needed urgent but expensive treatment in the United States. He even praised DJ's integrity before outlining how Carey needed 'at least €25K' to receive 'treatment which is not available in Ireland but he urgently requires'. After Tommy drafted the email and sent it to DJ, he replied, 'Perfect Tommy Thank you' and included Ciarán Barr's email address in his response. The GPA did not reply to any requests for information on this matter.

After Tommy sent the email to the GPA, he started to become suspicious of DJ's behaviour. When playing a round of golf in Mount Juliet, he brought up the issue of DJ's cancer with another golfer. 'I was telling him about DJ and how sick he was. He just said to me, "You must be joking – there's nothing wrong with him – absolutely nothing wrong with him." I said, "Are you sure?" He said, "I am sure, there's absolutely nothing wrong with him."' Tommy later confronted DJ, but the hurler never flinched. He simply said, 'I'm surprised at that now, because I know him well. I was going out with his daughter for a couple of years.' Tommy told this author, 'I don't know if he went out with the daughter or not, but he never even blinked an eyelid. That's what a devious person he was, I think, that he was able to tell these lies. The lies just tripped off his tongue.' During this conversation, DJ showed Tommy the scars on the back of his head, but they meant nothing to Tommy as they were old, and he assumed DJ would have had many bad belts of the hurl over the years.

After the warning he was given on the golf course, Tommy decided not to give DJ any more financial assistance. His overriding emotion about what happened with DJ is disappointment. He was badly let down and felt humiliated by what happened. 'You'd think, after all he's done, all the lies he's told, he'd have the courtesy to apologise – it'd be something. I never expected to get the money back to be honest with you. I gave it to him because I got ten years of watching fantastic hurling. It's not much to give that to him when [I thought] he had a medical condition.' He did think about DJ often but didn't know what was going on.

Then, in early 2023, his phone rang. 'It was the call from the Fraud Squad in early January or February … They called me on a Thursday morning.' The detective said, 'I believe you're a friend of DJ Carey's.' The officer said the gardaí were investigating Carey's 'financial affairs' and Tommy's name had come up. Officers knew Tommy had transferred money to DJ because they had copies of his bank statements.

The following morning, Tommy Butler went to Waterford Garda Station to give a detailed statement. 'They were very nice and they went through everything, and I went through all the payments I made; they were looking for back-up statements from myself.' Tommy told gardaí, 'Look I don't want to be the one to bring him down' – he was nervous of reporting DJ and stated that, if he was to make an actual complaint, he needed to be absolutely sure that DJ had never received any treatment in Ireland or Seattle for cancer. 'They confirmed to me that there was no question that he received any medical treatment. I made a statement on that basis. As far as I was concerned then, he had totally deceived me, and I had a right to make a complaint.'

Just before DJ Carey's first court appearance, Tommy removed the photograph of the hurling hero that was hanging in his home. Although he didn't bin it, he finds it hard to look at today. Tommy didn't think his retirement would start out this way, having been scammed by DJ at a time in his life when he had finally come into some money. He is not a wealthy man and felt embarrassed at the position Carey put him in with his family.

While Tommy seems to have avoided being tapped for a substantial loan in 2021, DJ had his sights set on another victim. For a short period that year, he had a job as a sales rep with G.H. Lett & Company Ltd, based in Enniscorthy, County Wexford. The drinks wholesale company supplies products to customers in the south-east and Dublin. They were trying to expand their clients in Kilkenny and needed doors opened. DJ was introduced to them by an associate. He didn't know much about the business, but initially he seemed keen to impress his employers. Publicans were happy to see him coming, as DJ was a nice guy to deal with. They said he'd come in to get an order, sit down and reminisce over cups of tea about hurling – he never seemed to be in a hurry, and he'd sit in the back of some bars on the phone for lengthy periods.

During his time working for Letts, DJ had reunited with some acquaintances from his glory days. One day he rang Rachel (not her real name), an old friend and business owner in Kilkenny city, to ask if he could drop in to her premises. 'We started buying stuff off him after that. He'd come in and collect the order and we'd talk about hurling.' The pair also shared stories about growing up and their children. DJ once confessed he thought Brian Cody was ignoring his son, Mikey, in the changing rooms, or holding a grudge against him.

Then DJ started mentioning his health problems. Rachel had already heard stories about DJ's cancer, and he told her that he was travelling abroad for treatment. She felt sorry for him and remembered him telling her how he wasn't sure why he was named as being involved with the underage squads for Kilkenny, because he wasn't allowed to do anything that would cause him stress or get him too excited. DJ explained that he needed to be very careful with his health. Thinking back, Rachel said there were some contradictions in what he was saying, but it is only hindsight that made this clear.

While DJ confided in Rachel about his cancer, he was also happy to share news with her that he was anticipating playing in the Irish Open Pro-Am with Rory McIlroy in Mount Juliet in June 2021. A month before the Pro-Am, in May, the first frantic phone call came looking for help. DJ had a 'favour to ask': 'I'm very embarrassed now, but I'm going to ask you for a loan of money, because I need to go back to America for treatment,' he said. He explained that he had a medical negligence case pending with the HSE and was due to be compensated, so he would be able to pay Rachel back with a little interest on top as quickly as possible.

Rachel was eager to help and had no reason to disbelieve him, as he'd been so genuine in the past. In fact, over the years, at matches in Nowlan Park and elsewhere, DJ had always gone out of his way to say hello to her. Rachel also remembered the time he had contacted and engaged in correspondence with one of her relations in the United States, who was a huge fan of his. These were things she was thankful for, and now she was in a position to help somebody in need. Rachel thought DJ appeared to be genuinely uncomfortable asking for money and was in a terrible situation. She consulted her husband and they decided they had to help. That's the kind of people they are – a decent, hardworking family and respected in the community. They transferred a five-figure sum to DJ's private banking account.

It was a significant amount of money, so Rachel was taken aback when, not four weeks later, DJ was in touch again and wanted more money. He sent this text: 'I just finished treatment and will go into isolation later. I was unable to contact you during the week but the commercial court made a decision last Friday to overturn a decision of the bank to take compensation monies paid to me by the HSE. They made a ruling that I must pay AIB €150k in total full and final settlement by 4pm today June 11 and therefore can release funds to me on July 16th. This must be paid in full. They won't accept payment when it's drawn down so I'm desperately trying to see if I can come up with it. I'm very embarrassed again for asking and if it can't be done that's no prob but if so it would be a massive relief. Best regards, DJ'.

Rachel replied, saying she was thinking of DJ, as she knew he was abroad getting treatment. She was glad things were being settled so quickly, but she was away and suggested that he talk to the bank about delaying them on the grounds that he was undergoing cancer treatment. DJ responded: 'I tried to but it gets put back into the system and won't be heard again til October. They didn't give me much time.'

Rachel was sympathetic, but she started to feel uncomfortable and suggested to DJ that he might be able to think of somebody else who could help – what about his employer? DJ said, 'Unfortunately they're tied up with funds for stock and couldn't release anything for now. No worries. Thanks for coming back to me and enjoy your few days away.' Rachel's uneasiness grew, since this second request for money in such a short space of time had aroused her suspicions. Something seemed off, but she didn't feel comfortable questioning DJ's bona fides. She didn't doubt he had cancer, but she was concerned about his ability to repay his debt.

DJ got back in touch again in August – almost three months after borrowing the money – to apologise for not being in contact about their order with Letts. He explained that he had been getting bloods done and also gave more information about how his treatment was going in Seattle. 'He said he'd fly on a Sunday, get treatment maybe on a Tuesday and then he'd be in isolation for five days before he could return.'

Four months after he first appeared taking orders for Letts, publicans noticed he was gone. One of them enquired with the company and was told he was sick. On 8 September, DJ sent a message to Rachel at 10.30 a.m., replying to her order for supplies from Letts: 'I've forward [*sic*] text into office. I'm out of action at moment had tumours removed from spleen.' A source said his employer contacted him about coming back to work, but he chose not to return. On 5 October, DJ messaged again after Rachel inquired about how he was: 'Still in hospital trying to get back to Seattle, I'll be another few weeks'. DJ also promised to pay back the money he owed her, but several times thereafter he sent texts with excuses, such as 'waiting on a cheque to clear'. Then, DJ's father, John, died of cancer on 13 October.

Eventually, Rachel's spouse took over the conversation, thinking he might be able to get DJ to pay his debt. After several promises, DJ finally sent a message in December 2021 to state that the money had been transferred in full with an extra €1,000 to say 'thanks'. The couple were overjoyed but had not yet checked their account – they took him at his word and believed the money was now repaid.

It was January 2022 when Rachel realised that, in fact, no money had been transferred, despite the pre-Christmas promise. Rachel's husband had had enough of DJ's excuses and told him clearly, 'I want the money now' and to 'cut the bollocks acting'. 'I said to him, "If you have a claim against the HSE, show me the claim". We gave him the money to help him with treatment; he had said he had a big claim against the HSE over treatment he had that went wrong. He had showed us scars at the back of his head. It was like an L going backwards.'

Rachel and her husband warned DJ they would go to a solicitor about the matter. They also said they would contact his Aunt Peggy, whom he was very fond of, to tell her what had happened. Locals knew Peggy thought the world of DJ. Ultimately, they didn't carry out these threats, but DJ never seemed perturbed by anything they said. When he was put under pressure, he did start to make irregular repayments, but the sums were very small given what he owed. He paid them back in hundreds, explaining that he didn't have the money to repay the amount in full but promised to do so as soon as possible.

In February 2022 Rachel received a text from a relative to tell her Catriona Carey would be appearing on RTÉ's *Prime*

Time that evening and to watch the show. 'As soon as I saw the programme, I was smelling a rat.' Even though DJ was not the subject of the programme, the fact that his sister was now at the centre of an alleged mortgage scam spooked Rachel. 'I rang DJ on the morning of 15 February, after Catriona was on the television programme. He answered the call straight away, and he said, "I know nothing about it, it's absolutely nothing to do with me." But after that, I started talking to people about him and realised we weren't the only ones who were owed money.'

When the couple asked questions about DJ, they didn't tell anyone about their own situation, as they wanted to keep it private and, particularly, they didn't want to divulge how much they had given him. It wasn't long before their enquiries revealed that DJ was asking 'lads in Gowran' for money. The final message Rachel sent to DJ by WhatsApp was never delivered. It was sent on 23 December 2022 and said, 'I can't believe how much of a fool I was to help you out'. Rachel and her husband agreed they would still have helped DJ if he'd been honest from the outset and not lied about having cancer treatment. 'If he'd have just said, "Look, I haven't a pot to piss in, can you help me?", we would have gladly helped.' It was his lie about having cancer that hurt them most of all.

Despite realising that they had been conned, the couple decided not to contact the gardaí out of respect for DJ's family – they didn't want to embarrass his two sons and his ex-wife, Christine, who were innocent parties. However, gardaí in Waterford contacted the couple in early 2023 and urged them to make a statement. 'They wanted to see us as soon as possible, and we were told to bring as much information with us as possible.' The couple's details had shown up in DJ's bank transactions, so the gardaí knew they had transferred a substantial sum to him. Such was the stress of going through with the complaint that, at one point, the couple wanted to withdraw their statement, but the gardaí urged them not to do so.

Another of the people DJ approached for money around 2021 was former Fine Gael TD and European Commissioner Phil Hogan. The Kilkenny man, best known as 'Big Phil' because of his height and his political clout once upon a time, is a keen golfer who owned a residence at the K Club. He knew DJ from his hurling glory days, but still did his homework and asked around before he committed to anything. Carey had used the pending settlement from the medical negligence case story, saying he'd pay back the loan once the compensation came through. Hogan contacted a friend to ask about the matter. They did some research and advised Hogan that DJ most likely did not have a medical negligence case and not to give him the loan. The politician got back to DJ, saying he'd give him the money if he provided the necessary proof of the pending claim. He never heard back.

A second Fine Gael man who was approached by Carey was Kilkenny councillor and former mayor of the city Martin Brett. He recalled seeing DJ in action on the hurling field in Semple Stadium. He was at a match with his brother-in-law and had the privilege of watching the instinctive hurler change the pace of a game. Martin described how DJ scored two goals out of nothing that same day. He was in awe of DJ's profile and ability to hurl: 'An instinctive, iconic person, who had that incredible ability to change the whole process of any game when he turned on the style. A burst of speed that lifted people.' He found DJ mesmeric in how he could change the direction of any game and lift the people. He also admired his prowess on the golf course, where he occasionally bumped into DJ. They had each other's phone numbers, and texts were exchanged now and then. One time, Martin remembers there was a situation with DJ's dad, John. Martin recalled that DJ went to extraordinary lengths to try to help his dad, looking for assistance in getting a local authority grant for him. However, Martin recalls a strange dynamic between him and his family. 'The family just backed off. There was some sort of dichotomy between him and his siblings, and it didn't go through.'

In spring 2022 Martin met DJ at Kilkenny golf club. They were on the course when DJ's health problems were brought into the conversation. At this stage, Martin reckons stories were rife about DJ's health issues. DJ didn't beat around the bush. He told Martin he was having financial issues with his treatment and needed help. 'He touched on a figure,' Martin recalls. Martin didn't agree to give him any money, but he was polite and told DJ he'd meet him again.

About a fortnight later, Martin drove to the Newpark Hotel in Kilkenny, where he met DJ in the lobby. He was taken aback when DJ revealed that he'd just had a full-body blood transfusion. Martin said, 'Jesus – that's strange and you're walking around?' DJ just shrugged 'yeah' and didn't have much to say in response. He was more focused on telling Martin again that his cancer and medical problems came with costs and he needed money. He asked him for €15,000. Martin wanted time to look into his request, as he didn't believe everything he was hearing but also didn't want to shoot down the ask without due consideration. He told DJ he'd need time to mull it over.

A few days later, Martin saw DJ again, this time with a golf bag over his shoulder in Mount Juliet. 'I says, what? Jaysus – you're a mighty man. How did you manage to recover?' DJ told Martin that blood transfusions were no bother to him. He was used to them. The following week, DJ rang Martin to ask if he'd thought any more about the loan. Martin said he had made his mind up and told DJ he wasn't happy to go ahead. There was an awkward moment when Martin paused and said, 'If I'm not happy with something, I won't go with it.' DJ insisted he was telling the truth, and Martin assured him he wasn't accusing him of telling lies, but he was having problems coming to terms with how the hurler had been so ill that he needed blood transfusions yet was swiftly walking eighteen holes afterwards. 'I says, we will leave it at that.'

Instead, DJ pushed the issue, and Martin said he felt under some pressure, but he was convinced that something was not right. So he suggested that it would be easier for DJ to fundraise by holding a golf classic or getting a group involved, rather than targeting individuals. That way, he would raise more money, but everybody could give a smaller amount. DJ's response stayed with Martin, who remembered him saying he would prefer to 'keep it under the radar'.

Does Martin know anybody else who gave DJ money? 'I do,

yeah. There's a guy who did management courses with me. He gave him €27,000. He admitted straight out that he gave him €27,000.' Martin firmly believes DJ has been tapping people for loans for many years. The last time he saw him driving, he was in an old car, 'maybe a 2008 or 2010 reg Opel'. However, he noticed he always had the best of golf gear, clothes, clubs and accessories.

During his glory days, DJ travelled all over the country attending charity events and performing official openings, and one of the counties where he had many connections was Westmeath. In the mid-1990s, Mullingar man Bernie Comaskey met DJ through Brian Reidy, a good friend of his and a staunch Kilkenny GAA supporter. At that time, Bernie owned Mullingar squash and leisure centre, which he described as the 'best club of its kind in the country', with a membership of 1,000. He had a ladies-only gym before it was fashionable. The walls were very bare in one part of the sports centre, so he decided to turn it into a picture gallery. Bernie had an impressive collection of GAA treasures in his attic, and he used these on the walls, but he decided he needed somebody with a big profile to officially open the gallery. He asked Brian if he thought DJ would come along to do the honours.

Bernie recalled how DJ and his then wife, Christine, visited his home in Mullingar in 1995 after the hurler kindly agreed to attend the official opening of the gallery. The couple went to dinner with Bernie and his wife, and, afterwards, they attended the opening, which was a huge success. The Westmeath Minor footballers were the guests of honour, as they had just won the All-Ireland Minor final. Bernie remembered how DJ watched people playing squash at the sports club before he joined Bernie on the court and they started playing. 'I would have coached squash, but I've never seen anybody with such natural ability.'

There were five grades of teams, and Bernie reckoned DJ would have been playing premier squash, or in the top league, if he had been two or three weeks at the club. 'He was that good.' They moved from the squash courts to the upstairs of the club, where they had a snooker table, and DJ 'almost cleared the table'. Bernie recalled how his son, Ian, was in awe of DJ as he watched him signing autographs, shirts and jerseys. 'He was just so modest,' Bernie said of the superstar, who took the evening very seriously. 'He gave a brilliant talk. The gist of his speech, directed at the Westmeath Minor footballers, was that this was just the beginning for them. He told them not to think they had it all done now. It's fair to say that some of them were wild enough. He asked them to look on this as a stepping stone and get on with it.'

While very few of the team took his advice, according to Bernie, DJ's words left an impression on everybody else. The music and craic continued into the early hours. Bernie had breakfast with the Careys the next morning, and he got DJ on his own, telling him he needed to give him his expenses. DJ insisted that Bernie had already taken the couple out for dinner and owed him nothing. Bernie was conscious of the going rate for getting somebody of DJ's profile for an opening like this and had made his own enquiries. He was told that around

£600 (punt) would be expected. 'DJ wouldn't hear tell of it.' As DJ and Christine pulled out of Bernie's driveway, Christine's window was open. Bernie threw an envelope in through the car window. 'A couple of hundred quid,' he said, but he had to throw it, and it was not expected.

From that encounter, for many years afterwards, anytime anybody from Westmeath ever met DJ, they'd return and tell Bernie that the 'great DJ Carey' was asking for him. Bernie often wrote to DJ at his Gowran home, and he always got a response. 'It wouldn't just be "Thanks for that, how are things?", but the replies were thoughtful.' DJ's caring and empathetic side came out during his brief interactions with Bernie over the years. Bernie recalled telling him about the death of a young Westmeath hurler in a car collision. DJ was moved by the man's death, as he had known the hurler and would have liked to have attended the funeral but did not realise what had happened. 'What he said to me: "If only I'd have known, I would've come up to that funeral."'

Years went by, and although Bernie continued to closely follow the GAA, he and DJ fell out of touch. Then, early in 2022 – Bernie can't remember the exact timing – DJ phoned him out of the blue. He told him that he was suffering from cancer and mentioned multiple myeloma. Bernie had friends in Kilkenny who had told him that DJ was sick, but it struck a chord when he heard it from the horse's mouth. There were a few phone calls back and forth in early 2022, and, during the conversations, DJ told Bernie about having to travel to Seattle for stem cell treatment. As he had told others, he explained that he was getting the treatment for free because of his 'elite sporting status'. Bernie decided there and then that he had to help in any way he could. He phoned his son, Ian, to tell him about DJ, and the father and son agreed immediately that they would help.

Bernie decided they should give DJ €5,000, and he discussed this amount with Ian, as he was going halves with him on the donation. However, before they handed over any money, Bernie wanted to be clear with Ian – something was bothering him. He wanted to help DJ, but he had been talking to his friends in Kilkenny and they had cautioned him about DJ's illness, saying 'something's not right there'. Ian had GAA contacts in Spain – a close-knit community where people talk. Bernie asked Ian to check with them, to ascertain whether they had heard anything. Ian came back to Bernie and said it would be wiser to give DJ €1,000 and see how things went. He said they could always give more in the future, but you can't take it back if it's a bad decision. Ian also suggested that they could maybe explore the possibility of sponsoring DJ's stem cell treatment in Spain. Ian had good connections there, and it was possible they could come up with a way to pay for the treatment. He promised to investigate this possibility further and to report back to Bernie.

Bernie phoned DJ and told him he wanted to get a cheque down to him. DJ gave him an address in Kilkenny. When Bernie told DJ how much he was giving him, there was silence on the phone. 'I knew that he didn't consider that any good, and I felt bad.' Soon after the cheque was posted, it was returned to Bernie marked 'address unknown'. Bernie thought this was odd, so he checked the address with DJ and sent it again, but the same thing happened. His cheque had been returned twice. Bernie still has the cheque stub dated 11 March 2022, with the description: 'D.J. Carey charitable contribution towards medical expenses in America €1,000.'

DJ got back in contact some weeks after the cheque was sent and asked Bernie if he could transfer the money to his bank account instead of posting a cheque. He said he was going to Seattle the following week and was €3,000 short, and he asked him for the full amount. Bernie explained that he had agreed to give him €1,000 and suggested somebody else might help him with the balance. Bernie's doubts about handing over more money were compounded when he rang DJ the following week and discovered the hurler was still at home and there was no mention of Seattle. Bernie didn't question DJ on this – he didn't feel comfortable quizzing him because he liked him so much.

After transferring the €1,000 to DJ's bank account, Bernie heard nothing for a while. He texted DJ, because he was conscious that Ian had helped and he wanted DJ to send him a text to acknowledge that he'd received the money. DJ sent Ian the following message: 'Hi Ian, Thank you very much for your kindness. I really appreciate your help. Please God we'll meet up soon, Kindest regards, DJ Carey'. Meanwhile, Ian was making enquiries at a new private hospital in Spain. He found out they did stem cell replacement there, and he contacted DJ to tell him the good news. He offered to sponsor the treatment in Spain for him and help with any expenses and somewhere to stay for the duration. Yet DJ didn't seem interested. Instead, he suggested that Bernie was 'well got with the Westmeath GAA' and asked him if he'd get the GAA clubs to organise a fundraiser for him.

Bernie couldn't shake the thought that DJ was supposed to be in Seattle having treatment, yet here he was phoning him about running fundraisers. He was still conscious of the local talk in Kilkenny about him, and he also didn't like the fact that, after the trouble Ian had gone to, DJ had no interest in the idea of treatment in Spain. So he told DJ that any fundraising would have to start in Kilkenny, and he'd follow it with Westmeath GAA from there. In response, DJ told Bernie he was 'getting it very hard' in Kilkenny since allegations against Catriona were all over the newspapers at that time. He revealed he had never 'nurtured a network' in Kilkenny, that he just hurled and went home, so it was difficult to get people around him to fundraise. However, Bernie didn't budge and this was the last time he heard from DJ Carey.

Even though Bernie had his suspicions, he never confronted DJ – if there was a chance he did have multiple myeloma, how could Bernie accuse him of lying? He does not regard himself as a victim, saying that DJ didn't do anything wrong to him, and he has no interest whatsoever in seeing him punished. He did not give a statement to gardaí. Bernie wants DJ's legacy to be balanced. He believes a man should never be judged on his worst deed. Others may disagree.

10

TERMINAL ILLNESS

Tom Brennan left his native County Laois to attend secondary school as a boarder in St Kieran's College in Kilkenny city and did his Leaving Cert there in 1986. While Tom was a schoolboy at St Kieran's, the school had a vintage crop of young hurlers. Tom was a few years ahead of Adrian Ronan, Pat O'Neill, Charlie Carter and DJ Carey, but he remembers them well. It is no surprise, then, that he ended up being such a huge GAA supporter. Most of his friends were from Kilkenny, and they all followed the Cats very closely, especially in the 1990s.

While Tom didn't personally know DJ in school, he said hello when he saw him around. After leaving school, apart from seeing him on the field or on the television screen, Tom hadn't come across DJ for many years, until he got involved with the Laois Minor hurlers as part of their backroom team during the Covid-19 pandemic. Sometime in 2020, the team organised a conference call to come up with a plan to support the hurlers when they were unable to train during lockdowns. A group that included Tom decided to help them with other areas, such as education and college options.

Michael Dempsey, a Laois man himself, was lined up to do a Q&A with the panel on Zoom. DJ, who at the time was involved with IT Carlow, also joined to offer some advice. Tom remembers how laid-back DJ was. He was talking about how he had been cutting trees the previous day for some relations – a hard day's physical work. He gave brilliant advice to the young lads, speaking candidly and admitting that he sometimes regretted rejecting the offer of a handball scholarship for a university in the United States in his younger days. He said he often wondered what might have happened if he had taken up that opportunity. He talked about college and told the young men to work hard. The feedback on the session was excellent, and everybody was impressed with DJ in particular.

It could have been that day that DJ Carey noticed Tom Brennan, but Tom reckoned it was more likely another time. The businessman's name came up in off-the-record comments made by Eddie Brennan (no relation) at the end of an interview broadcast by Joe.ie in November 2020, when he mentioned that Tom Brennan was worth a lot of money. Tom said he can't be certain if this is how he came onto DJ's radar, but shortly after that interview, he heard from Carey for the first time ever. On 4 December, DJ texted Tom asking if he could give him a call. They shared text banter about the Laois manager's job, with Tom telling DJ he was too late, as 'Cheddar' (Seamus Plunkett) had got the gig. Five minutes later, DJ called Tom.

He got to the point quickly – he needed a loan. He explained that he was due an insurance settlement of €1.8m because of medical malpractice by St James's Hospital. This was in connection with the story that he had been given too much radium during a previous treatment. He said that he had cancer but had significant debts with AIB, with whom he had agreed to do a settlement or debt deal for €120,000. He explained that if he settled his debt with the bank before he received his compensation, then the bank would have no claim on the €1.8m he was due. In cases where debt deals are done between banks and individuals, the person's income is looked at and a detailed statement of means must be provided. Every source of income and expenditure must be given to the bank, and this is taken into account. DJ's story to Brennan was convincing – as he explained, the last thing he needed was the €1.8m landing in his account before his debt was settled, as the bank would be entitled to lay a claim on this.

DJ asked Brennan for a substantial sum. He said his compensation money was imminent, and he'd probably be in a position to pay Brennan back what he owed by the end of the year. Tom wanted to help but needed to make a call home first. He didn't promise anything but said he would 'see what I can do'. DJ's response is something that has stayed with Tom since. The hurler said, 'Oh, I'm here in the car and I have my head on the steering wheel, and I'm crying with relief.'

While stories had been doing the rounds for some time about DJ at this stage, Tom had never heard any of these rumours. He had only heard that he might be sick. DJ was so well known, Tom never doubted his credibility. The bottom line was, if he could help him, he would. There were no alarm bells ringing. He didn't leave DJ waiting for an answer for long. After discussing it with his wife, they both said, 'poor DJ', and quickly agreed they had to give him a loan for an undisclosed sum. Tom believed DJ was in a bad way and needed the money.

DJ sent his bank details, but Tom didn't simply transfer the funds. He had a detailed loan document for a substantial sum drawn up by his solicitor to ensure everything was above board. Tom's solicitor also spoke to DJ about the loan and believed him to be genuine. The story about AIB and the medical settlement sounded credible. DJ delivered it perfectly. He had indicated that he'd have the money back by the end of 2020, but Tom reassured him that it would be fine at the end of February 2021. He wanted to do the decent thing and give him some breathing room.

The loan agreement was signed in person in Tom's home during a follow-up meeting. There was even a discussion around how DJ would invest the €1.8m compensation money when he got it, and Tom recommended a firm that could advise him. He asked DJ about making an introduction, but DJ told him to hold off for the time being. During his visit, DJ talked about his cancer and the medical malpractice case. He pointed to a scar on his head and explained that the mark was from surgery. He also chatted about how he was in Laharts garage in Kilkenny earlier that day, as he was looking to buy himself a new car once the settlement came through – he already had it picked out. Later, DJ sent a text to ask for a screengrab of the notification that the money had been transferred. He seemed grateful for Tom's generosity and kindness.

After the transfer, Tom didn't follow up with DJ until February 2021. Then it was mainly texts back and forth, but there was an odd call, as Tom asked, 'What's the story?' In the beginning, DJ always responded. Tom exchanged numerous texts with him throughout that February. DJ claimed he was in hospital many times over the period. On 19 February, he said he'd have the final €1.8m in his account by Monday 26 February.

Tom started to get 'kind of suspicious' after the February 2021 deadline passed. On one occasion, DJ told him the €1.8m was on its way; on another, he claimed he was on his way to the bank to pay him back. Many times he said he'd pay, but when Tom checked his bank account there was nothing. Tom tried not to get stressed. There is no 'poor me' with him, but quietly he was seething. It was becoming apparent that the money was not going to materialise. 'It was obvious as time went on that you couldn't believe a word out of his mouth,' said Tom. DJ always had an excuse ready – he was getting surgery and couldn't make it to the bank, that kind of thing – but Tom could sense something wasn't right.

Towards the summer of 2021, he was running out of patience. He started asking questions and making calls. He heard through the grapevine that DJ was playing a lot of golf in Mount Juliet. On one occasion he had promised to pay Tom back, but he texted him to say he couldn't because he was playing golf with Rory McIlroy in Mount Juliet that day. It was 30 June, and the Pro-Am was taking place there ahead of the Irish Open. Big names in golf were playing alongside other sports stars and celebs. McIlroy teed off with his dad, Gerry, Irish rugby out-half Johnny Sexton and DJ Carey.

Tom couldn't get his head around this. How could a terminally ill guy play golf with McIlroy? Moreover, DJ was never able to make time to get to the bank, even though he said he had the funds. He claimed to be in hospital the whole time. Yet, suddenly, he could make it to Mount Juliet to play golf with these lads. DJ seemed perturbed that Tom didn't appear to be happy for him. Sure, wasn't he out there playing golf with the likes of Pádraig Harrington, Shane Lowry and Graeme McDowell? There were others there too, including Dublin football boss Dessie Farrell and former Kilkenny hurler Henry Shefflin. Tom was furious.

DJ was smiling from ear to ear when *Kilkenny People* reporter Siobhan Donohoe met him after playing his round at the Pro-Am. She asked him how he got on alongside his hero, McIlroy. 'Great. I'm a member here. It's just brilliant. The course is just phenomenal.' As DJ was beaming at the screen, talking about playing golf, some of the people he owed money to were watching. They were bewildered at his miraculous recovery from cancer treatment. Like Tom, they had been chasing him for their money back, yet DJ never seemed well enough to get to the bank. Now, here he was hitting balls on the golf course, being snapped with celebrities and doing interviews about his exploits.

In August 2021 Tom Brennan figured out where DJ was living in Kilkenny. He needed to see with his own eyes that DJ was not in Seattle. That's why he ended up parking near the house and watching the former hurler stroll up the road that sunny summer's day, clearly not on his way back from treatment in America, as he claimed he was.

That day, Tom just drove home. The texts continued. DJ agreed to meet him on 8 September in Kilkenny with bank drafts to repay him, as he never seemed to be able to successfully execute an electronic bank transfer. However, Tom had done his own investigating and had established that DJ had a tee time in Mount Juliet that same morning, so he was expecting DJ to call off their meeting or 'call in sick'. 'Right on schedule that morning, DJ texted me to say he was getting a blood transfusion in St James's Hospital and apologised for being unable to meet me. Moments later, a representative served him with a summons on the first tee of Mount Juliet Golf Course.'

Days after this incident, Tom texted DJ to let him know that he had expected to hear back from him about the summons. He told him he knew he had not been in Seattle at the end of August and he advised him that his actions constituted fraud. DJ replied looking for more time to repay. Later that month, on 21 September, DJ sent this text: 'Hi Tom I just want to keep you informed that I'm very close to being sorted and in turn can pass on payment. I do not want to give exact timeline until I am sure of date. Kind Regards DJ.'

Tom Brennan replied two days later, saying he had heard words similar to the above around '40 different times previously'. He then told a few friends what was going on. One or two said, 'I have DJ Carey's number in my phone. I got this message from him asking me how I'm keeping, and I only met him five years ago on the golf course.' Tom told his pals not to reply to him.

On 10 February 2022, Tom secured a judgment of €40,000 against DJ Carey in Kilkenny Circuit Court. Looking back now, Tom said getting the circuit court judgment probably wasn't worth the legal fees. He was also surprised at the lack of media coverage of the story at the time the judgment was published. Then, on 9 January 2023, gardaí contacted Tom asking him to make a statement about what had happened.

Giving DJ a large loan was Tom's effort to try and help a sporting legend in his hour of need. He had always admired DJ. He loaned him the money for what he felt were the right reasons. Today, he doesn't think about it too much. He's realistic about his chances of recouping anything. 'My understanding is there's very limited assets.' It was the first and last time he ever gave DJ a loan.

The most disturbing part of what happened was how DJ behaved in Tom's house. As he did with Tommy Butler, he went into graphic detail about his treatment and gave gut-wrenching information about his cancer. It gives Tom 'the creeps' thinking back, how he welcomed this man into his home. He is sickened at DJ's actions and how he behaved. Tom's main motivation for sharing his story is because he has a close personal friend in Belfast who has been diagnosed with a serious form of cancer. As a human being, this man has demonstrated exemplary personal values, and Tom has found himself reflecting on the deceitful nature of DJ's actions. Tom is also on the board of Cancer Trials Ireland and, through this, has witnessed the courage and hardship of patients genuinely battling cancer, and how the illness has taken an enduring physical, emotional and financial toll on individuals and their families. 'The knowledge that someone would fabricate such a condition for personal gain is appalling. It is a direct affront to the integrity of cancer patients and their advocates. More than that, I believe this fraud has done real damage to the broader ecosystem of cancer fundraising and public trust in charitable and patient-driven appeals,' he told me.

What about the hurler's legacy? Tom thinks it is destroyed. The amount of people he has tried to con was a revelation to Brennan: 'I've never met anyone that told lies like him, and I think his reputation is totally and utterly and deservedly in tatters, and that's the way it should be.' So far DJ has repaid Tom just a small portion of what he borrowed from him. From March to May 2022, he paid back five instalments of €1,000 – a fraction of his debt. 'This was a loan, not a gift and this was always made clear to DJ,' said Tom. 'I had heard DJ was going around saying he was paying people back, but that is just another lie.'

When DJ conned Tom Brennan, there is no doubt he was conniving in how he went to the businessman's home and put on an Oscar-winning performance about how he had cancer. But even while Tom was chasing DJ for his money back, the hurler had moved on to his next victim. This time, the businesswoman he targeted had recently been diagnosed with multiple myeloma herself. It wouldn't be easy to get one up on Mag Kirwan. She's a formidable woman who was reared by Kitty Donohoe, the driving force behind Goresbridge Horse Sales. The business was started by Kitty's husband, Ned. He died suddenly in 1978, leaving the forty-two-year-old mother of nine, who was pregnant at the time, without a husband and at the helm of what is now Ireland's biggest sport and leisure horse auction house. Mag, like her mammy, is decent, hardworking and straight-talking. She and her husband Ger run Goatsbridge Trout Farm from their home on the banks of the River Arrigle in Jerpoint, County Kilkenny. Mag is ambitious, but she always has a glint in her eye and makes time for banter when she's out and about in Thomastown or Kilkenny city. She's good-humoured and is well-liked by people in her area.

Mag's mother, Kitty, is a Carey, but they're not related to DJ's family – and Mag remembered growing up thinking 'it's a pity we're not', because he was their 'hero'. 'As I grew up, our family were into horses and that was our background, but, obviously, All-Ireland Sunday, the whole lot of us were sitting in front of the fire watching, and we used to get a big pint of orange with ice-cream in it. It was really special. Watching the likes of DJ Carey, and he was a superstar. I can still picture him on that TV, scoring the goals and going for the high ball. I can still see him, and he was God, absolutely God.

'As I grew up further and had my own kids, we were doing business with him. In Ireland, you do business with people you trust, people you respect, as long as you're getting a fair deal … I remember thinking these are the kind of people I want my kids to look up towards in terms of role models. DJ Carey was a good-living man; he wasn't a smoker or drinker; he was a serious athlete and a businessman. He was the ultimate hero and the ultimate role model for my kids, and for us as kids growing up. That's what I thought about DJ Carey.'

In February 2021 Mag's world was turned upside down after she was diagnosed with cancer. Just before the diagnosis, she had been training for the European Duathlon Championships but got a pain in her shoulder one day. She went to a physio, but exercises didn't relieve her pain, so she investigated further with another physio and then went to her GP. An astute locum picked up something strange in her bloods and advised further investigation. It was during the pandemic, so it was difficult to get a scan, but once she did, Mag was told that she had 'a mass' on her shoulder. She didn't yet understand the problem and there were further tests and scans before she got her diagnosis. Initially, Mag was told she could have a plasmacytoma, but a biopsy revealed full-scale multiple myeloma in her bone marrow. Mag needed a haematologist, and she went to see Brian Hennessy in Waterford. 'He spent a good hour with us talking to us and he was amazing … He was very normal, but he did speak about how surprised he was that in fact I did have full-blown multiple myeloma; it was worse than he anticipated and it would mean [intensive] treatment. The plan was to have chemotherapy for four months, then harvest my stem cells, then a further three or four months of chemotherapy and a stem cell transplant. That's how he explained the procedure.'

Looking back now, Ger knows his head was spinning when he bumped into DJ in June that year. Against his wife's advice, he had been googling multiple myeloma and wasn't thinking straight – he was surviving, functioning. At that time, Ger had been involved with the development squad in Kilkenny for ten years. There had been big plans to develop the Under-15 and Under-16 squads, to support the young hurlers with the training, but Covid scuppered these plans. The youngsters were 'chomping at the bit' to resume playing, but Ger and the committed four volunteers he worked with had to wait until they got the go-ahead to restart training. The first gathering of the young players came in Graiguenamanagh on the first Saturday in June.

On that first day, Ger was getting used to the young lads, figuring out their names and what was what, when DJ arrived on the field. He walked straight towards Ger. 'Looking back on it now, it was very strange,' said Ger. 'He had absolutely no interest in the young lads. He made a beeline for me.' The conversation started with DJ asking Ger how he was, saying he had heard about Mag being diagnosed with cancer. At this stage, the diagnosis was common knowledge around Thomastown and the broader county, where the couple are well-known.

DJ spoke in a soft voice, and there was empathy in how he approached the subject. Ger opened up and revealed it was multiple myeloma. He explained to DJ how they were trying to figure out what was ahead of them. They were working with a consultant, and Mag was about to face extensive chemotherapy, while also probably facing a bone marrow transplant and then further treatment. DJ listened intently before he responded, 'That's what I have.' He talked about how a well-known hospital in Ireland had been treating his cancer, and he gave Ger the story he'd told others of an accidental radium overdose and his legal case against them. He told Ger that he had come up against roadblocks with the Irish medical system. He also talked about his elite sporting status in the United States, which entitled him to free medical treatment there, where he was attending a revolutionary cancer centre.

DJ was willing to share details, and Ger typed notes into his mobile phone so he would remember it all, as he was eager to share the information with Mag afterwards. He still has those notes today, including the name of the Fred Hutchinson Cancer Center in Seattle. DJ talked about the clinic and getting stem cell treatment there. He pointed to his neck and described getting incisions as opposed to a full bone-marrow transplant. He told Ger about the process, being zonked for three or four days afterwards, and then the recovery. He then reassured Ger, talking about the great advancements in treatments. 'Would she [Mag] talk to me?' DJ finally asked. Ger did not know.

That first conversation lasted about ten minutes. They sat on a bench while the young lads were working away. But afterwards, when Ger mentioned the conversation to somebody else who was at the pitch, saying, 'DJ has the same thing as Mag,' the response came swiftly: 'I dunno, that's debatable.' It's only looking back that Ger remembers those words from another GAA man. 'I would tend to give people the benefit of the doubt; I'm that type of a person,' he said. On the day, Ger remembered only having a nice feeling. He thought it was good to share his concerns for Mag with somebody who had the same cancer. Ger went home and told his wife about meeting DJ; he asked her if she would talk to him. She refused.

Mag has a biochemistry degree, and her first decision was not to research the condition herself but to find the best consultant. She would take instructions on handling cancer the same way she takes instructions from her running trainer. She is disciplined and likes to seek expert advice and do what she is told by those experts. Mag's favourite piece of business advice ever came from a business mentor, Blaise Brosnan, and it was a mantra she would apply to tackling her cancer: 'I would only worry about the things that I could control.' Mag was determined not to engage with too many people about her illness, and her first thought when Ger mentioned DJ having the same cancer was: 'I'm not going to go there.' It's not that she doubted him or his credibility, but she didn't want pity from DJ or anybody else. 'I put his number in my phone, and that was it.' Mag had better things to do, like running her business and taking care of her family, and she wasn't going to dwell on her diagnosis.

Every second week, Mag attended hospital. The other patients became her friends and, for her, going for treatment was a 'social thing'. She drank the tea and ate the chocolate biscuit, but she didn't want to think about cancer once she left the hospital. Mag described herself as 'positive', and she wanted to protect this mindset.

While Mag initially had no interest in talking to DJ, Ger asked her one day, 'Did you make contact with DJ?' She had not, but some weeks later she was in Mount Juliet for a walk when she spotted DJ in the car park putting his golf clubs into a car. She gave him a wave and said, 'Hiya, DJ.' He came over. They had a brief chat and Mag agreed to give him a ring sometime. He seemed genuinely interested, so, about a week later, she made the call. She was in Mount Juliet again when the thought struck her. DJ started off by saying that he was so sorry to hear about the cancer. He then started telling Mag what she should do. He told her he found probiotics fantastic, but this made Mag feel a little uneasy. DJ had actually given her a packet of probiotics he had in his pocket the day they bumped into each other. With her biochemistry knowledge, Mag knew DJ wasn't giving her good advice. 'I wasn't going to take anything other than what my consultant told me to take.' Not even an Anadin would pass her lips without sign-off from her consultant haematologist.

Despite disregarding DJ's medical advice, she recalls how she felt reassured hearing his story about having multiple myeloma for ten years. She saw this as a positive, as she likes to surround herself with people who are doing well. DJ told her gently, 'It's okay to have bad days. Let yourself have bad days and feel those bad days.' He wasn't pushy on the phone that day – in fact, Mag recalled his soft voice, his lovely way of talking. He made sure she knew that if she ever needed anybody to talk to, she could ring him anytime. He offered to meet for coffee. 'He was lovely. I thought that was fine and left it at that, and didn't really think too much about it, to be honest with you.'

Mag didn't ring DJ for support again because she had started treatment and was getting through it. She was working, and she had bought a house in Tramore, where she enjoyed spending time with her family and getting away. However, later that summer, Ger got a call and the news from DJ was stark. His cancer was back and he needed to go for stem cell treatment. A window of opportunity had arisen in the clinic in the US, but he had to go in a few days. There was a slot and he needed to take it. DJ gave Ger the low-down on how his health cover wouldn't kick in for thirty days, but the clinic needed the money upfront and the treatment was expensive. He had some of his own money but was short five grand. He was a little bit embarrassed, as he didn't know the Kirwans that well, but he 'basically asked for €5,000 to get him there and get the treatment'.

Ger didn't know what to say, so he told DJ that Mag looked after the coffers. He would have a word and see if she agreed. He then told Mag the story, and she recalled the conversation: 'Ger came home one day and said, "Listen, I got a phone call and very strange request from DJ Carey looking for five thousand." Ger explained he had to go for some treatment, stem cell in the neck and whatever; I didn't think about any of that. I wasn't going there, I was on my journey and I didn't take notice of that stuff. I said to Ger, "You know what, the poor fecker, if he needs the money, that's fine." I was a bit surprised, but I knew his business had been in difficulty – the story around was that he had been embezzled by his sister and had lost everything … I remember saying to Ger, "Look it, give him the money." I remember exactly what I said, I remember saying, "We have to presume we're never going to get that money back," and I said, "It doesn't matter, it's five thousand, if he needs the money give it him." … I think I texted DJ and said, "Send me on your IBAN".'

TERMINAL ILLNESS

A couple of days later, Mag transferred the money. In the aftermath, she never doubted his cancer story, even though she doubted she'd ever get the loan back. DJ had told Ger it could take a month, maybe two, to pay them back. Once the insurance cover kicked in, he would return the money. Despite her initial acceptance that she was unlikely to be repaid, since DJ had insisted he would do so, 'I was about to get in touch with him to ask him about the money when his father died.' It was 13 October 2021. Instead of asking for her loan back, Mag wrote DJ a sympathy card.

Around this time, Mag was having a quick phone conversation with one of her brothers, a golfer who played around Gowran and Mount Juliet. 'I said to him, "Do you know what DJ Carey's like? I hear he's not well, he's sick." He just said to me, "Stay away from him, something not right there." I said, "You know he's very sick?" and he said, "Not at all, nothing wrong with him, be careful – stay away from him." Of course I wasn't going to tell my big brother, actually I gave him five grand, because then I would've felt like an eejit.' Mag realised there 'might be a problem', and she began to think it had been a bad idea to give DJ money, although she still believed he had cancer.

The couple decided to leave things for a while after John Carey's death, but then Mag started to get annoyed by the fact that DJ hadn't made any effort to contact them about repaying the €5,000. She started to think, 'Maybe I do want the money back.' Mag decided to ring Willie O'Connor, an ex-Kilkenny hurler she knew, who had previously worked for DJ and regularly called to Goatsbridge. Mag asked Willie, 'Is there something I should know about DJ Carey?' His immediate response was, '"Oh Jesus. How much did you give him?" I went "fuck" to myself,' said Mag.

She continued, 'I said, "Why, how much did you give him?" He said – his exact words were – "He looked for fifteen, I gave him all I had which was seven, that was seven years ago."' Mag told Willie she gave him 'five'. Willie responded, 'You can say goodbye to it. I can guarantee you, you won't get it back.' Mag, a woman who loves a challenge, responded to Willie, 'I can guarantee you, I will get it back.' She promised him he'd be the first person she'd ring when she did. Mag put the phone down and swore to herself that she'd get her money back if it was the last thing she did.

Mag decided she had nothing to be ashamed of, and she started to discuss openly how DJ owed her money with the network of businesspeople she knows, both in the south-east and elsewhere. One day she got a call from a 'very successful' businessman, who asked her about Carey: 'He said, "Hi Mag, how are things?" I said, "Great, how are you?" I won't mention his name. He said, "Do you know DJ Carey?" I said to him, "How much did you give him, you big eejit?" He mentioned the figure, which was a six-figure sum. I said, "You're joking me, oh my God." He said, "I heard your name was mentioned." I discovered this person had given well in excess of €100,000.' Mag said DJ made very 'savvy' businesspeople like this man feel 'stupid'. 'This is probably the reason why I am here [talking to the author], nobody was stupid. I'm not stupid. He [the businessman] certainly wasn't stupid. This is how brilliant DJ Carey was.' As with Willie O'Connor, Mag vowed to the businessman that she would get her money back.

Around this time, Mag attended a local wedding, where DJ's financial affairs were the talk of the place. Another attendee told Mag that he had been approached for €70,000. A relative revealed to Mag that there had been a whip-round for DJ in the car park of a local hotel to pay for his son's twenty-first birthday party. A group of men emptied their pockets and handed DJ €800 when he asked for money, but he had repaid them some days later. All of these stories made Mag more determined to get her money back.

A short while after John Carey's death in October, Mag had sent a text to DJ asking if there was any chance of 'that few bob now' as she had a tax bill looming. Over the next few weeks, she continued her back and forth with him, and he made numerous promises that the money would be transferred, but it never happened. 'He started to talk in riddles a bit but always took a call, always replied to texts straight away. Always very nice and very calm, and very charismatic and polite, and all of those things you thought about DJ Carey. I began to realise over time, something is not right here.' She knew she had to be calm and cool, but she turned up the heat a little when he failed to deliver on his promises. Her pursuit continued.

'I'll have it tomorrow,' he said.

Another time he said he could only transfer 1,000 at a time.

Then he was in for a blood transfusion.

Then he claimed he was in America for treatment.

Then he said his brother had given him Covid.

Mag could feel herself getting angry, so she forced herself to calm down. To be nice, patient, logical. But she wasn't going to let up. Then one day, she rang him. 'I said, "DJ, I have at least three people who tell me you're not honest. That's not true, I don't believe that. You of all people. We have so much respect for you, what an amazing sportsperson you are."' Mag told DJ she knew he was a man of honour and integrity, and that she wanted him to prove wrong the people telling her stories about him. 'So I said to him, "I know you're a good guy, DJ, and that money is going to come back. I told everybody, 'Stop talking ill of DJ Carey, one of our greatest sportsmen of all time.'" I was just plámásing him,' she said.

Mag held one trump card: her sister, Miriam, is a respected journalist, ex-*Irish Times* and ex-*Irish Independent*, so she had contacts in the media. Mag let DJ know about her family connections, and she suggested he wouldn't want to see his name splashed all over the *Irish Independent* or another newspaper. DJ was furious. It was the first time Mag had noticed this emotion in him. He responded to what people were saying about him as 'disgraceful'. Mag continued coolly, 'Sure we know it's not true DJ. But all you have to do is pay me back my money, and I'll be the one to tell all those people to cop on, that you are not dishonest.' She knew what she was doing – she was playing DJ at his own game. DJ assured her he'd have the money the following week, although it might be in cash. Mag said she didn't mind either way, that she was putting him under pressure because she had a tax bill to pay. Two, maybe three weeks passed. Mag got in touch with him again. Her phone rang; it was DJ saying, 'I won't have that until tomorrow.'

Mag was isolating in Tramore the next day. It was December 2021. Around 12.30 p.m., DJ arrived at the yard of Goatsbridge Trout Farm. Ger came out from the factory and accepted the envelope with cash. He offered DJ a coffee and they had a chat. Later, Mag rang DJ to thank him and to 'suss him out'. 'I said, "I'm actually in isolation now, I couldn't tell you this morning, I didn't want to upset our little plan." He talked to me about how "It [the treatment] won't be too bad, it'll be fine, if you ever need anything – give me a ring." "DJ," I said, "I knew you were an honourable man [despite] all the people who talked badly about you, you have to stick up for your reputation."

'I was playing a little game. I had actually, over the course of the previous couple of weeks, met a number of people. I had a phone call from a man who was literally in tears on the phone. He had given him two or three thousand, but his wife didn't know – all his savings. He never got his money back.' Mag said that what really surprised her was the 'reluctance' of people to talk about loaning DJ money. The man whose wife didn't know, told her, '"If she found out, there would be a divorce." He was petrified she'd find out, and he was busy saving to try and replenish that money.'

Mag Kirwan couldn't wait to ring Willie O'Connor after she got her money back. It wasn't about the money but the principle of what DJ had done to her. She didn't want anybody thinking she was an 'eejit'.

While Mag does not give DJ Carey headspace in her daily life, she felt a moral obligation to stop him in his tracks. In early 2023, she got a phone call from a detective in Waterford Garda Station, who had her name from Carey's bank records. It was only some time later, when she was in the garda station, that Mag realised he didn't have cancer. She knew he was swindling loans from people that he couldn't pay back, but she had never doubted he was ill. Gardaí broke the news to her: 'I asked the detective, and he said, "He doesn't have cancer," and I said, "Are you sure?" He said, "Yeah, I'm sure, he didn't have cancer." That was the day I stopped believing he had cancer.'

Mag couldn't believe 'anybody could be that evil'. She remembers 'trying to convince a few people to go and talk to the detective. I said, "They need to have as much evidence, as many stories as possible, because they need to present this and they need a strong case."' Mag felt DJ needed to be exposed for his fraud and stopped in his tracks, as she thought he was still 'at it'. She didn't want him to get away with it, and she started to talk about DJ's behaviour openly in Kilkenny, as well as taking calls from journalists. She explained that it was easy for her to be the 'whistleblower' because she got her money back. She felt 'it was really important that nobody for one moment felt stupid', because DJ was so manipulative and so 'brilliant' at how he told his story. 'Whatever it is, it's not mental health – it's pure badness.'

Mag told this author that she personally knows ten people who gave DJ Carey sums of money from €5,000 to €127,000. She said many people haven't looked for justice because they are 'embarrassed' to talk about what happened, and she also knows people who played hurling with DJ who would still protect him. 'I think, if you refuse to believe the truth, you're protecting him. I know the truth. I know, so I won't protect him.'

From summer 2019 to late 2022, DJ was trying to buy a property in Kilkenny, and he even made regular enquiries to auctioneers. Apparently, he wanted to set up home in Kilkenny city. In one instance, he told his friend Joan that his money was 'tied up for six months', and he claimed that he was due a settlement from AIB of over €3m. He said he had been given inaccurate financial advice and that he was due money back through a corporate solicitor. It didn't make sense to Joan, but she didn't want to pry to try to find out why the AIB money would be coming through a corporate solicitor.

DJ asked Joan to intervene and see if she could talk to the homeowners about stalling the purchase of No. 9 Lower Patrick Street to allow him to sort out his account. The property, built around 1780, was in the heart of the medieval city and came with an asking price of €585,000. Eventually, somebody else bought the house, and DJ claimed to Joan afterwards that, because the mortgage never came through, he and a female friend had lost a €70,000 deposit on it that he paid to a Dublin solicitor. Joan has no idea whether this was another figment of his imagination or if it happened.

DJ inquired about buying other properties in Kilkenny city, including houses for sale on Castle Road, an exclusive property at Rosehill Gardens on the Kells Road, and Kilcreene Lodge, the former home of Walter Smithwick. He also took an interest in properties on the Dublin Road and the Castlecomer Road. He put bids on homes in at least two cases but did not follow through with a deposit. During one of the viewings, DJ mentioned that he had to travel to America for treatment but didn't elaborate further. After he made an offer on one property, he gave the name of a Kilkenny solicitor and promised the deposit would come by post. The deposit never arrived. It's unclear what DJ's motivation was for all this, when he must have known he couldn't follow through with deposits and that he couldn't afford a mortgage. Possibly, he was trying to give the impression that he was a man of means, when, in reality, he was a man under serious pressure, particularly after he had to leave 10 The Avenue.

DJ's attempts to buy a house in Kilkenny became a 'running joke' among auctioneers in the city. An informed source who had dealt with him said, 'If a big house came up for sale in Kilkenny, the running joke was "DJ's buying that". It was bullshit. He was buying nothing, it was all pure fantasy.' DJ told the same individual that he had bought land 'somewhere in Africa or Asia with gold', and it was going to 'come good'. Some of his stories sound so far-fetched now, but unless you were in the know, DJ Carey probably came across as a straight-up guy.

From the time DJ moved out of the house on Granges Road in Kilkenny in late 2021/early 2022, he appeared to be homeless, and he checked into hotels for long periods, including the five-star Lyrath Hotel in Kilkenny. A hotel source confirmed this, saying he checked in 'for quite some time, maybe seven weeks' in 2022. At the Lyrath he got his meals delivered to his room, telling staff, 'I'd love to be able to come downstairs, but with my cancer, I can't.' He explained how he feared contracting Covid-19 as he was vulnerable. He later claimed he actually got Covid and remained in his room for a long period. When he left the hotel, he also left behind an unpaid bill, although it is understood that this was not for his entire stay.

As well as staying at hotels, DJ was spotted sleeping in his car in the car park at Mount Juliet Golf Club, where he used the men's locker room to shower and get dressed in the mornings. He was also seen sleeping in his car outside the Hoban Hotel, which is just off the ring road in Kilkenny, where he used to go for his breakfast in the mornings. A source said that a former hurler couldn't believe it when he saw how DJ was living and kindly offered to pay his hotel bill on a night-to-night basis for a short period. Neither the hurler nor the hotel confirmed this story to this author, but a number of sources reported seeing DJ in the hotel during this period and said he looked dishevelled, which was out of character for him.

From this point, DJ's attempts to 'borrow' money focused on people closer to home, and he often hung out in busy coffee shops, restaurants and hotels. In 2022 one shrewd businesswoman in the south-east regularly noticed DJ in her premises, where he'd sit for hours with a cup of tea. She didn't know him personally, but she knew who he was – DJ Carey, the great Kilkenny hurler – and she wondered why he was there so often. He stopped her one day and beckoned to her to sit down. She felt awkward but did so. DJ immediately told her he had cancer and needed to travel to Seattle for stem cell treatment. It was urgent. He needed €50,000. Could she help? She looked at her watch, made her excuses and left. In her opinion, it was a strange way to approach somebody he didn't know.

Around September 2022 DJ approached a man in the same premises. 'He came over to me, and I said, "Howya, DJ?" I knew him over the years. He said, "Not good, I have cancer and I need to go to America but need to get the money together." I said to him, "A man of your calibre, would you not go to the Kilkenny County Board?" He said, "No, they'd do nothing for me."' DJ explained that, since the story broke about Catriona, he was not getting any financial help for his cancer treatment. 'I said to him, I wasn't in business any more and I was struggling along myself. To be honest, I smelt a rat straight away.' Although this was a brief interaction, afterwards the man rang somebody who knew DJ to ask, 'What the fuck is Carey at?' When he explained what had happened, the reply came, 'Don't tell me he's down there now!'

Other businesspeople got phone calls, some regularly, but all at least a couple of times a year. It always sounded urgent. DJ would ask for a meeting, saying he needed to talk. He would follow up the call with texts. Some fobbed him off and didn't entertain his requests to meet because they felt there was something odd about the whole thing. One high-profile businessman who DJ called on, asking him to invest in his business before he ever asked him to help fund his cancer treatment, said he might have been inclined to give DJ a loan if he'd been more professional in how he conducted his business.

James Kehoe, owner of the Lord Bagenal Inn in Leighlinbridge, County Carlow, recalled seeing the former hurler in his hotel regularly in 2022. Before then, he had only been an occasional customer. James is an astute observer of people, having worked in the hospitality trade since he was a teenager, and he can spot when something is off. He told this author how DJ would come into his hotel almost daily from the spring of 2022. He would sit with a pot of tea and biscuits, keeping an eye on everything. Initially, he sat in the lobby of the hotel, but he later moved into the main bar and generally sat at table 17 or 18, where his back was to the wall and he had the best view of the area. He always sat alone.

One day James said to DJ, 'Good morning, how are you?' The response was, 'I'm not well. I'm having cancer treatment in America. I don't have the money to finish the treatment … I don't know what I'm going to do.' James quickly realised what was happening: 'To be honest, I could read the story before it arrived. You become very wise to this type of thing [working in the hotel business for years]. Look, I get guys asking me for 50 euros semi-regular at the bar … I could see with DJ what was coming. He was telling me how difficult his circumstances were.'

Initially, James felt 'a bit sorry' for DJ when he talked about going to Seattle for treatment and how he needed a very specialised form of treatment that cost 'about 100,000 a shot'. DJ then started talking about money. James was standing for the entire conversation, while DJ remained in his seat. 'You can sense when a fella is going to touch you for money,' he said, and he quickly 'cut it off at the pass'. James changed the subject to the hotel industry and its difficulties since 2007/2008, and how he had had to work his way out of recession. DJ never raised the cancer story or his money problems with James again. There were many others who didn't have the same instincts as James and weren't as fortunate.

DJ regularly went to Gowran Park Golf Club, where he'd been an honorary member since the day it opened in 2001 and where he could play a free round of golf. He'd sit in the bar with a cup of tea, talking to people coming and going. Some days, he might have a slice of toast, before heading to IT Carlow for a session with the hurlers. Often he could be found golfing on his own on a Friday evening during the summer, which struck people who spotted him as odd. Visitors would point him out from the rooftop bar at Gowran Park racecourse (which overlooks the golf course) and ask each other, 'Is that DJ Carey down there?' Here was probably the greatest hurler of all time playing golf on his own. At other times, he sat in the rooftop bar himself with a pot of tea and struck up conversations with visitors to Gowran Park.

This author has confirmed the details of a story he told some visitors there who do not wish to be identified. He started by saying hello and asking if he could join them. Soon, he launched into a heartbreaking story of how he had cancer. It was 'terminal', and he needed specialised treatment in the United States. He mentioned how once he had been stopped by customs and excise officials in the States, who informed him that due to his elite sporting status he was entitled to free medical treatment. While this covered most of the treatment costs, there was a shortfall and he was stuck. It was a very serious situation. DJ gave the visitors, who were on a short break in Kilkenny, the full run-down on his health problems and then asked them for €10,000. They felt there was something strange about the whole thing, so they didn't agree straight away, but on returning to their home county, they rang a Kilkenny friend – they were swiftly told not to give DJ any money.

While Tom Brennan and Mag Kirwan were very clear in their assessment of DJ Carey after they figured out the truth, the betrayal was a little more complicated for another victim, Clare hurler Tony Griffin. When he and his brothers and friends played make-believe as they were growing up, the others were all Gretzky, Pelé or Jordan, but Tony imagined he was Jamesie O'Connor, Brian Lohan or DJ Carey. Tony loved to watch the Kilkenny man because he was daring and never afraid to go for the goal. As a youngster, he became interested in the shape and size of DJ's hurl, so he convinced his mother to drive to Kilkenny so that he could get a hurl made by Star Hurley. 'At a young age, you just emulate what you see.'

Tony recalled how, as a nineteen-year-old who had recently joined the Clare Senior hurling panel, he took a trip to Young Irelands of Gowran for a friendly. 'DJ scored two amazing goals that day; they were just unbelievable.' He remembered the heartache of playing in the 2002 All-Ireland final when DJ got the opening score – a goal for Kilkenny – and he saw how DJ's presence made 'such an impact' on the day. 'You somehow don't ever think you'll play on the same pitch as these guys. I was in awe of him ... There was something about DJ. I looked at him and thought he was on another level.' Former Clare hurling boss Anthony Daly once told Tony he was as good as DJ Carey. There was no higher praise you could give a young hurler.

While Tony continued to have huge admiration for DJ, the pair didn't have many interactions off the field over the years. However, a friend of Tony's in Kildare knew DJ through handballing circles in Ballymore Eustace, as he had visited to play over the years. 'He said to me, "I heard DJ is after falling on hard times, he's down in the dumps. Come here; we should have him up for dinner sometime." The fan in me said, "I'd love to meet him." My friend told me he was on to DJ, and he said, "Tell Tony I'm asking for him." Sure, when you're growing up admiring someone, you'd be glad to meet them.

'The dinner didn't happen, but [months] later I got a call from my friend again to say DJ was in difficulty.' In September 2022, Tony and his friend decided they needed to help DJ financially, as they believed he had cancer and needed treatment abroad. However, around the same time, DJ's name came up in conversation with another friend of Tony's, who cautioned him not to give money to Carey. 'He said, "Just be careful – I've heard that [his story] might not be completely true." He told me to check my sources as he had heard DJ was looking for somebody else's phone number who had recently sold his business.'

Tony went back to his handballing friend, who made further enquiries and assured Tony that DJ was unwell. The pair agreed that they'd suggest organising a fundraiser for DJ. 'My friend was initially the one in contact with DJ, and he

TERMINAL ILLNESS

came back and said DJ had refused any help, with a "no" to the fundraiser.' The explanation from DJ was that it was too difficult to fundraise with all the negative publicity about his sister Catriona's alleged mortgage scam that had broken in the media earlier that year. Tony understood that there was a backlash over this, so he offered to go to see DJ in person to give him some money. He took over the conversation himself and texted DJ to ask him if he wanted to meet for a coffee and a chat. 'He made it clear he didn't want to meet up. He said it was "just easier if you send it to this account". I made the transfer [of €1,500], and then three days later, I got a text back saying, "Thanks for that, I really appreciate your support, talk to you when I come back [from treatment]."' Although Tony had transferred the money, he had a 'funny feeling' about it all. 'I said to him, "We'll definitely come down and see you sometime," but there was no eagerness [from DJ] to take me up on this. I had some reservations.'

Two weeks after he gave him the money, Tony got a text from DJ saying 'everything went well' with his treatment. Tony had a lot on his mind while this conversation with DJ was going on, so he didn't think too much about the €1,500 and described the money as a 'donation' to 'help somebody out'.

One evening in December 2022, as Tony was sitting at home, he received a phone call from a detective in Waterford saying he was 'investigating a GAA star'. Somehow, immediately, Tony knew it was DJ Carey. There was a part of Tony that knew all along that something was off, but he just didn't want to believe it; there was also a part of him questioning, 'Why are they going after DJ Carey?' His first thoughts were, 'If this is true, this is very sad.' Shortly after the phone call, two detectives arrived at Tony's office and were able to explain that DJ was not in the United States receiving treatment in September 2022 when he told Tony he was away. 'It all seemed like a movie. I asked them, "Why do you think he did this?" I know everybody has the potential to do bad things, but my brain couldn't put it together that this was actually happening.'

Tony understands that the amount he gave DJ was small in comparison to others: 'If I'd given him 100k, I'd be really upset.' However, while he gave the money willingly, a month later Tony joked that he was a 'few quid short for a bill' himself. 'I was conned. I felt sorry and sad for the guy who was such a heroic figure to have fallen so far. Was I angry with him? Not really – that's human behaviour.' Tony wrote in his book, *Screaming at the Sky*, about his own grief after his beloved father's death from cancer in 2005, and how he had fundraised €1m for cancer charities in his memory. He is philosophical about what happened. His view is that there are different ways of dissecting what has happened. 'People with no appreciation for hurling, they'll only see the criminal. They won't see the mastery. For those of us who appreciated the hurler, we'll always appreciate the hurler.' However, he knows that people will question the person off the field, as 'that DJ' is not who we thought he was. 'What he did was not okay. People feel, what we thought we saw is not what we got.'

So how does he make sense of it all? 'He was such a good player that he was on another level, he was special, and when you're used to being told you're special, maybe the rules don't apply to you.' Tony said if DJ was to 'put his hands up' and say, 'I wronged a lot of people, I'm sorry,' many people would forgive him. On 15 February 2023 – a week before Carey's arrest – Tony sent him a text saying, 'Dear DJ, I just wanted to let you know there are no hard feelings and I forgive you for what has happened. I hope you are OK and you'll be in my thoughts. Tony Griffin.'

11

FAMILY DRAMA

Everything got much harder for DJ Carey from St Valentine's Day 2022. That night, RTÉ One broadcast to the nation claims that Catriona Carey had convinced people who were in mortgage arrears to put their trust in her. Catriona's dealings with her company, Careysfort Asset Estates Ltd, were outlined to the viewers who learned that people had paid tens of thousands of euro in return for the promise of saving their homes from repossession. Catriona pitched Careysfort Asset Estates Ltd – registered in England – as a 'friendly' Irish vulture fund, and reassured clients that she would buy their debt from a lender at a discount and sell it back to them at a lower price. First, though, a deposit was needed, either in cash or as a transfer to a bank account in Belgium or Germany, to secure the deal. She promised new loans with lower monthly repayments for clients, but these never materialised.

One of Catriona's clients was Colin Finnegan, who ran a successful haulage business and bought his parents' home, shop and coal yard in 2006. Some years later, he found himself in trouble after he lost a work contract in the financial crash. He was unable to make his loan repayments, and his property was about to be repossessed. RTÉ reported, 'In 2019, a barrister introduced him, and a number of others, to a Kilkenny businesswoman, Catriona Carey.'

Many months after Colin – and others in a similar position – had handed over a deposit to Catriona, there was still no sign of a contract for the new loan from Careysfort Asset Estates. When Colin was made aware that his property was on an auction site for distressed properties, he raised concerns with Catriona, who texted him: 'Our team put this up as part of our strategy. Please keep this to yourself and we do not want others to know how we work. We have this already bought as explained many times.' RTÉ reported that Catriona's reassurances 'were, in fact, a lie'. 'A neighbour had placed a bid on the property and was successful in buying it. The neighbour has reassured the Finnegans that they can stay in their home.'

Sharon O'Riordan, who worked as a chef for the HSE, was introduced to Catriona by a barrister she met while fighting repossession. Her lender had secured a possession order on her house in Castletown, County Cork. RTÉ reported that O'Riordan felt it was like being offered a lifeline, a 'path out of her financial rut'. 'The company was offering to sell the mortgages back to the original borrower for the same discounted price it had paid. On top of this, Careysfort Asset Estates would give people a new loan, usually at a rate of 5.5%, to allow them to buy back their mortgage.' Sharon O'Riordan liked the proposal and told RTÉ she thought Catriona was 'very likeable' and flexible.

Catriona initially asked for a deposit of €25,000 from Sharon to secure the deal, but when she learned that Sharon had no way of getting that sort of money, she settled for €5,000. Sharon had to go to her family to ask for the money, and they helped her. In November 2019, she met Catriona and experienced what RTÉ called the 'builder's handshake' that the businesswoman gave to many others. O'Riordan felt like her problems were finally going away. As she explained in the documentary, 'I drove down that road the happiest person in the world. I thought, *I finally got there*. What could possibly go wrong?'

RTÉ recorded conversations with Catriona, in which she claimed her company was 'flush with cash' – she even stated that there was €8m in pending property transactions. 'However, *RTÉ Investigates* checked the filed accounts of Careysfort Asset Estates. There is no reference to €8m of property transactions. And the company's current assets, which include cash, show a net balance of the sterling equivalent of €34,000.' RTÉ also stated that it wasn't just the 'claim about a phantom €8m that didn't stack up'. Catriona signed her emails using the title 'FCCA' or Fellow of the Association of Chartered Certified Accountants. 'But the Association of Chartered Certified Accountants confirmed to *RTÉ Investigates* that she is not a member.' She used other acronyms after her name, for instance AITI, suggesting she was an Associate of the Irish Tax Institute. 'The Irish Tax Institute also told *RTÉ Investigates* that it has no such record of her.' She claimed her company office was at 25 Merrion Square in Dublin, but the owners of this property stated she was never a tenant.

The programme reported that Catriona had a conviction under the Criminal Law (Theft and Fraud Offences) Act, 2001. She had been convicted in February 2020 for theft and for forging a cheque from Kilkenny hairdresser Nigel Kenny, who had hired her as his accountant; however, she avoided jailtime. When *RTÉ Investigates* doorstepped her to ask about her fraudulent behaviour, she declined to answer questions. In response to a 'detailed list of questions' from the programme about her recent business activities, 'she said that she could not speak about any client due to "strict confidentiality clauses". She also said her company had funds to "cover all clients deposits" but said, "We are not advised to refund clients at this point."' At the time of writing, a date of 27 January 2027 has been set by the Dublin Circuit Criminal Court for the trial of Catriona Carey, who has been charged with three offences contrary to Section 7 of the Criminal Justice (Money Laundering and Terrorist Financing) Act 2010. The case is expected to take four to six weeks. Catriona Carey is denying all the charges against her.

After the RTÉ documentary aired, DJ was under pressure – he mentioned during phone calls with people such as Bernie Comaskey that things had been tough since his sister appeared on RTÉ. He said he was 'getting it hard in Kilkenny' and nobody wanted to help him. DJ was looking for sympathy, but, from this point on, getting money from people for his bogus cancer treatment became more challenging for him. There is no doubt that many people on whom DJ was relying for money and sympathy had become more suspicious of his cancer claims since the allegations against his sister were made public. And the documentary was not DJ's only problem at this time. His brother Jack was concerned enough about DJ's actions that he was tipping people off not to give him any money.

Jack himself, at the time of writing, is also facing trial, charged with fourteen offences under the Companies Act. Seven of the charges relate to Careysfort Asset Estates Ltd, of which he was listed as a director for ten months. Other charges relate to a company called White Capital Trinity Ltd, where he was listed as director from February 2019 to December 2021. He too is denying the charges made against him.

DJ was the subject of many conversations in Kilkenny after the Catriona Carey documentary aired, with just as many people expressing an interest in his financial affairs as the content of the programme. People were talking about DJ borrowing money left, right and centre. 'Did you hear about DJ?' hissed one woman in the queue for Badger and Dodo coffee in Connolly's Red Mills on the outskirts of Kilkenny city. It was February 2022, and the woman's friend looked perplexed by her question as she answered, 'You mean Catriona?' The answer came, 'Nooooo … I mean DJ. He's up to his neck in debt.'

The local gossip was that DJ had left a trail of unpaid bills behind in local hotels, and he was the talk of the town. The woman mentioned names that were circulating: 'I heard Eamonn Langton [owner of Langtons Hotel] got stung as well.' Langton declined invitations to speak about his experiences with DJ Carey. There was also talk of DJ borrowing amounts varying from €10,000 to €50,000 from Kilkenny publicans.

They, too, did not wish to comment on this speculation, but this was typical of the types of conversations being had in Kilkenny around the time that Catriona's story hit the headlines. While elsewhere most people were focused on Catriona, the talk in Kilkenny was more heavily concentrated on her brother.

After the programme was broadcast, Mag Kirwan actually rang RTÉ journalist Paul Murphy to tell him about DJ. 'I said, "I just saw a fantastic documentary about DJ Carey", and he said, "What do you mean?" I said, "Surely you've come across lots of stories about DJ Carey when you've done your research on this?" He wasn't giving much, and I said, "Now I think it's time to talk about DJ Carey … you have my number, you know where I am." I said I want to tell my story.' Mag told Murphy that he needed to do a 'similar investigation' on DJ. However, Mag didn't think RTÉ seemed interested in her story at the time.

On 27 February 2022, Maeve Sheehan reported on the story behind Catriona Carey's fraud conviction for the *Sunday Independent* under the headline 'Revealed: The cheque forgery that brought down Catriona Carey'. Sheehan did an interview with Nigel Kenny, who had discovered that the name on his cheque for €6,948 made out to 'Collector General' to pay a tax demand had been altered to 'Catriona Carey'. He told the newspaper, 'I did feel sickened that I was robbed like that. I mean if anybody that you trust and you like takes anything off you, you're going to be disappointed, aren't you?'

Kenny knew Catriona when he hired her to do accounts for him. His business was doing well, so he was taken aback when he got demanding letters from Revenue. After writing the initial cheque in January 2018, he was surprised when, just two months later, Revenue sent him another tax demand, 'this time for €3,152'. Kenny rang Catriona, but she didn't answer, so he called Revenue, despite the fact that she had told him to 'never, ever, ever ring Revenue'. He spoke to a '"very nice man" who broke the news that his cheque for €6,948 had never been received …' Kenny still didn't suspect any wrongdoing, until he rang AIB's 24-hour banking line and discovered his original cheque had been cashed at a Bank of Ireland in Kilkenny. The next day, Kenny stood in that bank staring at the altered name and Catriona's initials on the back of the cheque. 'It was like something a five-year old would do. I don't know how it got that far.' At AIB's request, Kenny reported the fraud to gardaí and made a statement to detectives. Carey was convicted and received an eight-month suspended sentence. AIB reimbursed the money to Kenny – Carey did not pay back a cent. It was only when a friend told him about her conviction months later that he found out about it.

In 2022, Careysfort Asset Estates Ltd was not the only business in which Catriona was involved. On 10 June that year, Amy Molloy reported that a UK company registered in the name of 'convicted fraudster' Catriona Carey was 'on the verge of being struck off'. She wrote, 'The *Irish Independent* can reveal a notice for compulsory strike-off is pending for MP&P Private Commercial Investments Ltd, a company which lists its activities as "property unit trusts" … Carey is the sole director of MP&P, which is one of multiple businesses registered in her name in England.' The report stated that this followed a warning by the Central Bank of Ireland about Careysfort Asset Estates Ltd, which was 'at the centre of multiple fraud allegations' and was 'not authorised' to provide financial services. Molloy reported that Careysfort Asset Estates Ltd's registered address in Wenlock Road, London, was the same as that used by MP&P.

On 30 June, the *Irish Independent* reported that Bank of Ireland was suing Catriona 'over debts relating to a mortgage on a property. The bank first applied for a debt summary judgment against the Kilkenny woman in 2017, and the case is up for mention in the High Court next month. It is understood the property, which was previously held as security for the mortgage by Bank of Ireland, has since been sold and the bank is seeking to recover outstanding money owed.'

On 21 July, Catriona Carey gave her first in-depth interview after the *RTÉ Investigates* programme aired. In the *Sunday World*, she blamed an 'associate' for orchestrating the '€800,000 "Careysfort Asset Estates" mortgage scam'. She branded herself as 'the fall guy', yet admitted to spending tens of thousands of euro of clients' money on personal items. She said the €400,000 in client funds that were held in the bank were 'gone and not recoverable'. According to Catriona, she believed that the person she described as the 'ringleader' was purchasing her clients' debts from the banks, and that the contracts 'were good'. Catriona said, 'I'm sorry for the role I've played in this, but I need them (the clients) to understand I was being deceived also. The person behind all of this has been given a free role to live their life and they have not been exposed the way I have been exposed.'

In the same *Sunday World* report, she gave her response to an ongoing investigation by the Garda National Economic Crime Bureau involving complaints of fraud against her from more than twenty former clients. Carey said, 'I'm quite happy to be under investigation … I'm quite happy to face what I have to face.' She claimed to be 'very happy' to deal with the gardaí on anything they needed: 'I don't know why I wouldn't for my own sake. I have nothing to hide in what I've done. I have to date given [my associate] over €100,000 in assets to solve my own debt resolutions issues. I have wasted two-and-a-half years corresponding with a man who was deceiving me from the very beginning. I had no reason to set this business up to destroy people's lives. None whatsoever. Hopefully, everybody that was involved in this pays the price – including myself. If I deserve to pay a penalty for this, I will absolutely take that on the chin. I came into this with the best of intentions, to make some money and solve my own debt issues, solve other people's debt issues.' Carey claimed her 'associate' was the person getting debt deals through the banks. 'He had the contacts with the banks, he had the solicitor who was his friend for 30 years, he had contacts. He knew judges, he knew guards and he came across as a very legitimate person.'

One anonymous source, who met Catriona through Careysfort Asset Estates in 2019, googled her before getting involved and noticed there had been issues in the family business with DJ. 'I said it to her about DJ [and the fraud investigation previously into DJ Carey Enterprises], but she just said that was squared off. There was a big family row, and that was it, the family went with her. I looked it up and thought she was telling the truth.'

Catriona was due in court once again in January 2023 to contest a four-year driving ban, after initially pleading guilty to four road traffic offences, including driving without a licence or insurance. The *Sunday World* reported that in 2021 she had 'received 12 penalty points for speeding in a 50kmh zone, speeding in a 120kmh zone while twice she was caught driving while holding a mobile phone. She received a six-month disqualification from November 8, 2021 until May 8, 2022. However, she was stopped by gardaí on two occasions for motoring offences while the disqualification was active.' When she was stopped by gardaí driving her BMW on the Castlecomer Road on 10 December 2021 and informed that she had been disqualified from driving, Carey reportedly screamed at an officer, 'Do you expect me to get taxis?' The judge on the case 'took into consideration Carey's apology and guilty plea, but said it was difficult to offer an excuse when she was stopped a month later after getting into a car "knowing full well she's disqualified". She gave her a suspended sentence and a four-year driving ban.'

In a story published on 7 January Catriona answered queries put to her by the *Irish Independent*. She said she was appealing her driving ban because she believed there may have been administrative errors regarding the application of penalty points. When asked about Careysfort Asset Estates, she criticised banks for showing 'little or no interest in dealing with negative equity borrowers'. She said she 'had hoped that my company was plugging the market in this matter and also with a view to making a profit. More needs to be done for homeowners and little risk is taken by banking institutions globally as the system is completely set up against the individual. I have done massive research on all of this and genuinely hoped to be involved with debt restructuring for the long haul.' She claimed to have paid sums to her associate to clear her debts, but there was no proof given for this. In the case of the driving ban, she eventually withdrew her appeal in November 2023.

While Catriona Carey's business practices were all over the newspapers, her brother DJ's own dodgy dealings were about to be exposed. Initially, he was not named when a story appeared in early 2023 about a 'GAA star' at the centre of a 'cancer fraud scam', but in his own county many people had already realised that the person being written about was DJ. The first story broke about an 'alleged cruel cancer scam' in *The Irish Sun* on 12 February. John Kierans wrote that up to a hundred people were believed to have been 'hit for cash over a period of eight years by a GAA legend'. He stated that many of the people scammed were 'prominent names within the Gaelic football and hurling world. The legend – who may have allegedly accrued up to one million euro in the fraud – was still making begging phone calls up until four weeks ago even though Gardaí had begun a probe into the scandal. The star claimed he was suffering from cancer. One businessman who gave him a new car thought he was in the US having treatment but discovered from one of the player's friends he was actually holidaying in the Tropics. The businessman took the car off him on his return.'

Kierans also reported that the sports star had asked for thousands of euro to help pay for 'so-called cancer treatment' in America. In another report, he quoted a 'GAA insider who turned him [Carey] down. He [DJ] uses the same modus operandi and asks for a figure, quite often it is €15,000, and rolls out the cancer and stem cell treatment story. Many people who gave him money are just too embarrassed to speak publicly and have just written it off and vowed never to have anything to do with him again. People are now queuing up to make complaints and statements to the Gardaí. My understanding is the final figure involved is close to a million quid. He had a whole list of different American hospitals where he had treatment. My understanding is he never was in any of them.'

On 17 February, a few days after this story broke, RTÉ's *Prime Time* reported that DJ Carey had secured a settlement with AIB in 2017, 'through which a debt of over €9.5m was written down to €60,000'. There was a public outcry that he had received preferential treatment and there was a backlash against AIB's actions online. Many social media posts showed the extent of public anger. In one, David Hall, co-founder of the Irish Mortgage Holders Organisation, said, 'Some country. Who you are and who you know still works.'

On 20 February, the *Irish Examiner* reported that AIB was set to be 'hauled before the Oireachtas finance committee over a "jaw-dropping" settlement it made with former GAA star DJ Carey'. Elaine Loughlin reported on Carey's debt agreement, stating: 'Junior minister Dara Calleary said he had been contacted by many people in recent days who are furious that they "haven't had access to this kind of settlement". The Fianna Fáil TD said: "AIB should appear before the finance committee, they need to provide the details of this, the context of the agreement, it's a very jaw-dropping settlement." This was echoed by Employment Affairs Minister Neale Richmond, who described the scale of the write-down as "worrying". At least five members of the committee, including Green Party TD Steven Matthews, are now calling on the bank to appear to explain how it signs off on such settlements.'

Journalist Shane Ross told this author it was not unusual for AIB to do this for a person of influence, but for an ordinary individual it is not the norm. He cited examples such as previous taoisigh who had received preferential treatment. A tribunal heard how AIB wrote off almost £400,000 of Charlie Haughey's £1.14 million debt in 1980. A retired AIB manager told the Payments to Politicians Tribunal that the bank did not want to force the sale of Haughey's home because he had just become taoiseach. The bank feared the repercussions of selling his property or lands, suggesting they could have lost loyal customers given Haughey's popularity at the time. 'Haughey put them under duress,' said Ross, who also cited an interesting case of another former taoiseach, Garret FitzGerald, getting his debts written off by AIB. In 1999 FitzGerald admitted that the bank had written off a bad debt of up to £200,000 for him six years earlier. He said he sold his house at Palmerston Road in Dublin 6 to raise money to pay off the debt, which he incurred after borrowing money to buy shares in Guinness Peat Aviation.

Ross said, 'I would conclude, without any doubt, that this followed a pattern in AIB which was State owned at the time, of them being prepared [to help] individuals in powerful positions.' He believed that because Irish society is small, people have friends in high places, such as on the boards of banks and elsewhere. 'I suspect, although I have no evidence of it, that there are occasions where somebody gets a tap on the shoulder and says, "Go easy on X, Y, or Z." That's the way it operated in Ireland for a long time. It's more transparent now, but people did get preferential treatment.' He said DJ Carey had an 'aura' around him, and AIB, many years ago, were likely to be 'very glad' to have him as a client. There was a time when they'd have loved the association given their long-term sponsorship of the GAA championships. Ross said he thought the former hurler fell into a pit or a fantasy world of borrowing money to bring on great riches. 'I can't believe nobody said to him, stop this – this is madness. People at the time [of the Celtic Tiger] were living in make-believe. They saw eternal riches around the corner.'

In October 2023 this author asked Catriona Carey to give her account of what happened in DJ Carey Enterprises years earlier, when she resigned as company director. Catriona confirmed that she was placed 'under an investigation for misappropriation of funds, namely €1m, at the time'. She stated that she spent three years 'speaking with local detectives which culminated in my arrest to answer yet more of the same questions in Kilkenny Garda Station. It transpired that the DPP was not going any further as there was no misappropriation of funds.' Gardaí did not comment on Catriona's claims when asked by this author to clarify what happened with the 2009 case.

In our correspondence, Catriona said, 'I was and still am very disappointed at how DJ handled this matter. Perhaps it's was [sic] cowardly behaviour to satisfy Sarah Newman and he should have stood tall and told her the truth. She was his fiancé [sic] at that time and this suggests a very close relationship. I have to understand that and accept that this happened.' Catriona wrote that she will 'forever feel scarred' by what happened after she left DJ Carey Enterprises, especially the actions taken by Newman, 'who decided to run to gardaí, media, revenue and my accountancy body instead of clarifying where her investment had gone, which ultimately had gone back into her and DJs [sic] properties at the time and not to myself and was falsely reported. I have forgiven DJ for his weakness in handling this matter, and subsequent behaviour, of which I don't really know much about and would rather deal with any family issues in private.'

In a follow-up email, on 27 October, Catriona offered more information on what she meant by her comment as regards the money going back to Newman and DJ's properties. She stated that DJ had used a 'large portion of the money she [Newman] put into DJ Carey Enterprises to pay for Mount Juliet instalments on the build and didn't inform her'. Catriona also claimed DJ 'took some money for himself too' but 'it was not my business to query'. Catriona reiterated that DJ did not tell Newman about taking money out of his company to pay for Mount Juliet 'instalments on the build' or taking money for himself. 'So when she went to look for this money as her own cash flow was dwindling, it was not there. Of course she was angry. Hence I come into this. I did not know she was not aware of this. Said nothing as I am now very good at doing to my own fault! It landed on my door. She was informed of the truth as I engaged a solicitor to write to both of them way back in 2011. So she knows the reality.'

Catriona questioned if having a 'salary, company car' and expenses amounted to 'misappropriation' – as she believed in Newman's eyes, she was 'just a minimum wage person'. 'The company, when I walked away was paying its obligations,' she stated, adding that 'they [Carey and Newman] ultimately closed it down 18 months later as it was not a glamorous business but hard work physically with a living but not a living to compare to the lifestyle she needed to keep up. It was a comedown [from running a travel empire to a modest cleaning company]. I worked it with my family. It would still be here today. We worked hard and kept our heads down. It was not always easy. She created havoc and it may not have been her intention. We stole or took nothing from her. She stole my name and respect … I didn't really recover ever from it but I'm not playing victim I'm just stating a fact.'

In 2023 this author contacted Sarah Newman in relation to what happened at DJ Carey Enterprises and subsequent claims made by Catriona Carey, but she did not respond to any of the questions put to her. She simply stated that her life was 'now elsewhere and I broke up with him 10 years ago, so that's in my past'.

When asked about DJ's actions in borrowing money for cancer treatment, Catriona claimed she did not know about her brother's issues. She believed there were creditors after him who were 'angry and making threats', and she said she had heard mention of 'tough-style debt collectors' going to DJ's workplace. She suggested that some of his creditors went to RTÉ journalist Paul Murphy 'to get another programme aired' – 'brother and sister conmen'. 'I guess he [DJ] saw the destruction I got, so he would have even worse. So perhaps it drove him to some crazy state.' Catriona claimed she was told her brother's behaviour looking for money was 'out of character … Again I don't know, I guess it will unfold, and I would like to read the book of evidence so a full understanding of what happened could be established.'

Catriona's claims do not take into account the fact that DJ had been asking people for loans for his 'cancer treatment' for years before the RTÉ broadcast about her troubles, and had been pursuing his fraudulent activities for quite a while – conning people around him who trusted him.

12

FULL-TIME

A week after John Kierans broke the story about a 'GAA ace' targeting victims for money in a 'cruel cancer scam' in *The Irish Sun* in February 2023, DJ drove a car he had hired around the County Cork coastline. He was alone and spent a long time looking for a place to go – somewhere to think about his next move. The lid was about to be blown open on his cancer fraud. Details of his debt write-down by AIB were already national news, and DJ knew people were figuring out that the GAA star at the centre of a garda probe into a cancer scam was him. Indeed, Kierans had been writing about what the people of Kilkenny had already known for some time and which had been talked about in GAA circles for many weeks before the story was printed.

After hours of driving, DJ parked the car at Cork University Hospital. The car remained there for a few days until a family member had to go down and collect it, as it needed to be returned to the car hire company. On 19 February, the *Sunday World* reported that a family member of a 'GAA star under investigation for fraud has claimed he was placed in a mental health care facility this week after he tried to take his own life'. The family member said, 'We are trying to prevent a suicide – the facts are not being presented correctly. He attempted suicide and is in hospital under the care of the mental health professionals.' When the family member was asked if there was any statement the player or the family would like to make, they said, 'To be honest, giving statements and worrying about all of this now is not our priority.'

The newspaper reported that pressure had been mounting on DJ Carey since December, when the property at which he was staying was searched by gardaí. 'Following the search, it's understood the GAA player voluntarily presented himself to gardaí for interview, but he was not arrested. It's further understood he answered a number of questions put to him by officers in relation to the investigation. At the time gardaí carried out the search, judgement [sic] for debts of in excess of €80,000 had been registered against the player. These included a significant judgement obtained against the player by an individual who had loaned him in excess of €100,000 and further judgements of in excess of €30,000 to Revenue.'

On the same date, 19 February, Maeve Sheehan reported in the *Sunday Independent* that billionaire Denis O'Brien had been contacted by gardaí investigating 'a former GAA star who allegedly sought hundreds of thousands of euro from people under false pretences'. She stated that O'Brien was understood to be one of a number of people who were tapped for money by the sportsman in recent years, 'claiming it was either a loan or to pay for his cancer treatment'. Sheehan reported that O'Brien 'provided the funds according to a source who declined to put a figure on the amount. However, the sums involved are believed to run to tens of thousands.' She also stated that there were growing concerns for the health of the sportsman, 'who has been hospitalised since the news of the garda investigation broke last weekend. A relative told the *Sunday Independent* he has been receiving medical care as a result of the strain and his recovery is now the priority for his family over the coming days and weeks.'

Sheehan's report stated that O'Brien was understood to have provided financial support of 'various kinds' to the sportsman over the years, including 'allowing him to stay in his properties at different times'. She stated that the investigation had begun in 2022 after financial institutions were 'alerted to unusual transactions in the sportsman's bank accounts. A number of people subsequently came forward complaining that he had allegedly duped them into giving him money, either for cancer treatment he never availed of or as a loan that was never repaid.' It was also reported that gardaí had searched a hotel where DJ was staying in December, and that he 'relinquished his mobile phone and his passport and has also presented himself for interview'.

Detectives were examining the former player's messages and trying to trace people who had given him money but had not made official complaints. 'Statements have been taken from a number of those tracked down. It is not clear whether Mr O'Brien has met yet with detectives.' The probe into DJ's affairs was being coordinated in Kilkenny and Waterford, with assistance from the Garda National Economic Crime Bureau. Sheehan said that detectives had not divulged how many complaints they had received, but sources put the value of the alleged fraud to date 'in the high six figures'.

In another report from 19 February, Conor Gallagher wrote in *The Irish Times* that Denis O'Brien had provided gardaí with 'extensive information' on a former GAA star under investigation for 'widespread fraud'. Gallagher said that O'Brien was 'eager to help the man' and 'did not seek proof of his illness or the treatment costs'. He also reported on how the 'Garda National Economic Crime Bureau is investigating whether the retired player deceived friends and business acquaintances into lending him money for medical and other bills. Detectives are examining whether or not he falsely claimed that he had cancer when he approached people looking for money. The prominent former player is understood to have agreed loan arrangements with those from whom he took the money.'

One of DJ's victims who did give a statement to gardaí revealed to this author that an officer told them DJ had confessed he had 'begged, borrowed and stolen, and never had cancer' during a voluntary statement in the early stages of the investigation.

Gallagher's report referred to a story that had a familiar ring for those who had given DJ money over the years: 'It was known within his local community that the former star regularly claimed to own land overseas and that he was about to sell it netting him a financial windfall.' The reporter stated that the sports star had told people who loaned him money 'in more recent years' that 'he was due to receive an insurance payout on a medical negligence claim'.

On 22 February, *The Irish Times* reported that a 'former top GAA player' had been arrested by gardaí over a series of alleged fraud offences. Although he was not named, the news travelled fast of DJ Carey's arrest under Section 6 of the Criminal Justice (Theft and Fraud Offences) Act 2001. He could be held for up to twenty-four hours and, if convicted, would face a maximum penalty of up to five years. The Garda Press Office confirmed to *The Irish Times* that gardaí in the 'eastern region have arrested a male in relation to an ongoing investigation into an alleged fraud'. The newspaper reported: 'According to the Irish Statute Book, a person will be found guilty of a Section 6 fraud offence if they are found to have dishonestly, with the intention of making a gain for himself or herself or another, or of causing loss to another, by any deception, induced another to do or refrain from doing an act.'

On the same day, *The Irish Times* also reported on the arrest of DJ's sister Catriona. A report by Conor Lally stated the former international hockey player was being questioned as part of an investigation 'into alleged breaches of company law'. She was detained as part of 'an inquiry by the Corporate Enforcement Authority (CEA)'. The CEA has an investigative and enforcement role to ensure that businesses comply with the Companies Act. Lally noted that this 'inquiry is a separate investigation to the Garda investigation into allegations Ms Carey received money from mortgage holders to do deals on distressed loans and kept the money without the promised arrangements being struck with lenders. *The Irish Times* understands the alleged breaches of company law under investigation by the authority relate to Careysfort Asset Estates.' The report went on: 'The authority's inquiry into Ms Carey's alleged activities linked to Careysfort Asset Estates has been ongoing for some time. It is understood information about the running of the company has been gathered in recent months and that some of those details were being put to Ms Carey by authority investigators on Wednesday.'

Catriona was released without charge at the end of several hours of questioning by the CEA. On Thursday 23 February, the day after his arrest, DJ Carey was also released without charge. In his case *The Irish Times* reported, 'A file, including the responses he gave to questions while in custody, is being prepared for the Director of Public Prosecutions.'

It was an extraordinary coincidence for the brother and sister to be arrested by separate authorities around the same time. Perhaps it was a ploy by investigators to encourage more people to come forward with information about the Careys.

While the pace of the investigation into Catriona's alleged mortgage scam frustrated her victims, gardaí moved quickly to charge DJ. On 29 September, he appeared before Blanchardstown District Court, having been arrested by appointment earlier that day and charged with twenty-one fraud offences against twenty-five people – nineteen of deception and two of using a false instrument over an eight-year period from 2014 to 2022. DJ was granted free legal aid after his solicitor, Edward Hughes, told Judge John O'Leary that his client had 'no income whatsoever'.

A report in *The Irish Times* by Colm Keena on that day said that Mr Hughes described how the case was likely to be a 'heavily documented prosecution' with 'very difficult charges to defend'. Carey got bail on the condition he sign on at a garda station and follow certain conditions. He was told to tell gardaí where he would live, and to inform them if he intended to travel outside the country – Mr Hughes suggested his client might travel to the UK for potential work. As it happens, a friend of DJ's was desperately trying to get him work on a building site in the UK, but the publicity generated by the case made it difficult for anybody to take him on, and it fell through.

DJ looked weary, with bags under his eyes and his face was expressionless as he walked out of court in a grey beanie and a black puffer coat emblazoned with the IT Carlow logo. He was driven away from court by his solicitor in a black Maserati. Notably, the addresses given by both DJ and Catriona Carey, which appeared in all media reports alongside the charges for their separate cases, were not the actual addresses where they were residing. This was another sign of how the Careys seemed to think the normal rules did not apply to them, and they clearly didn't want journalists arriving at their respective doors.

At this point, DJ was relying on the generosity of a small group of charitable men, one of whom had given him a temporary place to reside in Maynooth, County Kildare, where he was sharing a home with other men. This man had also tried to help DJ get social welfare, but it appeared he was not entitled to anything. The friends who were helping to take care of him were paying for food and bills, but even they were reluctant to give him cash. They knew DJ had made huge mistakes, yet still felt sorry for him. When asked why they would help DJ, given his bogus cancer scam, one said, 'The man is in a bad way. It's very sad, he owns nothing. Imagine after all his years of hurling and working, he doesn't own a house or a car.' The source had tried to get an explanation from DJ as to what had happened to all the money he borrowed, asking him, 'Where is the money gone?' DJ seems to have been largely in complete denial, which was shown by his rare reply to this friend. Rather than take any sort of responsibility, he instead tried to blame someone else, claiming, 'A woman spent it, she spent it all.' Despite this, when confronted by gardaí, he did not repeat this claim and had no credible explanation for the fraud.

DJ's case was sent forward to Dublin Circuit Criminal Court on 3 November 2023. On that day, he was very early as he entered the Criminal Courts of Justice building in Dublin alone. Before he met his legal team, he quietly walked around the lobby in an open-necked white shirt, navy suit and black trainers. Most people walked by him without taking any notice. Eventually, he went to stand at the back of the courtroom, waiting for Judge Orla Crowe to mention his case. When the registrar called his name, his barrister, Richard Downey, told the court that a jury would be needed for the case, which would take three to four weeks to be heard. As there was a potential for overrun into a fifth week, the first available date for the trial had to be discarded over concerns that there wouldn't be enough time for it to play out before the courts' summer break. In the end the judge allowed a long period of time before his trial hearing, which made DJ's supporters happy, as they hoped it would give the former hurler time to 'come to his senses' and plead guilty. After agreeing to change the address on record for Carey, as well as the garda station at which he was signing on, Judge Crowe adjourned the case to 2 July 2025. DJ did not speak once during this brief appearance.

Once he was facing trial for his actions, DJ Carey started keeping a low profile. He lived in rural properties, firstly in County Westmeath and later across the border in County Offaly, a short distance from Moate. As he had done in the past, he would frequent a few select haunts for a cup of tea, as well as dining locally, and he became a regular at the Grand Hotel in Moate, where people passing through often remarked that he talked to them. He sometimes looked for sympathy from those with whom he interacted, by bringing up his plight in conversation without directly mentioning his upcoming trial. There were times when he told people it was 'all being sorted' and they were left believing his victims had been paid back. In March 2025, he walked into Frayne's coffee shop in Mullingar for a full Irish breakfast with a blonde female companion. All the men already there eating breakfast looked up, with one remarking afterwards, 'He just came in, like nothing had happened and said, "How are ye lads?"' The man explained that DJ was still 'well got' in Westmeath, meaning he had good friends there who were happy to support him. In spring 2025, DJ was regularly holding court in the Tuar Ard Arts Centre with older men who were enthralled by being in his company. There were suggestions that DJ was washing dishes in the restaurant at one stage.

Just after 9.30 a.m. on 2 July 2025, DJ Carey, dressed in a black suit, a blue pinstripe shirt, a patterned tie and dark shoes, once again stepped inside the Criminal Courts of Justice building. He grinned briefly as he talked to his solicitor, Edward Hughes, in the large open downstairs lobby ahead of his court appearance. Word had filtered out to some journalists two days earlier that a deal had been done to avoid a trial.

There was a moment before DJ slipped quietly into the dock when this author wondered if he would actually face up to his crimes and admit his guilt, or whether he would, instead, expose his family to up to five weeks of evidence. As he stood in the dock of courtroom number 7, his face seemed drained of any colour. His eyes and body hardly moved and he displayed no visible signs of emotion. He looked straight ahead with his hands clasped in front of him, the only word coming from his mouth, over and over, until he had it said ten times in response to each of the charges put to him: 'Guilty.'

The first of the ten charges that DJ pleaded guilty to was that he, dishonestly and by deception, induced the businessman Denis O'Brien to give him money to pay for cancer treatment on unknown dates between January 2014 and September 2022, contrary to the Criminal Justice (Theft and Fraud Offences) Act 2001. The other nine guilty pleas were for the same offence in relation to Owen and Ann Conway, on unknown dates between 25 March 2021 and 3 November 2022; Mark and Sharon Kelly, on unknown dates between 26 May 2021 and 10 December 2022; Aidan Mulligan, on unknown dates between 1 June 2022 and 22 September 2022; Edwin Carey, on unknown dates between 21 December 2021 and 12 November 2022; Tony Griffin and Christy Browne, on unknown dates between 1 September 2022 and 26 October 2022; Thomas Butler, on unknown dates between 1 October 2019 and 11 November 2022; Jeffrey Howes, on unknown dates between 1 February 2022 and 8 August 2022; Noel Tynan, on unknown dates between 1 January 2017 and 12 October 2022; and Aonghus Leydon, on unknown dates between 14 March 2022 and 21 March 2022. The amount involved in each individual case, or the total of the deception, was not disclosed in court.

Dominic McGinn, SC, for the prosecution outlined that all pleas were accepted and a *nolle prosequi* would be entered on one count of deception, while there were a further ten outstanding charges that would be taken into consideration. Eight of these are for deception, with two for using a false instrument 'with the intention of inducing another person to accept it as genuine' between 1 January 2014 and 18 September 2019. These charges were made under Sections 6 and 26 of the Criminal Justice (Theft and Fraud Offences) Act. The penalty in relation to a person guilty of an offence under Section 26 for using a false instrument, can carry a 'fine or imprisonment for a term not exceeding 10 years or both'. The packed courtroom was told that victim impact statements would be required before sentencing could be carried out.

On the day he pleaded guilty, some of DJ's victims were long distances away, as they had been eager not to change their travel plans, stating that Carey had already taken enough from them. Instead, they kept their phones close to them, waiting for an update. When it became known that he had pleaded guilty, there was a palpable sense of relief for the people he had conned. Some of his victims had simply wanted him to be held accountable for what he did, and for them, the sentence does not matter as much as people knowing the truth.

Before the brief hearing ended, Judge Patricia Ryan was told how DJ had undergone surgery for a 'heart condition' in Galway and was continuing to receive care for 'genuine' and 'serious' health issues. His legal team applied for an extension of his legal aid to allow for a one-page report to be drawn up on this heart condition. An associate of Carey's had mentioned to this author previously that DJ had been recuperating in a nursing home after having stent surgery, but it was hard to know if this story was 'genuine' – a word used by DJ's own defence when they described his health issues in court – or just another ploy to gain sympathy. Mental health issues were also mentioned in court.

DJ was remanded on bail. After he walked out of the packed courtroom, he went into a huddle with his legal team outside the door. Then, as he turned to make his way downstairs, this author took the chance to ask DJ to share some insight into his guilty plea. Although given the opportunity, DJ failed to offer an apology to any of his victims. He showed no remorse, no answer was offered for his behaviour, and he appeared to be quietly seething. Carey clenched his jaw and his body stiffened when he was asked if there was another side to the story. He walked briskly while this author walked alongside him pleading with him to give context, if there was any missing, that would explain his crimes. DJ often complained about being hounded by banks and Revenue to strangers, but when given a chance to speak after his guilty plea, he had nothing to say. As he approached the main doors of the courts, other reporters were in pursuit of him to ask the same questions. He never uttered a word and got into a BMW parked nearby. At the time of writing, DJ Carey was due to be sentenced on 29 October 2025.

13

DJ THE MALINGERER

DJ executed his skills on the hurling field to perfection. So much so that he wasn't known for his physicality. He didn't need to get physical – he could flick the ball here and flick the ball there. It was genius. An old rival, former Offaly hurler Brian Whelahan, once said, marking DJ was the ultimate challenge. If you weren't on your game all the time, he could destroy you in a few seconds. These skills that he honed on the hurling field, he used in real life as he manipulated the people who worshipped him to get his hands on their cash. DJ shaved his head and his eyebrows regularly, and he pretended he was in the United States getting treatment when he was in Ireland. Did he get a kick out of conning people, did it make him feel excited to take money from people who believed him? He never seemed particularly perturbed when people refused him cash; instead, he just moved on to the next person, as if on a sales cold-call.

After he pleaded guilty to deceiving people, the GAA community and people in DJ's wider circle of acquaintances made calls back and forth to each other as they swapped stories about his strange behaviour. A businessman called a former

Kilkenny player to ask, 'What about the marks on his head? What was that about?' before a reply came from Kilkenny: 'They were from a fucking failed hair transplant.' Another man, when out playing golf with friends, told them how he had worked with Carey in Dunnes Stores in Kilkenny in the late 1980s. They became friends, so, naturally, when the man was getting married in 1993, he invited DJ to his wedding. 'He rang me and said he'd like to go but he'd need a £15,000 [punt] appearance fee to come.' Carey was uninvited and the pair are no longer friends.

Under one of the many articles published online in July 2025 about DJ, there was an interesting comment from Frank Murphy, owner of a popular filling station in Mullingar, County Westmeath. 'Hi [sic] never paid for 65 euros at my petrol pumps in Mullingar, just drive [sic] away, he just said sorry.' There are also question marks over whether or not he was paying green fees during his evening rounds at Moate golf club while he awaited sentencing.

To understand what happened, we need to first understand the huge esteem in which we, the Irish public, held DJ. What happens to sports people like DJ after they retire? It is often said that sports stars die twice – the first time at retirement. The transition from being celebrated and at the top of their game, to joining the rest of us mere mortals, can leave a sports star struggling. At the end of DJ's intercounty career, he went from being a celebrated All-Star travelling to Croke Park on the team bus with a garda escort, revered by Irish people the world over, to joining the ordinary fans in traffic. The walk to Croke Park after parking in Clonliffe College was a far cry from being able to park outside the dressing room on All-Ireland final day.

This kind of comedown is a scenario that can lead a person like DJ to feign or even induce illness. Dr Marc D. Feldman, Clinical Professor of Psychiatry and Adjunct Professor of Psychology at the University of Alabama, Tuscaloosa, believes somebody who was as celebrated and much-loved as DJ Carey is at risk of needing to keep the adulation coming. Dr Feldman is an international expert on Munchausen syndrome, also known as factitious disorder. Although he has never examined or treated DJ, his opinion is based on vast experience. Feldman believes that DJ is the type of person who needs to be seen as a warrior fighting a battle. He wants to be seen as strong and brave, being a victor. 'Everyone needs attention … Factitious disorder patients draw attention to themselves by being (or appearing to be) sick. If convincing enough, this deception can become a career.' Although Munchausen syndrome is defined as a mental illness, Dr Feldman stresses this doesn't mean they don't know what they're doing or that they're helpless victims.

The second reason somebody would lie about their health is malingering. This is not a mental illness, and while similar to factitious disorder, the goal is usually different. They want something tangible or external, such as money. 'The difference is when you look at malingering, you can usually figure out if you know their life circumstance and their stressors, why they're doing what they're doing,' said Dr Feldman. It is possible for a person to have factitious disorder and also engage in malingering. The two conditions can co-exist and change over time. Somebody can start by seeking money but find the attention so gratifying that factitious disorder becomes prominent. Then they may want medication or money and go back to malingering. In many cases, it is not straightforward.

A symptom of such conditions, according to Dr Feldman, is high-visibility behaviour that does not ring true. Inconsistent stories or continual pleas for money or attention with an illness like cancer can mean there's some medical deception involved. Medical deception, whether it's factitious disorder or malingering, is deliberate, conscious and wilful behaviour. There is considerable planning involved. There are no limits to the resourcefulness of the person who is medically deceiving others. They are limited only by knowledge, creativity and motivation.

In April 2023 there was a selfie image circulating on WhatsApp of DJ Carey looking the worse for wear with what appeared to be a phone charger cable crudely taped to his nose with a plaster. The image does not have the normal hallmarks of a photoshopped image or a fake. It's presumed DJ sent it to somebody from whom he was trying to get money and sympathy. People circulated the image to their contacts and joked that DJ had finally been 'charged'. Whatever the reasons for feigning illness, Dr Feldman said it is almost always an 'act of desperation'. This photo certainly looked like an act of a desperate man.

One of the stories DJ told consistently, was that his world handballing titles meant that the cost of his treatment in the Fred Hutchinson Cancer Center in Seattle would be covered. In

September 2023, this author contacted the clinic to ask them if they have a treatment scheme to cover elite athletes. The email response came swiftly: 'No, Fred Hutchinson Cancer Center does not have such a program.'

It may be hard for those who have never met DJ to understand just how convincing he was when feeding his victims a tissue of lies. People may think it now looks obvious that Carey had a phone charger inserted in his nostril, but when a person is told their hero is dying, their default position is to help – not to question the person's motivation. Many of the people DJ targeted are lifelong GAA supporters who would have done anything for him. When his lies started to come to light, they agonised over giving a statement to gardaí, as they felt devastated about what transpired. Some of his victims, like Tommy Butler, even demanded to see proof from gardaí that he never had cancer, as DJ was so convincing. Tommy, a volunteer driver for the Irish Cancer Society, couldn't understand how he could lie about having such a devastating illness.

There were many rifts and fallouts in DJ's family, but blood is still thicker than water in Gowran, County Kilkenny, and it was Jack Carey who tried to clean up his brother's mess after the initial arrest. It is understood that, in spring 2023, Jack paid back a sum of around €5,000 to Wexford hurler Larry O'Gorman. Larry then contacted gardaí to say he wanted to withdraw his previous statement. Although, for some reason, his complaint wasn't withdrawn, in October 2023 he told this author, 'It's sorted and I'm happy.'

We don't know if DJ and Jack ever had a confrontation

over the fact that Jack had rumbled what his brother was doing and had been warning people not to give him money when his borrowing was getting closer to home. Jack had gotten word that DJ was frequenting well-known establishments in Leighlinbridge, County Carlow, and asking anybody in his path for money. Jack was also the one who tried to get DJ legal advice on his predicament. The Kilkenny County Board were asked to help the former hurler after his arrest. They were approached to see if there was any legal assistance they could offer, but they explained they were unable to do anything. Jack contacted victims after the case got under way to ask about what had happened. He knew that his brother had been telling his cancer story about Seattle over and over, and he was trying to get to the bottom of the extent of the problem. He did not appear to realise the scale of his brother's fraud.

The mural with DJ Carey is no longer on the wall in Gowran. There are now fresh layers of paint covering where the hurler's figure was once dominant. By the end of summer 2023 there was talk of the need for a monument to commemorate the great Michael 'Ducksie' Walsh, the most successful Irish handballer in history, who had died in 2016. Ducksie was a hero to younger generations, growing up in Butt's Green in Kilkenny city, and there was mounting pressure on the GAA and the local authorities to recognise the world handball champion. In the debate about the need for a monument in his honour, there was no mention of DJ Carey, his famous doubles' partner, whom Ducksie often called 'a man of mystery'. For years, whenever handball was mentioned, the conversation quickly turned to the great 'Ducksie and DJ', but since DJ's cancer scam was exposed, to even utter his name is too painful for some of his greatest fans. The conversation about the monument has shifted to how it should recognise all handballers in the county, similar to the hurlers' statue situated by the banks of the River Nore on Canal Walk in Kilkenny city.

Yet there are still hurling fans who will aggressively defend DJ, no matter what is said. On Sunday, 6 July 2025, Kilkenny were beaten by Tipperary in the All-Ireland Senior Hurling Championship semi-final on a scoreline of 0–30 to 4–20. This was a bitter disappointment for Kilkenny and there was no shortage of match post-mortems over what was dubbed the 'ScoreGate' controversy. The scoreboard in Croke Park showed that Tipp were on 4–21 instead of their actual total of 4–20. Some argued that Kilkenny had been misled into hunting for a goal in the last few minutes, when they only needed two points. Asked outside the stadium after the match how they felt about DJ's guilt, many Kilkenny fans actively defended him, saying he was the greatest hurler who ever lived. There was also admiration and support shown for DJ's son, Mikey, who played for Kilkenny that afternoon despite his father's court appearance in the days leading up to the match. Others refused to talk about it, much like the GPA, the Kilkenny County Board and the GAA, who were all invited to answer questions in relation to the research for this book, but each of which chose to remain silent.

One of the people who has always been in DJ's corner is his former primary school teacher John Knox. To him, what has happened resembles a Shakespearean tragedy. He described DJ's actions as a fatal flaw in a grand person, who still has a lot of his life to live. John was delighted that DJ pleaded guilty because he felt he wasn't living in the real world until now. He is well aware of the seriousness of the deception perpetrated by his former student – his own mother died of cancer – but he knows how hard it is for GAA fans to condemn their hero. Knox gained some insight into Carey's mindset when he talked to him on the phone some months after his arrest. He admitted, 'He was painting the good picture, sorrow didn't enter into it.' Knox confessed that he thought DJ had an addiction problem. When asked what he thought he was addicted to, he answered, 'Telling lies to people to get money.' He concluded, 'You have to face the truth yourself; hopefully he will.'

On the same weekend as the All-Ireland semi-final, Sarah Newman's interview with Niamh Horan appeared on the front page of the *Sunday Independent*. In it, she outlined her personal trauma over Carey's actions, advising others to 'listen to the red flags'.

Before throw-in at Croke Park on All-Ireland Sunday, 20 July 2025, the Kilkenny jubilee team was honoured a quarter of a century after its famous win over Offaly in 2000. Man of the Match that day was DJ Carey, but he was noticeably absent from the stadium for the jubilee ceremony. There had been much speculation in the lead-up to the event about Carey's potential attendance. When the day came, there was no sign of him, but boos were still heard from Hill 16 when his name was called out. The announcer declared, 'At full-forward was DJ

Carey from Young Irelands, he scored 1–4 on the day, claiming his third All-Ireland of five in total and he would end the year with his eighth of nine All-Star awards.' No reason was given for his absence; it was simply stated at the end of the factual round-up that 'DJ is not with us today.'

One of the main outstanding questions in all of this is how much exactly DJ stole. Because he pleaded guilty, his bank transactions were not made public. Figures attached to his individual victims were not read out in court either during his arraignment. While his victims were relieved about that, it is known that they had handed over various amounts from €1,000 up to six-figure sums. On 13 July 2025, journalist Maeve Sheehan revealed for the first time in the *Sunday Independent* that Carey was originally charged with 'scamming €415,000 from 23 people'. Sheehan reported that DJ had 'admitted to fraud to the value of €250,000, involving 13 victims'. 'The biggest victim financially speaking was Denis O'Brien, the billionaire businessman who was approached numerous times by Carey for money to fund his bogus cancer treatment. According to a source, Carey was charged with deceiving Mr O'Brien out of €150,000.' Sheehan wrote that the total figure is believed to be higher, as O'Brien had also allowed DJ to stay in his properties. She also reported that gardaí suspect the 'true cost' of Carey's fraud is 'far higher than the €415,000 that he was prosecuted for', with detectives contacting 'close to 50 people whom they believed Carey approached for money'. This is hardly surprising, given that the €415,000 figure does not cover any loans given to DJ prior to 2014, or cash handed to him. There are also others, like Bernie Comaskey, who did not go to the gardaí but gave DJ money on the basis that he was fighting cancer. Some speculate that even DJ himself does not know the full amount he has taken from people over the years, but they believe €2m would not be wide of the mark.

If he did defraud people of this kind of sum, where did the money go? The life DJ has been living since his arrest would indicate that, whatever he took, there is nothing left. Yet years of spending on trips to the US and other places, dining out frequently, hiring cars and checking into five-star hotels on weekends away could account for a serious amount of expenditure. Although the sum of €2m might seem like a lot of money, it would be easy to burn through over the course of an extravagant lifestyle lived for nearly two decades.

What is perhaps most upsetting for DJ's victims is the sense that he does not recognise the harm he has done. Even when his crimes were exposed, he appeared to be in denial and, at the time of writing, there was no indication that he felt bad about his crimes. While his hearing in July 2025 was pending, he discussed his case with many strangers during rounds of golf, carvery dinners and pots of tea in the Midlands. His explanation to all of them was that the entire situation had been blown out of proportion, the media was printing lies about him, and it would all soon be sorted out. He regularly blamed others for his downfall, particularly the banks. It is understood he told his two sons about his decision to plead guilty just days before the hearing. In the months before his sentencing, he continued to tell stories in an attempt to elicit sympathy about his health, showing one man a scar on his chest, mentioning a heart condition and claiming he had to go for regular blood tests. He described to another friend how he didn't have the correct number of valves in his heart and was having ongoing issues. Sadly, even people who remain on good terms with DJ aren't certain if his latest health issues are genuine.

When interviewed by Ray D'Arcy in 2015, in discussing his financial problems DJ Carey said, 'I would be one of those people that would be very conscious of what I would do … I'm not one of those that would turn around and say I don't care. You borrow money, it should be paid back.' Yet, on the day when he finally admitted his guilt in court, he did not even offer an apology to his victims, many of whom were more hurt by his cancer lie than the fact that he stole from them. This author has given DJ Carey many opportunities to explain his actions, but he has never cooperated. At the time of writing, it seems that, having betrayed the fans who worshipped him and having been convicted of fraud in a court of law, DJ Carey still believed that he had nothing to explain or apologise for – only time will tell if he changes his mind. It is a sad end to the storied career of a once-great man.

BUÍOCHAS

I am surrounded by good people who have supported me throughout this journey. I married a patient man, Alan O'Reilly, who champions everything I do. My daughter, Róise, brings so much fun and laughter to our home that it is an immediate antidote to everything else that is going on in the outside world. My parents, John and Madeleine, better known in our family as 'daideo' and 'Lala', gave me so many opportunities in life. Every woman needs a village, and they are mine.

Míle buíochais to Enda McEvoy for all your advice and guidance.

Many thanks to my publisher, Conor Graham of Merrion Press, for his foresight throughout the process. Editors are unsung heroes, and I am so fortunate to have been able to work with Wendy Logue and all the team at Merrion Press. Conor also introduced me to Trevor Birney, Jim O'Hagan and the talented crew at Fine Point Films. From the moment I started working with the crew on filming the story based on the book, there was a gear shift for me. I thrive best when I'm working in a team, so it was a huge asset to have Fine Point Films behind me.

There were many times when my texts, emails and calls were unanswered, or doors closed as I arrived. But for all the rejection from people who were wary, there were many more who understood I had a job to do and were willing to put the kettle on and tell the truth about DJ Carey. Journalism relies on sound sources, and I am very fortunate that this project introduced me to so many decent people. You know who you are. *Go raibh míle maith agaibh.*